The Homosexuality Debate

Fides quaerens intellectum ...

Anselm, Archbishop of Canterbury, 1093–1109
from the preface to the Proslogion

The Homosexuality Debate

Faith Seeking Understanding

Catherine Sider Hamilton
editor

ABC Publishing
ANGLICAN BOOK CENTRE

Anglican Book Centre
600 Jarvis Street
Toronto, Ontario
Canada M4Y 2J6

Text typeset in Janson and CgLisbon
Cover and text design by Jane Thornton

National Library of Canada Cataloguing in Publication
The homosexuality debate : faith seeking understanding /
Catherine Sider Hamilton, editor.

Includes bibliographical references.
ISBN 1-55126-397-1
Printed in Canada

1.Homosexuality—Religious aspects—Christianity.
I. Hamilton, Catherine Sider

BR115.H6H63 2003   261.8'35766   C2003-904619-2

Table of Contents

Contributors   7
Foreword   11
Editor's Acknowledgements   13
Introduction   14

Scripture

1. Same-Sex Eroticism and the Church: 37
      Classical Approaches and Responses
      Edith Humphrey

Church and Culture

2. Human Rights: 97
      The Concept of Rights in Christian Moral Discourse
      Joan Lockwood O'Donovan

3. Evangelical Freedom   109
      John Webster

4. The Authority of Experience Among Anglicans
      in Moral Debate   124
      Christopher Lind

5. The "Appeal to Experience":   136
      Biblical Roots and Critical Developments
      Carroll Guen Hart

Church Polity

6. Our Differences Need Not Destroy Us   171
   Rowan Williams

7. Conflict and Communion: 176
   Homosexuality and Church Practice in Anglicanism
   Eric Beresford

8. "Patience Leads to Character":   216
   The Polygamy-Homosexuality Analogy in
   Contemporary Debate
   George Sumner

Pastoral Care

9. Homosexuality and the Anglican Church in Canada: 229
   A Pastoral Approach
   Patrick Yu

10. "The Gladness of the Gospel":   250
    A Traditional Perspective on Pastoral Care
    David A. Reed

Contributors

The Rev. Canon Eric Beresford has been Consultant for Ethics and Interfaith Relations for the Anglican Church of Canada since 1996. In this capacity he works on a wide range of ethical issues including those related to human sexuality. In 1999 he was seconded to work part-time with the Anglican Consultative Council on ethical issues related to the environment and biotechnology. He has worked also as an ethics consultant to Health Canada and for the Ontario Human Rights Commission. Canon Beresford studied at the Universities of Liverpool, Oxford, and McGill, and holds degrees in science and theology. Before taking up his current appointment he was Assistant Professor of Ethics in the Faculty of Religious Studies at McGill University.

Dr. Carroll Guen Hart (PhD 1993, Free University of Amsterdam) has published articles on the calling of the intellectual, the nurturing of public life, and the uses of scientific knowledge in human situations. She has an enduring love for nuance and complexity, for history, for patterns of meaning, and the texture of human journeys. She was one of the founders, with her husband, Willem, of An Adhoc Group in the Diocese of Toronto that sought to explore and promote the full acceptance of homosexual persons in the Anglican Church. The group gave rise to The Bishop's Dialogue Committee on Homosexuality, of which Carroll remains an active member. A former Director of Worldview Studies at the Institute for Christian Studies, she lives with her husband in Toronto.

Dr. Edith Humphrey is Associate Professor of New Testament at Pittsburgh Theological Seminary. An Anglican layperson, until her appointment at PTS she was musical director at St. George's Anglican Church, Ottawa, and Professor of Scripture and Dean at Augustine College, Ottawa. She is the author of numerous academic and popular pieces, including *A Solid Foundation? — The Seven Pillars of the Jesus Seminar Re-Examined; Joseph and Aseneth*, and *The Ladies and the Cities*. She is also a co-author of *Longing for God: Anglicans Talk about Revelation, Nature, Culture, and Authority*. As an advocate of "charitable orthodoxy," she is a popular ecumenical speaker, a member of the Primate's Theological Commission, Anglican Church of Canada, and a member of the Commission on Ministry of the Episcopal Diocese of Pittsburgh. She and her husband, Chris, make their home in Stanton Heights; they have three daughters.

Dr. Christopher Lind currently serves as Director of the Toronto School of Theology. Before coming to Toronto he was President of St. Andrew's College and St. Stephen's College in Saskatoon and Edmonton. He is a member of the Primate's Theological Commission of the Anglican Church of Canada and has worked extensively with the World Council of Churches on issues related to justice, peace, and the integrity of creation.

Dr. Joan Lockwood O'Donovan is an Oxford theologian who has lectured and tutored in theology and political philosophy for theological colleges, the university and adjunct programs. She has written numerous articles in political theology and philosophy and two books: *George Grant and the Twilight of Justice* (Toronto: University of Toronto Press, 1984) and *Theology of Law and Authority in the English Reformation* (Atlanta: Scholars Press, 1991). With Oliver O'Donovan she edited *From Irenaeus to Grotius: A Sourcebook in Christian Political Thought* (Grand Rapids: Eerdmans, 1999), and is about to publish a joint book of essays entitled *Bonds of Imperfection: Christian Politics Past and Present*.

The Rev. Dr. David A. Reed is Associate Professor of Pastoral Theology and Director of Field Education at Wycliffe College in Toronto. Ordained in the Episcopal Church, he pastored for eighteen years in Massachusetts and Connecticut. David received his education at Barrington College, Andover Newton Theological School, and Boston University, where he completed his PhD in Systematic Theology. David has a continuing interest in current trends in church and culture, including issues relating to marriage, family, single life, and sexuality. He served until recently on the Canadian Primate's Theological Commission. David and his wife, Carlynn, have two sons and live in Unionville.

The Rev. Catherine Sider Hamilton (editor) is a priest in the Diocese of Toronto and is pursuing doctoral studies at Wycliffe College in the Toronto School of Theology. She has published a sermon ("Remembrance Day") in *Best Sermons 5* and has written for various church publications, including *The Anglican* and *Incourage* magazine. She and her husband, David, have four children.

The Rev. Dr. George Sumner is the Principal of Wycliffe College in Toronto. He has a doctorate in theology from Yale University, where he studied with Dr. George Lindbeck. He has served as a missionary to Tanzania and in Navajoland in the USA. His theology of other religions, *The First and the Last*, will be published by Eerdmanns. He is married to Stephanie Hodgkins, and they have a son and a daughter.

The Rev. Dr. John Webster is Professor of Systematic Theology at the University of Aberdeen. He has also taught theology at Oxford and Toronto; he was the Lady Margaret Professor of Divinity in the University of Oxford and Canon of Christ Church, and he was Professor of Theology at Wycliffe College in the Toronto School of Theology. He served the Anglican Church in Canada on a variety of ecumenical, liturgical, and doctrinal commissions. His research and writing are in the area of dogmatics and the history of modern theology.

The Most Rev. Rowan Williams is the one hundred and fourth Archbishop of Canterbury and Primate of All-England. He comes to Canterbury from Wales, where he served as Bishop of Monmouth and Archbishop of Wales. Before being elected Bishop of Monmouth, he was Lady Margaret Professor of Divinity in the University of Oxford. His many publications include *Lost Icons*, *The Wound of Knowledge*, and *The Making of Orthodoxy*. He is married to Jane and has two children.

The Rev. Canon Dr. Patrick Yu was born in Hong Kong. He is a priest in the Diocese of Toronto and has served in urban, rural, and multi-cultural parishes. His special areas of interest are interfaith issues and supervisory ministry: he coordinates summer internships for Wycliffe College students. He is currently the incumbent of St. Timothy's Church, Agincourt. Patrick has been a member of the Archbishop's Sexuality Dialogue Group from its beginning.

Foreword

Since its inception in 1994 as a study and resource group on questions of Christian ethics in the Anglican Church of Canada — in particular, on the controversy surrounding homosexuality — Fidelity has sought both a fair hearing for the church's classical teaching and a fair understanding of the arguments for change and of those making the argument. In the process, we have hoped to carve out some neutral territory for creative thought, consistent with the gospel, and fair and sensitive in an embattled area of the church's life. This essay collection is intended to provide just such a territory: a place for fair hearing and understanding, a place where creative and faithful Christian thinking can happen.

That said, I'm ever mindful of one member's warning that, given the times, our work could be compared to a peace conference in the midst of a raging battle. The possibility of war is ever lurking, threatening to overwhelm and undo anything that the peace conference might have to offer.

Such may be the case for this collection of essays. Nonetheless it is offered to the church as a means of understanding more clearly both the church's tradition on human sexuality and the challenge to that tradition presented by the present controversy. It is intended also to inspire a bold proclamation of the Christian vision of life and the pursuit of that place where righteousness and mercy kiss.

To that end, we could not be more pleased with this collection or with the group of distinguished writers who agreed to contribute. We are grateful for the advisory committee who first set the wheels in motion. They were the ones who insisted that the collection resist the temptation of responding to immediate quarrels, taking the long view instead, so that it might be a collection that would help people understand the history and the roots of the controversy. This committee included Peter Mason, George Sumner, Ajit John, Kim Beard, Catherine Sider Hamilton, and Patrick Yu.

We wish to thank Robert Maclennan, Publishing Manager of ABC Publishing, for his support of this project, for his gracious oversight, and for the work of the readers and designers.

We are deeply indebted to our editor, Catherine Sider Hamilton, who painstakingly drew the collection together, patiently bore numerous delays and complications, and all the while gathered the parts that would contribute to the cohesive whole now before you.

Finally, we wish to pay special thanks to two individuals. The late Master Douglas Peppiatt, former Vice-Chancellor of the Diocese of Toronto, and the Rt. Rev. Douglas Blackwell, retired Suffragan Bishop of Toronto, were each instrumental in the founding and establishment of Fidelity and in guiding our efforts in the formative days. We miss Douglas Peppiatt. We wish Douglas Blackwell the very best in his retirement. To them both we dedicate this volume.

I appeal to you, therefore, brothers and sisters, by the mercies of God, to present your bodies as a living sacrifice, holy and acceptable to God, which is your spiritual worship. Do not be conformed to this world, but be transformed by the renewing of your minds, so that you may discern what is the will of God, what is good and acceptable and perfect (Rom 12:1, 2 NRSV).

F. Dean Mercer
President, Fidelity

Editor's Acknowledgements

This collection owes a great deal to many people, not least to the authors themselves, whose wisdom and passion have made the book compelling and whose patience with its long gestation I have appreciated. Special thanks are due to Dean Mercer and the executive of Fidelity, whose project this book was, and who generously entrusted its editing to me. Dean has been the driving force behind the work of Fidelity since its beginning; by his vision, not least for this project, the church has been blessed. The book itself began to take shape one morning at Wycliffe College in a rather remarkable meeting of minds. To those who were there — Dean Mercer, Patrick Yu, George Sumner, Peter Mason, Kim Beard, and Ajit John — we are indebted. Dean Mercer and Robert D. Sider read the whole manuscript and offered valuable suggestions for the Introduction; for their critical acumen and support I am grateful.

It has been a pleasure to work with ABC Publishing: Greig Dunn's editorial suggestions were most helpful, and Robert Maclennan, Publishing Manager, was both astute and always gracious.

Finally, my thanks to my family: to my children, Caitlin, Nicholas, Sarah, and Robbie, who, as deadlines approached, met flex-meals, flex-laundry, and flex-bedtimes with good humour, and were always ready with a hug, and to my husband, David, who keeps me laughing in a busy life, and whose love abides.

Introduction

For more than two decades the debate about homosexual practice has held the Anglican Communion, especially in North America, in its grip. How do we understand homosexuality? What is the moral basis for homosexual practice? What is a sexual ethic for the twenty-first century? These questions and others like them are at the centre of what has become a fierce and often bitter controversy. They are not only provocative questions but necessary ones too, precisely because they deal with issues of sexuality and ethics, issues that are central to the life of the church in our time, as they have been for the living church in any age. Ethics, those principles of right and wrong conduct that govern our actions, are the point at which faith meets life. Our manner of life says a great deal about how we conceive our Christian commitment. This conjunction of faith and life meets us with particular force in the matter of sexual behaviour. The compelling power of sex, and its profound moral implications, has always made sexual ethics a flashpoint for Christian living. And the time in which we live, with its highly sexualized and material culture, has only intensified the force with which the issues of sexual behaviour confront us. Given the priority our society gives to sex, given too the high value it places on both self-realization and a whole range of personal freedoms, it is not surprising that the question of homosexual practice should have arisen, and arisen with intensity.

That the question is important, both to our time and to our Christian living, does not yet imply that it should be divisive. Yet the debate about homosexuality seems likely to tear the church apart. The divisiveness of the debate invites reflection. Why should it be this question out of the many questions that have arisen in the life of the church that threatens to burn down the house? The church has always faced difficult debate. Why, when we have survived the controversy over divorce and remarriage, a new Prayer Book, women's ordination — to name but a few — does this one seem both intractable and lethal?

Part of the answer lies, of course, in politics. The history of political manoeuvring in this debate, of dialogues manipulated and educational events weighted in favour of one side or the other, is unedifying.[1] But political machinations on the part of people with power are not the whole problem. The source of the debate's intractability lies deeper, in the nature of the question itself. This is a debate that pushes us back upon our fundamental presuppositions. It touches on the foundations of the faith — on the authority of scripture and how we conceive the Christian "story," on the doctrines of creation, fall, redemption, and kingdom hope. It touches also on how we understand the relation between the faith and the context in which it is lived. It touches, that is, on the old question of Christ and culture, church and world, and the relation between them. What is the relation between the tradition of the church, for instance, and its contemporary wisdom, or between our own lived experience and the inherited formulations of the faith? The debate about homosexual practice drives us back to these underlying questions, so that it is not just our understanding of homosexuality that is at issue, but our whole conception of the faith. It is little wonder that the struggle is fierce and the disagreement apparently irresolvable.

Precisely because it concerns the fundamentals of our faith, this is a debate worth having. Insofar as it forces us to articulate the presuppositions on which our faith rests it is invaluable — not because we will thereby find a compromise between convictions that are essentially opposite, but because we will have a better sense of the gospel. This collection of essays hopes to seize the opportunity the debate offers. Each essay goes to the root of some aspect of the debate, whether the question is broadly speaking a matter of the authority of scripture, or of church and culture, or of church polity or simply — but urgently — of "how then shall we live?" In the course of the essays, we begin to see the essential points of the two opposing arguments[2] and also the faultlines between them. The shape of the debate, that is, as well as the foundations of its two different visions, begins to come clear.

It is in large part the sheer variety of the essays that allows the debate thus to take shape before us. These essays are written by authors deliberately chosen to represent a cross-section of the church, so that the debate might appear here in the various aspects it has assumed in the different milieu it has penetrated: academic, popular, lay, and ordained. Our authors are scholars, clergy, and lay people who reflect in their different styles of writing and argumentation their different contexts. One characteristic, however, they all have in common. They write, each one, with deep feeling and with a passionate concern for the welfare of the church in this time of crisis. This common concern, expressed in a diversity of perspectives, is a sign of hope in a debate that threatens to tear the church apart. Accordingly, these essays are offered to all who share in this passion for the church and to all who find the struggle for Christian truth compelling, in the hope that this volume may, both in the intensity of its statements and in the variety of its perspectives, be a useful tool in the continuing debate. For the debate will go on, whatever political solution is found in the short term. It is our fundamental Christian convictions that are at issue and, as these essays demonstrate, such convictions are not lightly put aside.

The collection begins with scripture. Here is the centre of the argument, for revisionist and traditionalist alike. Both turn to scripture as a — indeed, *the* — primary authority in the debate, seeking to ground in scripture the argument either for the church's classical teaching on homosexual practice or for change. Both claim that scripture is on their side. The struggle for the authority of scripture suggests that most voices in this debate care about the Bible and about Christian authenticity. Very few revisionists (though there are some) desire to jettison scripture. On the contrary, they find in scripture itself, in its story of creation and wide redeeming grace, confirmation of the call to change. This common concern for faithfulness and authenticity is reassuring. On the other hand, the cacophony of competing readings has the potential to be unsettling. Certainly it represents an intriguing display of hermeneutical pyrotechnics and a challenging exercise in discernment. It may also suggest an interpretive chaos that calls into question precisely the authority of scripture. How, exactly, is scripture authoritative in this debate? Given the array of different interpretive perspectives, given the plethora of readings of a single passage, how are we to decide among them?

It is with this question that Edith Humphrey begins. Before we can read scripture in any debate, Humphrey says, we need to ask how it is authoritative. She situates authority in the matrix of scripture and tradition, with reason and experience as the tools by which we read. In fact, she says, we do not and cannot depend on scripture alone as our guide. We read it willy-nilly through the lens of our own experiences and presuppositions; we ought also to read it under the guiding authority of tradition: the common, approved, and living experience of God's people and the pattern of reasoned reflection on scripture that has shaped the church's understanding.

With this hermeneutic in place, Humphrey takes us on a grand tour of the classical reading of scripture from the days of the early church to the present day. She begins with a re-telling of the "story" of scripture, classically conceived, and then shows how this story, and the place of sexuality (and homosexuality) within it, remains the church's standard reading of scripture for eighteen centuries. It is a story in five acts, comprising creation, fall, the calling of Israel, the coming of the Christ, and finally the birth and ongoing life of the church in the Holy Spirit. In this drama human sexual identity has an important place. Indeed, sexual difference is key to our identity, both as beings created male and female in the image of God and as beings redeemed in Christ whose marriages can imitate the unity of Christ with the church. Then, too, our sexual identities are caught up in the story's arc, from creation to fall to redemption and kingdom hope, so that we are not, as sexual beings, simply good, but stand between the distorting power of sin and the healing grace of God. It is in this perspective, Humphrey says, that the Bible treats homoeroticism (as she calls it) negatively. It is one part of the world's brokenness, one sign of the distorting power of sin and the way that distortion is not chosen, but woven into the fabric of our lives.

Though the church's discipline varies, this remains its reading of scripture on homoeroticism until the twentieth century. It is only then that revisionist voices appear. They do so, Humphrey shows, roughly at the same time as laws and government policy toward homosexual practice are liberalized and public opinion shifts. Here the public mind, with its changing social mores, and the Christian mind work in concert, so that the church begins to produce readings of scripture that are in harmony with the changing attitude toward homosexual practice. This phenomenon offers us an intriguing glimpse into the relationship between the mind of the culture and the mind of the church; we can also see the potential for conflict between the public mind and the tradition of the church. The question of the relationship between church and culture, as well as its role in shaping Christian thinking, is one that will continue to surface not just in this essay, but throughout the collection.

Humphrey concludes with a survey of current readings of scripture, both classical and revisionist. Her survey, while it defends the traditional reading, also opens a window upon the debate. Points of difference between revisionist and traditionalist readings here stand out. While traditionalists tend to understand texts in light of the classical "story" about God and humanity as Humphrey sketches it, revisionists measure the texts against the truths of contemporary culture and experience. So, for instance, John Boswell (among others) argues that the present-day understanding of homosexuality as an orientation calls into question scripture's pronouncements against it (since scripture did not know homosexuality as an orientation).

In juxtaposing the contemporary traditionalist and revisionist literature, Humphrey begins to draw out the faultlines that run through the debate. One has to do with the relative weights we accord to our own individual and contemporary experience on the one hand, and to the "official" experience of the church as defined in its tradition on the other. Do we privilege contemporary experience or do we privilege tradition in our reading of scripture when they conflict? The other, and related, question concerns our orientation to the culture: In what sense does the public secular mind reveal the purposes of God? Is the public mind transparent to those purposes? To what extent is it friend or foe, kin, or alien? And how do we weight the authority of the public mind when it conflicts with the teaching of the church?

The next two essays in the collection address explicitly the second of the questions Humphrey's essay has posed: that of church and culture. John Webster and Joan O'Donovan take up two concepts, both central to the contemporary Western mind. One is human rights, the other is freedom. Both authors argue that these ideas as popularly understood run against the grain of the gospel. Good ideas when informed by a Christian vision, they have been bent to the service of a self-referential and atomizing point of view that has no root in the good news of Christ — even though it has sometimes been the church that has promoted it. Here the authors position the good news over against culture, suggesting that at least in regard to these concepts, the Christian view is properly shaped by presuppositions quite different from those that prevail in our culture.

Dr. O'Donovan faces us with a startling question: Is the concept of human rights after all the best foundation for the public good? Or does it in fact undermine the very ideals of community, equity, and public trust that it claims to serve? O'Donovan lets the history of the concept of human rights speak for itself. Here is a concept that is fundamentally atomizing, based in rights of ownership — the individual's ownership of his own being and capacities and of everything he makes with those capacities — and requiring therefore a contractual relationship to others (so that our public relationships, as in economic transactions, are determined by "calculations of self-interest"). Can such a concept create the community and public trust we desire? Does it not in the end create a society locked in an endless struggle between competing personal freedoms, in which the individual will is the only measure of good and all good is both individual and self-referential? Seen in this light, the concept of human rights seems a surprising choice for the organizing principle of a Christian society. And yet it is more and more the principle of choice, not just for the secular state, but for the Christian church within the state.

O'Donovan suggests that the Christian appropriation of rights language has been made possible by certain interpretations of God and our relation to God. These interpretations are formed by "classical liberal anthropological premises" that stress above all God's "rational, self-positing freedom" and our sharing in that freedom. So self-determination, the *sine qua non* of our culture, becomes the essence of God and of the individual as the creature made in God's image. Perhaps, this essay suggests, it is time to think about alternative understandings of the *imago Dei*, ones more in keeping with both the ancient wisdom of the church and our own hope for true community.

In "Evangelical Freedom," John Webster considers further the concept of freedom, challenging the contemporary belief that freedom is self-determination and offering an alternative and gospel-oriented vision. To be human, we believe, is to be autonomous: a law unto ourselves. This concept of freedom, Webster argues, carries with it a misperception of God. It sees in God absolute freedom and absolute power, set *over against* our own. But this is not a specifically Christian understanding of God. Webster proposes a dogmatics and an ethics of freedom that will return to the inner structure and content of Christian teaching. There we find a God whose nature is revealed in his works, in who he is *toward* his people. He is Father, Son, and Holy Spirit, creating, reconciling, perfecting: his freedom is always also an act of relation and an act of grace. It is freedom to be *for* us.

Even when we turn away from God, in our mistaken attempt to be free, God's freedom demonstrates itself "not as freedom to withdraw from fellowship, but precisely as an utter determination to maintain fellowship," a determination that culminates in the life and death and resurrection of the Son. In Christ we see "the fulfilment of the free divine resolve and promise: I will be your God, you will be my people." And as free Spirit who perfects the creature, drawing us always back into relation with God, God works toward the consummation of his fellowship with his creature.

If this is divine freedom, what is human freedom? It is to be what we have been made to be, creatures in the image of God. It is not autonomy at all, but always freedom in relation — to God, to each other, and within the givenness of our human situation. And it reflects the grace of God: our freedom is to be reconciled creatures, set free from self-absorption for fellowship with God, set free from anxiety and self-responsibility to rest in the purposes of God, set free from the concern for our own self-preservation to be radically for the other. In true freedom we are free to live for the other, to seek our neighbour's good and to find that it is here, in this act of fellowship, that we become most truly what we are. Precisely in the absence of self-determination, in our care for others' ends and not our own, are we most truly free.

It is a moving vision, startling because it cuts across the grain of our cultural presuppositions, the now almost automatic assumption that freedom is autonomy, inspiring because it rings with a passion for the gospel.

Two essays on experience follow the essays on church and culture. These essays are critical to the collection as a whole. If the tension between church and culture is a constant theme running through this debate, the role of experience is perhaps the debate's central faultline. It is in the revisionist argument that the appeal to experience flourishes, so here we listen to a revisionist analysis of the authority of experience. Christopher Lind situates the question of the authority of experience within a discussion of the different categories of experience itself and the different moral languages in which these categories are used for ethical decision-making.

Lind names four categories of experience. Experience, he says, can be religious (as in Wesley's "heart strangely warmed" or in the experience of the numinous). It can be the experience we identify as conscience — the "gut feeling" about right or wrong that we associate with a divine command. Or it can be communal, a collective experience of oppression or liberation, for instance, in which the suffering and saving God becomes known. Finally, it is often, especially now, the feelings and events of our own lives and it is authoritative because it is our own.

Lind here raises a salutary caution against a simplistic view of experience. He points out that the appeal to experience is not a new phenomenon but an ancient one, and that it is in one way or another authoritative for all of us. He points out too that it is not simply true; there is a need to decide between the competing claims of experience. One way in which we attempt to adjudicate such claims is by an appeal to the wisdom of the contemporary Christian community (as for instance in the process of determining appropriate candidates for ordination). Group experience, therefore, provides a check for the experience of the individual. Here is a variation on the old appeal to tradition: in both, the judgement of the church guides the judgement of the individual, though in this case it is the present community rather than the historical church that is authoritative.

Furthermore, experience does not stand alone. When we use experience in moral deliberation, we use it always in the context of a particular "moral language," a particular way of ordering and speaking about the world. We read our experience through the lens of a deontological or teleological or utilitarian or feminist world-view. Experience has different weights in these different languages. The point here is not the relative value of the different types of experience or of the different moral languages in which we speak from experience. It is rather to recognize the differing assumptions on which our arguments are based and the differing languages in which they are expressed. Lind suggests, too, that in a world of many different moral languages, the crucial question is which type of moral language is most useful for settling the question at hand. For the most part, the language that is most useful will be the language of the day. If we are in France, we speak French. If we are in an age of commerce, we speak the language of utilitarianism.

Here is an interesting view of the relationship between the church and the age in which Christians live. Lind recognizes that our thinking is inevitably shaped by contemporary values. Unlike O'Donovan, however, he does not object to this shaping. The wisdom of each age is neutral, the given context in which the church exists, to which and from which it speaks.

Carroll Guen Hart, in her essay on experience, goes further. She makes a strong argument for the presence of the Spirit in the wisdom of the age. It is here, in the crucible of lived experience, where the felt truths of our own lives collide with the traditional teaching of the church that the Spirit is at work. Here the Spirit draws us out of a limited vision into a new and truer one, one that speaks the gospel for our time. She hears truth in the experience of her gay and lesbian friends and she asks the church to listen.

But she asks the church to listen as it has always done: by hearing the Word of God through the combined witness of experience, scripture, tradition, and reason. The appeal to experience, while it pushes us in this instance toward a new way of seeing, in no way demands a departure from the scriptures and the tradition of the church. Rather, "experience is part and parcel of both scripture and tradition; the same complex dynamic is at work wherever we find the people of God in all ages." But the appeal to experience is specifically an appeal to the "contemporary working of the Spirit in God's creatures and in creaturely situations." It keeps us open to real life and to the new edge of a living faith.

Guen Hart supports this definition of experience as the place in which the Spirit is particularly at work with an understanding of Spirit as that which animates all beings, that breath of life that we recognize in each other as "personhood."

In our spirits, God's spirit is at work. In particular individuals, Jesus of Nazareth above all, God's spirit is at work. Spirit works to lead the church and ultimately the world into truth — that glorious freedom of the children of God in which the bonds of cult and nation, rule and law, are broken and all people come together to seek, "with and for each other," God's reality. That leading may be felt in individual and concrete experience, for the Spirit, after all, animates all things. So experience is an essential part of God's Word to us and so God's Word is always partly new. The Spirit moves in the world now as it did in the past, and the church, if it is to be true to itself, must be open to its present leading.

The life of the church is thus always lived in the tension between the old and the new. "In religious experience," Guen Hart says, "the felt experience of 'annunciations,' of possible new moves by God, exists in tension with the tradition, challenging and being challenged by it; such contemporary, felt experience is the instrument by which the inherited faith becomes new and true in our own time."

Guen Hart describes this process in the history of the church, and especially of Anglicanism. The early church's experience of the Spirit being poured out upon the Gentiles led to a new thing in the history of Israel: the inclusion of the Gentiles in the circle of the clean. In later centuries, Christians have responded to the prompting of the Spirit in their struggles against slavery and Nazism and in their openness to Darwinian science, even when it meant challenging other Christians' interpretations of scripture.

Anglicanism itself, as Guen Hart describes it, is a history of creative tension between respect for tradition and openness to the Spirit. Guen Hart points to the Methodist revival and the Tractarians, both movements that were in their own time rejected by many in the church on the grounds of scripture, tradition, and reason, but in which we now recognize the truths of scripture and the working of the Spirit.

Guen Hart suggests that this moment is a similar one: here in the voices of gay and lesbian Christians the Spirit leads the church into a fuller realization of the gospel. It is, in our time, the voice of the Lord, asking us to "step out in faith" into a new and truer understanding of the gospel, one that lives out for our day Jesus' call to healing and inclusion. In the call to bless gay sexuality, Guen Hart concludes, we see the shape of the kingdom: "the lame walk, the lepers are cleansed, the eunuch has a portion and the unclean ones are given an honoured place at the banquet."

Guen Hart's comparison of the gay movement to other developments in the church's history, such as the Oxford Movement, raises for us a new and important question: the problem of the analogy. This is a problem that will surface again in George Sumner's article on the analogy with polygamy. How do various changes in the church's practice, various historical movements, compare? In what ways, other than the fact that they represent change, are they similar and therefore mutually illuminating? Attention to detail, to "the facts on the ground", Sumner will argue, is essential. He will also suggest that analogies work in a certain way. They do not stand on their own as witnesses to the truth. Rather, they "help to shape our imagination as we read scripture." To a mind steeped in the scriptures, analogies suggest new connections that may enrich our understanding of God's word. Here Guen Hart would concur. In the interplay between the reading of scripture and the history and experience of God's people, the Word is heard.

And yet, we do not agree. In part we disagree because we weight that interplay differently: for the revisionist, as Guen Hart describes it, our own experience can bear the truth of the Spirit as fully as does the Bible. Sumner, in concert with Webster and O'Donovan, would disagree. It is possible, they would say, and indeed necessary to give the scriptures priority. For scripture is foundational, a kind of potter's wheel on which we are formed. By a constant influence it shapes us and shapes our understanding, of experience as of anything else.

In part also, we disagree because we position ourselves differently in respect to our culture. Guen Hart sees the contemporary experience of sexuality and the contemporary stress on values such as inclusion and freedom in an essentially positive light. Where the essays on church and culture charge that we have in our time — precisely, for instance, in our understanding of freedom — distorted the gospel, Guen Hart sees in our time the living Spirit, leading us into all truth.

These are different worlds, and they lead us to read the phenomenon of homosexuality quite differently. It is not surprising that the debate proves difficult.

If it is important to parse the deep and hidden differences between points of view in this debate, it is important also to ask how we shall then live. The remaining essays address the questions of church polity and pastoral care raised by an intractable debate.

That this debate threatens the unity of the church is increasingly clear. Schism and rumours of schism afflict the Anglican Communion as bishops move independently to bless same-sex unions or to consecrate roving traditionalist bishops. Archbishop Rowan Williams examines both the stresses on the Communion and the sources of its unity. Reflecting on the Primates' meeting in Porto after the irregular consecration of bishops in Singapore for American traditionalists within another bishop's diocese, Williams points out that the Primates clearly had no wish to see that consecration, or the debate about homosexuality, divide the church. They were, in typically Anglican fashion, willing to define church unity in the broadest possible terms so as to hold dioceses of differing views together. The test they proposed was acceptance of the Lambeth Quadrilateral (scripture's supremacy in doctrinal matters, the major sacraments, the creeds of the undivided church, and the historic episcopate). "Anglicanism," Williams says, "has worked on the assumption that a common ecclesial language and theological method take you a long way, and its authority has been a mixture of authoritative texts and a process of rather untidy corporate interpretation of them." It continued to work in this way at Porto. And it worked at Porto in large part because there both restraint and forbearance were the order of the day.

This is key. The classical Anglican method, which finds its unity in common prayer and corporate reflection and a common theological method, and which allows the greatest possible range of interpretation within the broad parameters of the Quadrilateral, depends upon patience and mutual respect. It depends upon collegiality. When there is no central authority other than the authoritative texts of the church and its common mind, then everything depends upon the willingness of individual bishops to speak and listen honestly, disinterestedly, and with a sense of their place in the centuries-long conversation of the church … and then to wait for a common mind to emerge.

When collegiality fails, the structure that depends upon it may fail also. For in the Anglican Communion, it is precisely that collegiality — the willingness to listen to each other and to the saints who have gone before — that is our defence against error. Williams's article leaves us with the hope that "the classical Anglican method [is] not dead yet," that we do not need the central executive power of which we have always been wary, that our peculiarly rich brand of biblical reflection and theological conversation may yet save the day.[3]

If Rowan Williams asks how Anglican Church polity works in general, Eric Beresford and George Sumner examine how it works in the specific instance. Beresford treats the current debate; Sumner the African churches' response to polygamy and the analogy often drawn between that response and the questions raised for the church by homosexual practice.

Beresford sketches the political history of the debate about homosexuality. He frames this history in terms of a distinction between debate and dialogue. Debate, he says, is necessarily oppositional. It seeks truth and wants to separate truth from positions that obscure it. It works by a process of argumentation and produces in the end winners and losers. Dialogue, on the other hand, begins from and seeks community. It assumes a shared history and a common ground, and it works by the telling and hearing of the community's story.

This particular story, as he tells it, is one marked more by debate than by dialogue, one marked also by acrimony and division. Though each country in which the question of same-sex relationships has emerged has handled that question differently, each one, and indeed the whole Communion, finds itself to some degree embattled. On the national level, the debate has sometimes taken the form of both guided conversation and the introduction of more or less official liturgies for blessing same-sex relationships. Both the process of conversation and the liturgical acts have created controversy. This tension is reflected on an international level in the Primates' continuing discussions, especially at Lambeth in 1998. There the discussion was fractious and its tone often harsh; there too the geographical divide that characterizes the debate became clear. The call to bless same-sex relationships hails from the global north; bishops of Africa and Asia not only have other, more pressing concerns (poverty, civil war, famine and AIDS, crippling national debt and government corruption, for example) but also resist what they see as a challenge to scripture. The conservative motion that eventually passed at Lambeth reflected in part this perspective. Although the motion passed overwhelmingly, Beresford points out that it has done little to secure the unity of the Communion. Both events that have been most obviously damaging to the church's unity — the Singapore consecrations and Motion 7 and its aftermath in New Westminster — occurred after Lambeth 1998.

Since then the Primates have shifted their attention from the specific question of homosexuality to questions about the nature of the church, its structures, and the theology that shapes its common life. Beresford suggests that it is these broad questions — the search for the meaning of community — that are the most fruitful for the Primates, who have in any case no real international jurisdiction. To expect the Primates at Lambeth or the Anglican Consultative Council to settle the specific disputes of the church is to ask more from these structures than they can deliver. The Anglican Church is loosely organized, with each province having its own structure and an authority residing in its particular constitution and canons. At its most recent meeting the ACC recognized this loose structure and also its hope for communion, asking that dioceses avoid unilateral actions without reference to the province, and that provinces act with the wider Communion in mind. They asked, in other words, for mutual respect and for a sense of community.

It is not by *fiat* from above that we will be held together, Beresford suggests, but by a common concern for the Communion in which we all share. It is with this plea for a sense of community that Beresford ends. The debate, he points out, and the fissures that threaten the church, would not be so painful if we did not care for the Communion that is now at risk. The church's hope, he says, lies in this care. If we can remember our underlying community, that common life in which we all share, we may find the will to preserve it even through the conflicts that arise within it.

George Sumner, in an article offering insight into many aspects of the debate, takes up the question of church polity through the lens of the analogy with polygamy. The moral analogy has been, as he puts it, a "weapon of choice" in the battle over same-sex unions. It has been used to determine how the church should act as well as how it should think about homosexual practice. Sumner argues that in the case of polygamy, the right analogy has been used to draw the wrong conclusions. Liberals propose that, as the African church has changed its view of polygamy, so we now can rethink homosexual practice. But this misreads what actually happened. The change in question was a softening of pastoral practice, not a rethinking of doctrine. The question was not, "Is polygamy a positive good?" but rather, "What is the best pastoral response given this human situation (the widespread African practice of polygamy)?" The answers varied, but looked to a care for the people involved and to patience with the vagaries of human sexual conduct.

Thus the comparison with polygamy, Sumner argues, does not

suggest that we should rethink the doctrine of marriage so as to encompass homosexual practice within it. It suggests exactly the opposite: that from a position of doctrinal clarity on marriage we are free to respond to the pastoral exigencies of the human situation. The real fruit of the analogy, Sumner suggests, lies not in doctrinal debate but in the nurture of the virtues. It calls us to patience and humility: a humility that refrains from the politics of power and a patience that bears with the brokenness of the world.

Beresford calls us to a rediscovery of community. Williams and Sumner both call us to patience and humility. The church works, they seem to say, when it practises these difficult virtues. It is these virtues and an accompanying call to community that inform the two visions of pastoral care that follow. The authors, Patrick Yu and David Reed, see the situation of the church in which pastoral care must be offered somewhat differently. But they both propose a program to which patience is fundamental: the honest patience that recognizes the real disagreement within the church, a disagreement stemming from different underlying theologies, and the deep patience that "welcomes sinners ... to [the] table."[4]

Patrick Yu situates the question of pastoral care within a divided church. We live between two sexual ethics and two ways of understanding homosexuality. How, in this tension, do we practise pastoral care? His answer respects the tension insofar as it calls people to the kind of friendship and demanding ethical discussion that may lead us into truth, and in the meantime will reflect the grace of Christ.

Friendship is the first task of pastoral care, a friendship that imitates the wide welcome of the Christ. Drawing on the biblical image of God as shepherd and on the stories of Jesus' life — his capacity for meeting people where they were, his patience with human failure, and his tendency always to let grace come before judgement — Yu calls for a pastoral care that is equally flexible and responsive to the human situation. Let grace, he says, precede judgement and so (like the shepherd) draw people in, let the church's message be good news as well as challenge. It is only in friendship that we can both support and challenge each other in the practice of Christian living, so that the good news can be not only welcoming but also redemptive. And friendship is the task of the whole people.

A concomitant task, in a church that disagrees, is that of conversation. Dr. Yu charges that we have abdicated our responsibility as Christian individuals and as a community to take ethical questions seriously. We are, he says, afraid to discuss controversial issues in our churches and ill equipped to deal with the theological questions such issues raise. He suggests a program of honest conversation in parish settings by which the church may come to a true common mind on homosexual practice, rather than leaving the question to the essentially political forum of General Synod. This engagement with the gospel and with each other as fellow Christians, the patience and mutual respect it requires, and the risk it involves, is one part of what it means for the church to practise pastoral care in the present situation.

David Reed sees the situation in which the church must offer pastoral care rather differently. While Yu describes a church divided, Reed presents a church not so much divided as embattled, within and without. Christians in the church have little sense of their own history and little knowledge of the Bible; they lack a Christian mind. At the same time, the culture surrounds the church with values and presuppositions that have no root in the gospel. We live as Christians, he says, in a foreign culture.

In this context the task of pastoral care is partly a missionary one: to reclaim for the church the Christian vision of life and to proclaim it by word and deed to a culture that does not understand it. It is a ministry in four parts — healing, sustaining, guiding, and reconciling — that challenges at the same time that it welcomes and offers comfort. Both discipline and friendship are its tasks. It takes seriously, that is, the divine purpose as well as the human situation, and seeks to draw all people into God's reign. In the case of sexual ethics, a truly pastoral church will proclaim the now counter-cultural Christian vision of chaste living for all, as well as the hope that in such a discipline we may find "the gladness of the gospel."

Reed leaves us with two challenges. He asks us to be the kind of caring community in which alone real sustaining and real reconciling are possible. Like Dr. Yu, he asks us to be friends to all who come in. Secondly, he asks us to *be* the church, to have a Christian heart and mind, to understand that in Christ we follow a different vision. In this way we can uphold the normative Christian vision for sexual living as for anything else, while also being patient with the human condition, that condition in which we so often fall short of the mark. He would have the church offer a wide mercy to the individuals who come its way without giving up the vision that informs its doctrine and liturgy. It is in its doctrine and liturgy that the church can exercise the discipline that draws people into God's purpose. And it is in its communal life that the church can practise the sustaining friendship that draws people into the love of God. In this joint practice of patient discipline and humble love we are most truly the church.

With this call to be the church we come full circle, back to the problem with which we began. For we do not agree on what it means to be the church. We do not agree on what exactly is broken in the church and in our sexual lives or on the shape of a church that is a fitting harbinger of the kingdom. Ought we to be patient with homosexual practice, seeing it as one manifestation among many of a fallen world, or ought we to bless it, seeing in it the presence of the Spirit and the holiness of the good creation? In the pages of this collection we see something of the different visions and the reasons for the differences.

Catherine Sider Hamilton
Advent 2002

Notes

1   See Jeffrey Satinover, *Homosexuality and the Politics of Truth* (Grand Rapids, MI: Baker, 1996), for a disturbing description of the political process behind the decision of the American Psychiatric Association to remove homosexuality from its list of disorders.

2   I have chosen, for the sake of clarity, to use the shorthand terms "traditionalist" and "revisionist" for the two arguments, although neither term does justice to the nuances of each approach. The strength of these terms, as opposed to "liberal" and "conservative," for example, is that they locate the disagreement in the realm of authority, where I believe it belongs. The traditionalist, while not seeking merely to preserve the tradition but to proclaim a living faith, nevertheless finds in the shape of the tradition the governing paradigm for that proclamation. The revisionist does not seek merely to revise the faith, but to represent it in terms consistent with contemporary experience and values so that it is contemporary wisdom that provides the touchstone for interpretation.

3   The Archbishop's hope offers an encouraging contrast to the less sanguine vision of Cardinal Newman, whom Anglicanism was unable to hold. Newman concluded that we are not capable of finding the truth, no matter how rich our theological conversation. The church, he suggests, must possess in her very structure the authority to defy that assault of evil upon the truth that reaches even into the mind of humankind. (See J.H. Newman, *Apologia Pro Vita Sua* [London: Penguin Books, 1994].)

4   *Book of Alternative Services* (Toronto: Anglican Book Centre, 1985), p. 191.

Scripture

Same-Sex Eroticism and the Church

Classical Approaches and Responses

Edith Humphrey

There is good reason to query the need for another discussion of the church's traditional understanding(s) of the scriptures on same-sex eroticism. We can anticipate an irritated response from the revisionist: "Here we go again!" Alternately we can imagine, from the traditionalist, an echo of the dominical exclamation: "They have Moses and the prophets. If they will not listen to them ...." Yet, it must be admitted that there is today, even in the church, an anti-historicism and a resultant amnesia regarding the words of the ancients, our older siblings in the faith. Despite lip-service paid to the importance of common ecclesial experience, fewer and fewer Christians know church history (especially the history of the patristic period) well.

In view of our generation's ignorance of the past, and because it is difficult to hear the contemporary conversation from within what seems to be a situation of urgency, this chapter is offered as a summary of classical approaches to the reading of scripture on this issue from the first century until today. For the sake of clarity, we begin by discussing methodological questions regarding the interplay of scriptures and tradition, next consider the scriptural texts and related ancient writings, then look into how scripture has been read in the past, and finish with a sampling of contemporary traditional interpretations of the Bible on this issue.

Approaching the Question

Before looking at the classical readings of scripture on homosexuality, it is important to consider how Christians have variously approached the entire question of authority. Scripture is key in the debate about homosexuality precisely because the church has, since her beginning, understood the Bible to be authoritative for both theology and ethics. But how do we hear the Word of God in scripture? Various traditions have given different answers as to the manner in which scripture is related to the Word of God, and therefore authoritative. *Sola scriptura* is the Protestant cry, so that the Word of God and the scriptures are commonly seen as identical; Roman Catholics hold to the two separate but complementary rules of scripture and tradition. The Anglican Communion is more diverse, including under its roof those who hold to both the Protestant and Roman views. Frequently Anglican theologians have spoken of scripture as one leg of the famous "three-legged stool": scripture, tradition, and reason. Even more recently, theologians within the Anglican Communion have added experience to that stool, citing the so-called "Wesleyan Quadrilateral" (of which, in its contemporary formulation, the Wesleys would have been most skeptical). There would appear, in these different approaches, to be a conflict about how exactly scripture is authoritative. Ought it to stand on its own (the Protestant *sola scriptura*) or is it properly coupled with tradition (the Roman emphasis on church together with scripture)? Does it make sense to speak about reason and experience as additional sources of authority? Can experience, for instance, trump scripture?

This dilemma about "which authorities" may well be a false one. Reflection upon the four elements of scripture, tradition, reason, and experience will disclose that they are related, but not symmetrical in their interplay. After all, reason is the human tool by which we read and understand scripture, by which we discern and transmit tradition, and by which we interpret and classify experience. Experience is, it seems, the personal (and often prereflective) raw material for what passes into the church's common tradition: or, put the other way, tradition is the common, approved, and living experience of God's people. It is also that pattern of reasoned reflection upon scripture that has, over time, shaped the church's understanding. This is surely the case in both Protestant and Roman approaches to authority, although the first leans formally upon *sola scriptura*, while the latter accepts two authorities. At the very least, then, tradition is the matrix within which the scriptures are received, read, passed on, and understood. Consistent or "holy" tradition would then represent the continuing thought and practice of the people of God, who seek to have the mind of Christ. This approach, representative of much Eastern Christian thought, may be of help in moving Western Christendom beyond its impasse of "which authorities."

Much attention has been devoted in the past few decades to the scripture as "narrative" or "story." Frequently this trend has been understood as a movement away from an oracular approach, and toward a "freedom" that befits God's people. But even as story, scripture has power to shape our lives. Narrative is not unconnected to proposition; it is false to suggest that story has no message. In reading the biblical stories, and its overarching narrative, we must not solely ask, as the aesthete might of a poem, "How does it mean?" since "What does it mean?" is also a significant question. Some have assumed that, if scripture is mostly narrative, it cannot be responded to as an authority: but this would be simplistic. A narrative's authority is different from that of a mere precept, for it appeals to the imagination as well as to the mind and will. Indeed, a story held in common, and most particularly, God's story embracing humanity, sets an authoritative pattern that gives life, changing the person and the community from the inside out. In this survey, it will become apparent that sometimes the scriptures have been approached more as sheer law than as narrative, and tradition more as bare precept than as the continuation of the divine story. To admit the hermeneutical failings of our forebears is not, however, a substitute for our faithful judgement today. We too are called to discern the pattern of God's story, and respond to its direction of the church.

Earliest Treatments:
The Scriptures and Related Literature

Before we look at the classical readings of scripture on homosexuality, let us begin by sketching out the classical story itself. The story of scripture can be understood in five great acts.[1] Act One tells us about a creator God. Act Two speaks of a good creation gone askew by death and sin. Act Three presents the call of the nation Israel to be a light to the world. Act Four is the central episode that questions, illuminates, and transforms the drama: it shows how the calling of Israel and all humanity was fulfilled in a surprising and crucial way in the coming, life, death, resurrection, and ascension of Jesus the Christ. Act Five, in which we find ourselves, describes the ongoing life and healing mission of the church through the Holy Spirit. We await the finale of this drama, but are given intimations of God's purposes for his people and the entire cosmos. This drama of God's coming to be with us, for us and in us, is presented in the Bible's many forms — narrative, law, gospel, psalm, epistle, apocalypse.

We learn this story intimately, so that we can play an authentic part in it. Particularly important to a faithful reading of scripture is the recognition of this "we" factor: the scriptures insist that God's Word is to be heard not privately, but by the whole community, past and present. To recognize that the human authors of the scriptures wrote in particular historical contexts says nothing in itself about how the Bible is to be used in any particular controversy in the church today. The problem of moving from the context of the original writer to application today should not be used as a pretext for bypassing explicit teaching or perspectives that we find difficult or "quaint." Rather, in each case, we are to read all the pertinent texts carefully, with the voices of earlier Christians and creedal discussions in our memory. Even where we see that a prescriptive passage is particular to a moment in the history of God's people (e.g., prohibition of pork or head coverings for women), we must respect the underlying theological/ethical truths. Some prescriptions have an enduring claim (e.g., the command not to murder) because they are inextricable from what has been revealed to us about the world, our nature, and the nature of God. A faithful reading of scripture thus means that we seek to understand how the passages that we are reading at the moment, and the questions that we are presently asking, fit into this forgiving, healing, and life-giving drama that has been initiated by God himself.

Human Sexuality in the Scriptures

Before considering how same-sex eroticism is understood in the biblical texts, we must consider what they say about human sexuality in general. Though "sexuality" is a recent construct, a working definition can be offered: sexuality is, in part, what makes us both distinct and inherently inter-related as male and female. Thus sexuality would include, but not be limited to, physical aspects, and biological "sex" would be a component of "gender." Several clues to the complex nature of our sexuality are given in scripture itself.

From the creation narrative or narratives we learn that our human sexual differences are key to our identity. Genesis 1:27 stresses both diversity and unity: "So God created Adam in his image, in the image of God he created him, male and female he created them." Again in Genesis 2 and 3, God is said to have created Adam and Eve with equal dignity, in a complementary but asymmetrical relationship. This relationship is presented as part of the initial and perfect will of God: "It is not good for the man to be alone"; "Therefore a man leaves his father and his mother and clings to his wife, and they become one flesh." Sexual distinctions are thus part of God's good (very good! 1:31) creation. Yet sexuality has also been deeply affected by sin and by divinely imposed limitations. The judgement declared for disobedience — "You shall surely die" — is partly fulfilled in their complicated inter-relations, in which healthy interdependence becomes authoritarianism or co-dependence. Yet the bond created in the beginning between husband and wife still retains its original stamp of goodness. Eve becomes the "mother of the living," and in their harsher surroundings human beings learn the wonder of inter-dependence and dependence upon the One who has made them in two sexes.

Clearly, sexuality is not tangential, but a great gift and a powerful instrument for good or ill. Here, in our most common and most demanding relationship, we see a powerful symbol of the relationship that God desires with us as the body of Christ. Single and married people alike know that the relationship between male and female is a "given" in life, but also that it is difficult. So the epigram: "Marriage is the only war in which you sleep with the enemy." The popular recognition of a "war of the sexes" sits uneasily side by side with expressions of the "religion of love" found in practically every age and tirelessly promulgated in pop culture. The one view grasps disharmonious sexuality without acknowledging its fundamental integrity. The second lays on human love a burden it cannot bear, romantically ignoring human fallibility. Among other scriptural witnesses, Hosea, Ephesians 5, and Revelation 21–22 teach us that the highest purpose of human sexuality is to serve in marriage as an icon of God's relationship with his people. This perspective is lost in our society's idealization of romantic sexual encounters.

In contrast, the Bible presents sexuality as a divinely prescribed mode of being for human beings, valuable in itself and in its iconic representation of divine-human relations. From the beginning, sexuality entailed interdependence, companionship, and procreation; the distortion and strained fulfilment of these good things, subsequent to the Fall, has not completely thwarted that original intent.

In the New Testament marriage becomes more than a simple pictorial reminder of God's desired intimacy with his people (as in the Old Testament), and takes on a "sacramental" significance. Now, the relationship between husband and wife tangibly indicates the life of Christ with the church, and actually partakes of it, as does voluntary and devoted celibacy. Thus, Jesus affirms both the complementarity of man and woman in God-ordained marriage, and celibacy as faithful lifestyles under God's rule (Mt 19:3–13). Indeed the whole New Testament values the single life as a sign that human sexual relationships are less than the final or ultimate good, given humankind's more foundational need for a right relationship with God. It finds in celibacy a witness at least as potent as marriage. The glory of marriage is such that an unbelieving partner may mysteriously be touched by a godly spouse (1 Cor 7); singleness has its special place in the healing of humanity and is a gift to the community of the church. The glory of marriage — and celibacy too — is to share in the shape of the life of Christ. In this sense, acts of toil and sacrifice, such as a husband's toil for his partner, and a woman's pain in bearing children, take on dignity: they are glory-tinged by the toil and pain of the incarnate Jesus. And the celibate joins Jesus in single-minded witness to the coming kingdom. In the "last Adam" the curse of sin, sorrow, pain, and death has lost its sting. Amid other signs of healing and reconciliation, the barrier or strain between the sexes is lifted in Christ ("there is no male and female"). Yet we still await that new age in which there will be no mourning, pain, or death. Until that new age arrives our lives (in fullness and in deprivation) are being worked into God's plan.

So we see that marriage, as well as other forms of communion, is a demanding relationship: dependence and trust are seen as essential to our being. Because we are fallen creatures, these lessons will involve pain, and sometimes will be taught inversely (that is, by our experience of the opposite of trust and dependence), yet they are invaluable. As with our membership in God's church, we should not approach marriage simply as a "voluntary association," but as an inviolable covenant in good times and in trouble, when the other is strong in fidelity or not. Similarly, a faithful decision to be celibate and yet in dynamic and life-giving relationships with persons of both genders is an arduous calling of great benefit to both the celibate person and the community of God. Both godly lifestyles, when lived out consistently, are potent expressions of the surprising truth that in Christ God has done something about "hardness of heart" (cf. Mt 19:8, 11–12). This perspective renders faithful marriage and celibacy a creative adventure in which God's grace is enacted, rather than an abhorrent or impossible lifestyle choice that impinges upon our freedom.

Amidst current assumptions that sexuality is for the purpose of self-gratification, the church's different attitude toward this great gift is bound to be a strong sign in the world of God's love and righteousness.

The Scriptures Speak on Same-Sex Eroticism

As we consider the biblical meta-narrative, and our place as sexual beings within this story, we are led to a dual response — we celebrate God's good creation and saving work in the world, while fully admitting the sin and disorder within us and the world at large. We must understand any problem that we face in light of this entire story: God is completely truthful and utterly tender-hearted toward humanity. Any discussion of the scriptures and same-sex eroticism should consider both this pattern of God's story and several specific biblical texts. It is interesting that none of the relevant scriptural texts tackle the issue as a primary topic in itself. Yet the pertinent passages are found in different genres and are spread throughout both testaments: one Old Testament narrative (probably) refers to homoerotic activity; short legal texts condemn it; two pastoral texts list it among other vices; and one longer New Testament passage treats it within a larger theological discussion. We need to situate all of these texts within the overall story of God's creating and recreating work.

On some matters, such as female ministry and slavery, scripture speaks with various voices. But there is no internal tension among the passages that speak of homoerotic behaviour. The Genesis narrative, the "Holiness Code" of Leviticus, the lists of dark behaviours in the epistles, and the more extensive illustration of Romans 1 all register disapproval. Moreover, the New Testament material cannot be dismissed by an appeal to cultural conditioning, as in the question of head-covering for women in Paul's first letter to the Corinthians. The biblical teaching regarding homoerotic behaviour is not unconsciously coloured by cultural norms; rather, the New Testament in particular adopts a decisive countercultural stand against behaviour frequently condoned and sometimes idealized in the surrounding Hellenistic culture.

The first pertinent text is the narrative of Genesis 18:16—19:29 (and a similar story in Judges 19) in which the men of Sodom demand that Lot hand over his guests (angelic visitors, as it happens) so that they may "know" them. Some, following Sherwin Bailey, have argued that the sin of Sodom was not a sexual one, but a breach of hospitality. Bailey argues that the Hebrew verb *yada* (to know) does not always carry sexual connotations.[2] While this is true, this observation is beside the point in a passage that clearly has to do with sexual intercourse (Lot rather chillingly offers his daughters as a substitute, inviting the men to "do with them what you wish"). It is true, however, that gang rape is the specific intended sin in this story. Thus, one cannot speak from this story alone about homoerotic behaviour *per se*, although the story of Sodom has frequently been used to condemn it. Wherever the biblical tradition mentions Sodom (Isa 1:10 ff., Jer 23:14, Ezek 16:49ff.), it speaks more about hypocrisy, falsehood, arrogance and the like, than it does about sexual sin.[3] As Judaism and Christianity later encountered Hellenistic acceptance of homoeroticism, this latent element in the Genesis story was highlighted: several second-century BC texts (discussed below) cite Sodom as an example of sexual perversion, and are probably echoed by Jude 7 and 2 Peter (though these do not discuss homoeroticism directly). At any rate, it is from these texts and the continuing tradition that we derive the term "sodomy." The story of Sodom, then, became a colourful illustration of sexual sin among both Jewish and Christian communities, although this was not its most obvious point.

To derive ethics from narrative is a delicate business. Equally complex is the use of Old Testament injunctions by the new covenant community. Though prescriptive, Leviticus 18:22 and 20:13 must be read carefully, for they form part of the Holiness Code, many of whose prescriptions or prohibitions have to do with cultic practices of ancient Israel no longer binding on Christians. That many of the Levitical laws are no longer binding on the church, however, is no grounds to dismiss all its instruction.

The question to ask is, How does the general pattern of the scriptures direct us to understand this Levitical prohibition? Do we place homoerotic behaviour in the same category as the prohibition of non-kosher foods and the twining together of two types of thread; or, do we hear it, like the prohibition of incest (18:6–18), addressing our behaviour today? The distinctions of "cultic" and "moral," "culturally-specific" and "general" are helpful here.

Amidst its understanding of a new covenant, the early church continued to follow the lead of the Hebrew Bible with regard to sexual ethics. For example, when the first-century Corinthian church assumed that their status in Christ (i.e., their spiritual maturity) gave them license to misbehave, Paul challenged them: "Do you not know that evildoers will not inherit the kingdom of God?" (1 Cor 6:9). The letter then illustrates by reference to those who steal, get intoxicated, scorn what is holy, pursue general sexual immorality, and practise two types of homoerotic behaviour. These, Paul comments, were the practices of some Corinthians, but these people have been transformed by God.

It is the two words used by Paul for same-sex behaviour, *malakoi* and *arsenokoitai*, that should give us pause. The latter term *arsenokoitai* is a compound word derived from our Levitical texts. The Septuagint translates Leviticus 20:13 ("[If] a man lies with a male as with a woman ...") with the Greek words *meta arsenos koiten gynaikos* (literally, with a man lying as with a woman). *Arsenokoitai* thus means, following Leviticus, "those (men) who lie with a male." Paul's judgement that homosexual behaviour is immoral therefore derives from and continues in the Levitical tradition. The term *malakoi* is less technical, and means literally "soft ones"; it is found in other Greek documents, usually with a slur intended, to refer to those exhibiting various types of sexual indulgence, but often refers explicitly to the passive partner in a homoerotic relationship.[4]

Romans 1:18–32 provides the longest and most significant treatment of our subject, since Paul pursues in this text a serious theological argument. His canvas is very large (as it is throughout Romans), for he depicts the human situation. His chief aim in chapter 1 is not to teach ethics, but to describe the human condition of sin, idolatry, and rebellion. He begins with our God who creates. A wonder of the created order is that by its nature it provides a window through which God's glory can be seen (verse 20). This open window, however, has been rejected by humanity. Thus in verse 21, Paul depicts the foundation of human sinfulness as wilfulness that gives neither honour nor thanks to the creating God.[5]

But true atheism is not possible for a creature made to worship: loyalties are simply exchanged by the suppression of truth, so that "creatures" rather than God are worshipped (verse 23). God's response to this senseless idolatry is to "let go" ("therefore," verses 24, 26) and permit the natural consequences. Paul gives a first, vivid example of this fallout: human passions are disturbed and the primary created relationship (male and female) is distorted. This distortion is played out in homoerotic behaviour, by both male and the female (verses 24, 26–27). Paul thus uses homoerotic behaviour as an example of what has happened to humanity in terms of the body and the passions. He then goes on to consider disordered mind, and the sins that spring from that locale (verses 28–31).

Thus Paul presents homoerotic activity (including lesbianism) as symptomatic of the primal rebellion against God, alongside other symptoms such as covetousness, murder, strife, gossip, deceit, disloyalty, and pride. It indicates a primary breach between the two partners designed for each other. As an act, homosexual relations dramatize the human rejection of God's purposes that affects all of us in various ways. It is a pointer, or diagnostic tool, of the human condition.

The primal sin, then, is the refusal to thank God and worship: homoerotic behaviour is one of the consequences, pointing back to that first mis-step. Some have pleaded that since Paul simply uses homoeroticism as an illustration, it is inappropriate to derive ethics from his argument. This can hardly be so. Would anyone apply the same logic to the other signs of depravity (evil, murder, and so forth) cited here? Paul assumes agreement that homoerotic activity is not right because of the way that God has created humanity — what he has to say about a fallen and judged world cannot be followed if the reader does not agree with him here. In fact, Paul treats homoerotic activity in terms of the overall story of God's dealings with humanity — which is the method that we have enjoined for the Christian community when tackling specific issues.

Paul's story is told with passion and with pathos in order to point to the profundity of depravity, shared by all humanity, Jew and Gentile. He then goes on to establish the utter justice and mercy of God, who has triumphed over sin and death in Jesus. Though the passage is theological, pointing to God, and not primarily ethical, it has strong words to say about the condition of human beings, who need both forgiveness and healing. Those who have a sober view of their disorder and sinfulness, as exemplified in all these signs, are those who can also receive God's medicine.

Biblical texts, then, need to be read in terms of their genre, and in terms of the overall story of the scriptures. The Genesis narrative, because of its nature, and the Levitical passages, because of their possible qualification by the new covenant, must be considered alongside other passages. The lists in 1 Corinthians and 1 Timothy indicate that the early Christian communities retained Old Testament views regarding sexuality immorality. They did so, as Paul shows us in Romans, not simply out of habit nor because they had a limited knowledge of God's ways, but for theological reasons: they understood God as creator, whose nature and purposes are visible in the created order. And they understood sexual immorality of this kind as a sign of the disruption of the good created order.

As Larry Hurtado notes, "no one should expect an easy affirmation of same-sex relationships by anyone sensitive to the Christian tradition and biblical witness."[6] This is because the scripture, both in its overall presentation of creation and in its explicit passages, does not approve same-sex erotic behaviour. There is something more to be said, however. In the past, some Christian writers have noted the clear disapproval of homoerotic behaviour, and the fire of Paul's discussion (as well as the language about "abomination" in Leviticus). They have assumed that Paul's passion is directed solely toward homoerotic behaviour, and missed the overall thrust of the apostle's argument. A careful reading of the beginning of Romans will not stop short at a mere proscription of homoeroticism. Paul indeed goes on in Romans 2 to pull the rug out from under any who would use his list of vices to take pride in their own "righteousness."[7]

Homoerotic behaviour may be fallen and sinful, but so too is the self-righteous condemnation of others by those who are not so tempted, yet are prey to other sins. For Paul, both self-righteousness and sexual sin are to be abjured; fidelity requires holding together God's justice and mercy. Paul's treatment of the issue within his letter to the Romans, then, serves as an apt conclusion to the scriptural metanarrative, in which we learn about how a faithful God has taken the initiative to forgive, and to give new life. All, Jew or Gentile, male and female, are called in Jesus to join God's new community of light: to answer that call means to repent, to be forgiven, and to accept healing, wherever that is needed.

Related Early Documents, Jewish and Christian

In addition to the Bible, there are other Jewish and Christian writings that deal specifically with same-sex eroticism, written during the four hundred years surrounding the "turn of the eras" — that is, from about 200 BC to AD 200. While one cannot easily look to such documents to establish an authoritative "tradition" of interpretation for the church, they are essential in helping us to understand how these Jewish and Christian communities handled the issue. In fact, because many of these texts were written at a time proximate to the widespread practice of homoerotic behaviour in the Greek period, they deal with this more squarely than either Hebrew Bible or New Testament books. Again (cf. "Naphtali" and Romans 1), some have actually made a mark upon texts that did become authoritative in the Christian tradition.

The Wisdom of Solomon (first century BC–mid first century AD) is accepted as authoritative by some Christian traditions. Like Paul, the author of this book links confusion about God with the confusion of good and evil. Like Paul, the author was surrounded by a society of those who knew neither the Torah nor the character of the God of Israel. Chapter 14 details various types of "godless" behaviour, including child sacrifice, breaking the sanctity of marriage, and sexual irregularity (literally, "changing of kind," *geneseōs enallagē*, verse 26), alongside other "foreign customs" and "disorders" (see especially verses 22–31.) The term *geneseōs enallagē* used here is one that includes same-sex eroticism, but also alludes to other "genre confusions," including bestiality and the strange story of the angelic "watchers" who had concourse with human women. (There is a whole tradition on the latter story that grows out of, or alongside, Genesis 6:3). During its litany on depravity, Wisdom of Solomon also recognizes the "mercy" of God. However, throughout this section there is a marked difference in tone from Paul's letters, as the author of Wisdom consistently distinguishes clearly between "them" (pagans who act unnaturally and sin) and "us" (who "will not sin," 15:5). Here is a writer keenly aware of the distinction between Hebrew Bible morality and what he sees in Hellenistic culture. For him, acceptance by God seems to rest more upon human effort than it does for Paul, who emphasizes God's mighty redemptive act in Jesus: the book knows about creation and the true God of Israel, but not yet about the critical turning point in our great story. It is clear that Paul was informed by this passage, or by other very similar arguments, for he uses the same language. In going further than Wisdom, Paul does not "correct" the traditional abhorrence of sin. Rather, he places the discussion of the Fall in a larger context — that of the gospel's cross and resurrection. "They's" are transformed by God into "we's." And "we's" are placed in that category only by the mercy of God, not because of any innate difference in character from those originally outside of the household of God.

The ancient apocalyptic corpus *1 Enoch* fills in the Genesis 6 tradition of the "watchers," those celestial beings who transgressed Torah boundaries by uniting with human women, producing "unnatural" offspring (10:9ff., 106:14–17). The conceptual link with the story of Sodom is obvious here (angels "knowing" humans; humans seeking to "know" angels), and this idea of mixed categories is found in books roughly contemporary with the Enoch corpus, including *Jubilees, The Testaments of the Twelve Patriarchs,* and *3 Maccabees. Jubilees* 20:5, "The Testament of Naphtali" 3:3–5, and *3 Maccabees* 2:3–5 explicitly link the transgression of the watchers with that of Sodom, emphasizing uncleanness and bold self-confidence. One quotation suffices:

> You destroyed men for their wicked deeds in the past, among them giants relying on their own strength and self-confidence, upon whom you brought an immeasurable flood of water. When the inhabitants of Sodom acted insolently and became notorious for their crimes you burned them up with fire and brimstone and made them an example to later generations.[8]

The link between sexual transgression of boundaries and arrogance may be obscure to us: these are connected because transgression requires a disregarding of God's created order, and therefore of God's will. Other pseudepigraphal writings proscribe different kinds of homoerotic behaviour without mentioning the watchers story, namely *Psalms of Solomon* 2:3; 2:13–15, *Aristeas* 151–153, *Sibylline Oracles* 3:185, and *2 Enoch* 10:4. Of these, all are confidently dated prior to the writing of the New Testament, with the possible exception of *2 Enoch*, whose dating is uncertain. They give us insight into Jewish attitudes in the Second Temple period concerning homoerotic behaviour, with which much (though not all) of Hellenistic society was comfortable. As the books were transmitted through the early Christian tradition, they set up a tradition of interpretation that became widespread in the early church. Christianity redefined the ideas of what was clean and unclean (Mark 8, Acts 15) but never abandoned the basic concept of created boundaries and sexual appropriateness.

There is, however, a difference in tone and in the definition of God's people between these writings and the New Testament. Paul, for example, does not wax eloquent about hell-fire. More foundationally, God's people are constituted by inclusion in Christ, in his death and resurrection, rather than by birth and adherence to Torah. 2 Peter 2:6–10 is the closest in tone of the New Testament documents to these writings, linking the stories of the watchers and Sodom in the traditional manner, and speaking of "licentiousness," "lawlessness," "indulgence of the flesh in depraved lust," and "despised authority." Yet the unequivocal critique ends this way: "The Lord is ... patient with you, not wanting any to perish, but all to come to repentance" (3:9). The tone differs, as does the longing for complete human redemption, but the judgement upon homoerotic activity, alongside other practices that harm the flesh, remains consistent.

Roughly contemporary to the New Testament writings are those of Philo (20 BC–AD 50) and Josephus (AD 37– c. 100). Philo writes a commentary upon the Torah (*Laws*, Book 3) that applies the Levitical proscription of homoerotic behaviour to his own Alexandrian context. Sections 37–42 of this work are colourfully pejorative not only of the behaviour, but also of the character and mannerisms of those who follow the Greek habits. He uses the term "pederasty" to refer to these: it needs to be remembered that in his day this term did not refer to sexual abuse of children, but to the common association of mature males with teenaged same-sex lovers. His objection to the practice is not simply that the young are being preyed upon, but that the male is being made to take on the characteristics of the female in the sexual act. In another work, *Questions and Answers on Genesis*, Philo offers an imaginative description of life in Sodom that fills in the gaps of the more reserved Genesis story in such a way as to highlight the decadence of his own day. His appeal to the natural order *(physis)* is basic to his argument, but the treatment goes far beyond philosophy and ethics to unrestrained condemnation and exhortation.

The historian Josephus's treatment of homoeroticism is more measured, as we might expect, given his apologetic purpose — the commendation of Judaism to the Roman world. However, he is not prepared to conciliate his reader by misrepresenting the Jewish response to this issue; nor, indeed, would this have been an overwhelming temptation for the writer, since Roman society was less generally welcoming of homoerotic practice than Greece had been in its heyday. In *Antiquities* 1:199–202, Josephus tells the story of Sodom, first stressing the unsociability of the Sodomites, but then indicating the sexual character of their intention against the angelic visitors. He attributes Sodom's destruction to God's indignation against the citizens' atrocities (including sexual immorality). Both Philo and Josephus, then, read the story of Sodom as connected with homoeroticism, though Josephus does not sermonize. The consistency of their approaches, connected with other second Temple material, attests to a long-standing tradition in Jewish exegesis, one which is maintained vigorously in later rabbinic material (cf. *Midrash Rabbah* 50.5, a sixth-century work, and Rashi's eleventh-century commentary on Genesis 19). The earlier Mishnah, though it does not characterize the sins of Sodom as homoerotic, does proscribe same-sex activity as it upholds Levitical law (e.g., *M. Sanhedrin* 7:4).

This continuous position in Judaism was paralleled by the growing body of Christian texts that proscribed homoerotic behaviour, sometimes in harsher terms than the New Testament texts. The *Apocalypse of Paul*, for example, adopts language that recalls both Genesis and Romans ("those who committed the iniquity of Sodom and Gomorrah, the male with the male...") but situates its referents within a vivid apocalyptic tour of the abyss. Those who know the rhetorical style of Tertullian (third century) will not be surprised to find here another fiery invective against same-sex eroticism that belies St. Paul's words regarding restoration — "All the other frenzies of passions — impious both towards the bodies and towards the sexes — beyond the laws of nature, we banish not only from the threshold, but from all shelter of the church, because they are not sins, but monstrosities" *(De Pudicitia* 4). Tertullian, typically unhappy with the milder pastoral discipline of his contemporaries in leadership positions, found his place more naturally in the extreme asceticism of Montanism than in mainstream Christianity.

Lurid descriptions and thunderous judgements are, however, atypical of the early Christian literature. *Didache* 2 (second century AD) briefly forbids the "corruption of boys"; *Apostolic Constitutions* 7:2 (late fourth century AD) uses this same phrase to forbid "sodomy" in general, making an explicit link with the Genesis narrative. Although these codes are not as theologically developed as the Pauline treatment of Romans 1, they reflect a typical Christian concern for the new covenant law of love *(Didache* 1:1–3) and for lessons to be learned from the overall biblical story (Sodom's fate is considered archetypal in the *Constitutions)*. Again in the second century, Justin Martyr *(First Apology,* chapter 7) defends Christianity when he applauds the Christian eschewal of "sodomy" and respect for children. Justin is intent on showing how Christian morality far surpasses non-Christian standards, in the same way that Christian theology surpasses pagan religion.

The prohibition against homoeroticism is constant in these early Jewish and Christian texts: the implied or explicit reasons frequently differ, since Christian writers make no appeal to "clean and unclean," but relate the matter to gospel and to biblical narrative in general.

Fathers, East and West

As in the earliest Christian period, church documents and theologians remain firm in proscribing the behaviour without demonizing it as the worst of all sins. In the West, canons were passed at the Council of Elvira (Southern Spain, AD 305–306), which forbade the catechumenate, baptism, and communion to those engaging in same-sex erotic behaviour. Similarly, the seventeenth canon of the council of Ancyra (Asia Minor, AD 314) lists a certain behaviour (probably homoerotic, pace Bailey 86–7) alongside bestiality, and gives various penalties in view of the age of the offender, his marital status, and the persistency of the behaviour. In the East, the pastoral decisions of Basil (*Epist.* 217, can. 62) and Gregory of Nyssa (*Epist. Canonica*, 4) provide ready examples: both consider homoerotic activity to be equivalent to adultery and deal with it accordingly. Moreover, the disciplinary measures prescribed were most probably mitigated and qualified in actual cases. As Sherwin Bailey remarks, "it can hardly be said that the spiritual penalties imposed by these … canons … are marked by excessive harshness."[9] To modern ears, the required penitential periods seem long, but they are consonant with the disciplines imposed upon other offences. The impulse of Basil and Gregory, like that of the Western canons, seems to be pastoral restoration rather than simple punishment and deterrence through fear. Such an approach is consonant with Jesus' gospel of repentance and the Pauline epistles.

As representative of the central patristic period, we will consider the fourth- to fifth-century greats, St. John Chrysostom of Constantinople and St. Augustine of Hippo. Both men, writing well after the christianization of the Empire in AD 313 (Edict of Milan), are good examples of the church's attitude toward homoeroticism in that era. Along with the christianization of the Empire had come forgetfulness or laxity with regard to what had been the counter-cultural lifestyle of a Christian minority. In their sermons, we see both preachers working to reinforce Christian particulars in an age that they describe as increasingly decadent. Chrysostom's typical critiques of theatre and dance read eerily like twentieth-century pietistic polemic! Augustine himself had had intimate contact with other worldviews, notably the Manichaean, and so he is at pains to demonstrate the special character of Christian belief and practice.

St. John Chrysostom

St. John Crysostom's most extensive treatment of homoeroticism is to be found, as one might expect, in his homilies on the book of Romans. In *Homily 3* and *Homily 4*,[10] Chrysostom's words are unequivocal, though he goes beyond mere condemnation to explain Paul's logic, God's purposes, and the reasons for God's will in sexual matters. In *Homily 3*, when he comments upon verse 24 ("to dishonour their own bodies between themselves"), he indeed asks a question that might occur to us today: "How comes he [Paul] to mention no other sin, as murder, for instance, or covetousness, or other such besides, but only unchasteness?" Also, his answer is congenial to our own methods of exegesis, in that it shows concern for the original context of Paul's epistle: "He seems to me to hint at the audience at the time." Paul's emphasis on sexual misconduct, then, is an indication of the Roman situation.

The end of *Homily 4* suggests the prevalence of same-sex eroticism, especially among the well-to-do of Constantinople. His final words warn the congregation against admiring those who live a life of luxury, and who have fallen into an all-consuming lifestyle.

(Elsewhere in his homilies he objects to those who frequent church in order to gaze upon the bodies of boys, rather than the glory of God!) Chrysostom's intent, however, is not simply to declare these behaviours "unlawful," but to show why God has forbidden them, which he does by adducing sequelae in the bodily, personal, and societal realms. In the course of *Homily 4*, he shows how this behaviour is against nature, and so cannot be a real pleasure, claiming that it rather gives rise to a fivefold civil war. Male wars against male partner, (for they "burn in lust towards each other"); female is set against female for the same reason; male is in strife against female, and female against male (because they no longer desire intimacy with each other nor need to learn to live at peace together); both sexes are at war with nature itself when they act in this way. Most disturbing to Chrysostom is that those who are involved in such actions do not perceive that they "suffer such things" and so are "unable to be freed from this misery." In the course of *Homily 4*'s fire and judgement, Chrysostom characterizes those who believe same-sex eroticism to be lawful as "pitiable" and "objects for many tears." They "do themselves much injury" and "make themselves such objects of compassion that others weep over them." The one who acts in this way, according to the bishop, is both the victim of injustice and liable to judgement, for the soul and body have been "disgraced." In his usual homiletic manner, he closes by speaking of strong punishment for the obstinate. Though we may cringe at his colourful phrases ("How many hells shall be enough for this?"), we must temper our response by a familiarity with Chrysostom's style. Whenever dealing with sin (not simply with this expression of it), the bishop's language of warning is characteristically strong. He is, nevertheless, just as extravagant in praising a merciful God who does not give repentant human beings what they deserve. In all this, Chrysostom sees himself as following in the divine *modus operandi*, for he comments "God … keeps on threatening hell … that so at least He may get us drawn unto Him."[11]

Chrysostom's more pastoral side comes out in his *Homily 5* on Titus 2:11—3:7. There he also speaks explicitly of same-sex eroticism as being among the "divers lusts and pleasures" mentioned generally in the letter, recognizing that his congregants, in their milieu, are inevitably faced with examples of "this corruption of all that was right." In actually tackling the issue of converse with those outside the truth, Chrysostom does not suggest the harsh penalties adduced for rhetorical effect in his Romans homily. Rather, he recommends that his flock have regard for both non-Christian and for those of the community who have been "attacked by this dangerous disease" of soul-sickness. Thus he exhorts:

> Let us then give thanks to God [for his grace to us], and not revile them; nor accuse them, but rather let us beseech them, pray for them, counsel and advise them, though they should insult and spurn us. For such is the nature of those who are diseased. But those who are concerned for the health of such persons do all things and bear all things, though it may not avail.[12]

* * *

St. Augustine of Hippo

From St. Augustine of Hippo, the great patristic voice of the West, we might expect a harsher approach. Augustine is, after all, noted for his emphasis on ever-present "concupiscence" (erotic lust) and the role that he understands this to play in the transmission of original guilt. Moreover, unlike Chrysostom, in whose teaching heterosexual love took its natural place within Christian marriage, Augustine sometimes exhibits a certain reserve regarding the purity of sex within marriage itself.[13] We might, then, have anticipated a stringent and unforgiving attitude to homoeroticism, which by its nature is excluded even from the obvious positive fruit of sexual concourse (i.e., offspring, albeit flawed). Instead, however, we find in Augustine a dual treatment quite similar to that of Chrysostom. Firstly, he handles the issue briefly and categorically in his third book of the *Confessions:*

> Sins against nature ... like the sin of Sodom, are abominable and deserve punishment wherever and whenever they are committed. If all nations committed them, all alike would be held guilty of the same charge in God's law, for our Maker did not prescribe that we should use each other in this way. In fact, the relationship which we ought to have with God is itself violated when our nature, of which he is the Author, is desecrated by perverted lust.[14]

Augustine categorizes homoeroticism as one of the "sins against nature" (*contra naturam*), using the same idea of nature that we have seen in other contemporaries. His concern is twofold: such actions involve the "misuse" of one person by another, thus marring our horizontal relationships, as well as affecting our relationship with God, who is the "Author" of life as it should be. However, he concludes by emphasizing God's intent to heal:

> Your punishments are for the sins which men commit against themselves, because although they sin against you, they do wrong to their own souls and their malice is self-betrayed. They corrupt and pervert their own nature, which you made and for which you shaped the rules, either by making wrong use of the things which you allow, or by becoming inflamed with passion to make unnatural use of things that you do not allow....This is what happens, O Fountain of life, when we abandon you, who are the one true Creator of all that ever was or is, and each of us proudly sets his heart on some one part of your creation instead of on the whole. So it is by the path of meekness and devotion that we must return to you. You rid us of our evil habits and forgive our sins when we confess to you.

You listen to the groans of the prisoners and free us from the chains which we have forged for ourselves. This you do for us unless we toss our heads against you in the illusion of liberty and in our greed for gain, at the risk of losing all, love our own good better than you yourself, who are the common good of all.[15]

In the end, Augustine shows a surprising tenderness toward human entrapment in sin, and points decisively to the generosity of a good and liberating God.

Chrysostom and Augustine well display the general approach to transgression and to sexual transgression in the church prior to the Middle Ages: strong language or threatened punishments for the sake of deterrence, but a different tone where repentance and forgiveness are concerned. (The exception to the rule is Tertullian, a rigorist who followed a trajectory towards schism.) We can sum up this period in Wright's words: "All the evidence indicates that the teaching mind of the early church unreservedly condemned homosexual activity. Yet, although clearly viewed as contrary to God's will in scripture and nature, it was not singled out for special execration."[16]

Medieval Period and Reformation

In the medieval period, we see little discussion of the issue but much legislation against the practice. Although from time to time extreme penalties were imposed for infractions, for the most part same-sex erotic behaviour was treated with no more rigour than offences such as theft or adultery.[17]

Towering over the period is of course the great mind of the late medieval theologian, St. Thomas Aquinas (d. 1274), whose thinking is characteristically subtle and clear. In his *Summa Theologica* II.II.Q.Q.153–154, the issue is dealt with along both traditional and surprising lines. In harmony with those before him, Aquinas speaks about homoeroticism as *contra naturam* (against nature), but amplifies by placing it after bestiality in gravity. Characteristically, Aquinas is not content simply to appeal to scripture to mount his argument, but works at a philosophical explanation for the prohibition of same-sex lustful acts.[18] Aquinas argues from a creational foundation, assuming that the major function of the sex organs is to procreate, and therefore they must be used in such a way that the possibility of generation/conception is not excluded. Thus, all homoerotic acts, from mutual petting through to sodomy, are unnatural, though they may differ in gravity of harm that is done.

In the course of his argument, Aquinas counters the position of some of his contemporaries who thought that homoerotic acts (performed by consent) are not sinful to the same degree as adultery or rape, since there is no harm to the other. He refutes this by broadening the context of discussion: homoeroticism is a transgression of God's own law, and therefore God is offended, even where the partner may not be. Here Aquinas differs from Augustine, who insisted that God cannot himself be injured by our sin, but that in fact we harm ourselves. The difference may be only skin-deep, however, for Augustine did speak about such behaviour damaging the person's *relationship* with God. Both Aquinas and Augustine insist that homoeroticism makes an impact upon the vertical (human being-God) relationship even more than the horizontal (person-person). It is doubtful, however, whether Augustine would ever concur with what seems to be Aquinas's assumption: that homoeroticism could possibly leave the person-to-person relationship unscathed. Rather, he appealed to a wise and far from arbitrary God who has forbidden that "we should use each other in this way."

We finish our survey of the medieval period by analyzing two Italo-Greek documents made public by John Boswell in his book *Same-Sex Unions in PreModern Europe*. Boswell adduces two rites from the medieval period (twelfth and thirteenth century).[19] The Greek title for these church rites is *Adelphopoiesis*, which is translated literally as "the making of brothers." Provocatively, Boswell renders the title *adelphopoiesis* as "same-sex same gender unions," which to today's reader most clearly suggests an erotic dimension. The texts themselves do not refer to physical aspects in the relationship, however. Rather, they provide a formal setting for the creation of a spiritual bond between close Christian co-workers, that "linking ... by (the) holy spirit and in manner of faith" referred to frequently in Paul's letters (e.g., Phil 2:25, 2 Cor 12:18). Moreover, the liturgies contain petitions that the bond between the brothers be based on "unashamed fidelity" and that they not be a cause of scandal (perhaps to those who might misconstrue the relationship?). Given what we know about the civic, ecclesial, and theological statements made everywhere throughout the Middle Ages, it is highly unlikely that these rites made allowances for erotic activity between monks. What we can ascertain from these texts is that persons of the same sex pledged fidelity to each other as specially designated brothers, for the purpose of growth in faith and Christian mission, and that the church blessed such arrangements, dignifying the pattern of the apostolic and subapostolic coupled missions by means of a liturgy.

Although in the medieval church homoerotic behaviour was not usually singled out for special disapprobation, discipline during this period was severe. It could, however, be argued that our own attitudes are framed as much by an individualistic approach to ethics as they are by the ideals of tolerance or even kindness. Today those individuals who live in an ecclesial community that still practises correction feel the alien quality of the disciplines to which they submit, and struggle to understand their identity in a world that paradoxically frowns upon censure. For those who are part of the body of Christ, it should not be the disciplinary instincts *per se* of the medieval church that perplex us, though we may wonder at the extent and severity of the penances. Rather, we should pause over the difficulties inherent in a mixed situation of civil and ecclesial authority, and our age's own way of distorting the gospel story, remembering that we, too, have our blinkers! It is unfortunate that throughout the church's history, there has not always been a true pastoral concern for those involved in homoerotic activity. Frequently, concern for strong deterrence and for purity (two motives fed by fear, it seems) have triumphed over a deeper witness to God's truth and mercy. The spotted record of the church in this regard is a strong call for God's people to heed Paul's condemnation of self-righteousness in Romans 2.

Reformation

In the Reformation period, the popular imagination seemingly envisaged homoeroticism as an example of heinous sin, and worthy of forceful punishment. This is illustrated by two artefacts — Dürer's painting "Lot and his Daughters," which pictures the destruction of Sodom in great detail, and an engraving by Theodore de Bry in which the explorer Balboa oversees the execution of Amerindians by ferocious dogs, because of the crime of sodomy. The writings of Calvin and Luther, while maintaining a strong stance against homoeroticism, are more pastoral. Both reformers recoil from homoerotic actions, but characteristically refuse to consider this particular breach of chastity apart from general human sinfulness. Calvin, in his *Commentary on First Corinthians*, exegetes 6:9–11 by speaking of sodomy as "the most serious of all sins,"[20] but then adds that all sin, regardless of its type, is evidence of human corruption, and calls for repentance. He notes that Paul's treatment in Romans 1 goes beyond actual activity to consider the "passions" that lead to this: "By connecting the evil desires of the human heart with uncleanness, he [Paul] indirectly gives us to understand the fruit which our heart will bring forth when it is left to itself."[21] This concern for the heart as well as outward action is consonant with the Reformed emphasis upon heartfelt repentance. Calvin applies to this topic, as the Reformers did to every example of human fallenness, the Christian insights gained from Jesus' "radicalization" of the Law ("you have heard it said, but I say…") and Paul's denial of fallen human righteousness. Some[22] have assumed that Calvin is here condemning homosexual tendency ("the internal disposition toward homosexual acts") along with the activity. In fact, Calvin simply repeats Paul's words about "passions" and then explains this drive to sin by reference to other examples of human transgression. We cannot deduce from this that Calvin refused to discriminate between homosexual tendency and action. Rather, his concern is (as ever) theological. The upshot of his discussion is not to single out homoeroticism (though he considers it an abhorrent practice) but to declare "there are none who are not to be found corrupted by some vice or another."[23]

Similarly, when Luther comments upon passages that deal specifically with same-sex eroticism, he moves on to talk about sexual immorality in general. He is careful in his *Lectures on Genesis* to explain the judgement upon Sodom in terms of the general erosion of its moral fibre:

> If you do away with the marriage bond and permit promiscuous passions, the laws and all decency go to ruin....Therefore as an example to others the Lord was compelled to inflict punishment and to check the madness that was raging beyond measure.[24]

Luther, searcher and finder of the gracious God, is compelled to engage in theodicy; it is not his instinct to assume that sodomy in particular demanded such severity. The general condition of Sodom, which included widespread corruption of every sort, required radical action. A similar tendency to broaden the discussion is seen in his *Lectures on Romans*,[25] which mention homoerotic behaviour alongside other examples of unbridled or unseemly passion. God's mercy is such that forgiveness will be extended to any who are repentant. Muted in all Luther's treatments is the classic and medieval description of same-sex eroticism as "unnatural." This change of course reflects Luther's lack of enthusiasm for the category of natural grace, and his rigorous insistence that there is nothing pure outside of what has been redeemed.

With the Protestant movement away from penitential disciplines as a means to make atonement or to accrue merit, and the concomitant belief that a sinful disposition in itself (alongside specific sins) requires forgiveness, we see less specific attention to homoeroticism *per se*. Neither Calvin nor Luther belabour the issue, nor do many of the emerging confessional statements deal specifically with it. We see during this time two significant changes in the church's response, the first a strength and the second a weakness. On the one hand, human brokenness was emphasized as the global human experience, a condition requiring radical repentance on the part of every Christian: thus homoeroticism was placed in a larger context. For example, Question 139 of the Westminster Catechism (1647) includes as "forbidden in the seventh commandment" a number of forms of immodesty and immorality, beginning with "adultery, fornication, rape, incest, sodomy, and all unnatural lusts" and ending with "lascivious songs, books, pictures, dancings, stage plays." Homoeroticism is not singled out in this application of Puritan principles to daily life. On the other hand, the move away from penitential codes and personal confession before the priest left behind a kind of pastoral vacuum: thus, particular problems, including the inclination to homoerotic behaviour, were less likely to be squarely faced. The tendency not to single out specific sins for disapprobation was coupled, it seems, with a lack of reality in addressing particular weaknesses that must have plagued this age, as any other.

Beyond the Reformation to Today

Up to Wolfenden

In the period from the Reformation up to the second half of the twentieth century (especially the 1960s) three major shifts occurred that created the climate for a radical re-reading of scripture in some quarters so as to allow for same-sex eroticism: the separation of church and state, the restriction of capital punishment, and a new view of homosexuality as a predisposition rather than a sin. Beginning with the Reformation, we begin to see the separation of church and state, both on the continent and eventually in England, so that morality comes to be viewed as a matter of private rather than public concern. As early as the English Act of 1553, sodomy became punishable by the royal rather than church courts (a move that was ratified in the next generation by Elizabeth I), although the churches were involved in the establishing of the facts of each case. It would be two more centuries before the church was no longer required to be involved in any way, except in the case of its own clergy. All the same, it must be remembered that given the British political system, no complete severance of church and state would take place, since the House of Bishops continued to have a certain legal authority, and many politicians were leading members of the church. It is not unusual to read Hansard records of debates that include exegeses of scripture (good, bad, and indifferent) as this issue is tackled.

Second, after the rigours of the Reformation, we see less stomach for the capital punishment of a wide array of crimes, including the formal severe sanctions against "private" sexual activities that were difficult to demonstrate.[26] The royal courts, though empowered to exact death, frequently did not do so. By 1861, as part of a general mitigation of capital offences, anal intercourse was no longer punishable by death. This general move toward tolerance was interrupted briefly in 1885 by an amendment made to the 1861 legislation in which general homoerotic activity, conducted "in public or in private" was proscribed. The 1885 bill was intended to frustrate a growing market of child prostitution; it had been framed in order to act against the conditions made public by such reformers as William Booth, W. H. Stead, Josephine Butler, and Ellice Hopkins, who were concerned for the protection of women (and especially) young girls in the cities. At the last moment, a clause concerning same-sex behaviour was included, prescribing up to two years' imprisonment for any "indecency." The move was controversial, but justified at the time by the bishops in the House, who cited scripture in their efforts to enact a bill that would curb immorality.

Right up to the 1960s, the infamous clause of 1885 was to cause great consternation because of its general nature, and because it provided ample opportunity for blackmail by the unscrupulous. Meanwhile, from the churches sprang such groups as the White Cross League and the White Cross Society, which established shelters for young men and boy prostitutes, "based on the recognition that in each case there was a physical, a mental, and a spiritual factor."[27] Finally, in the 1950s, there was a decade of conservatism, which for various political and social reasons saw an abrupt increase in arrests for homosexual offences. The Wolfenden Committee report demonstrated an increase from 622 convictions in 1931 to 6,655 in 1955. Such statistics and the changing social situation in England led to the removal of homosexuality as a legal offence in 1967. The debate over this change makes the nature of the decision clear. Those in the church who approved the decriminalization of various sexual offences did so not because they had changed their assessment of homoeroticism, but because there had been a change in the contours of English society. It no longer seemed reasonable for some moral issues, especially those that fell into the class of "fornication," to be governed by the state. Hansard records the words of the Archbishop of Canterbury:

> I would uphold the belief that just as fornication is always wrong, so homosexual acts are always wrong. At the same time … I think there is a real cogency in the plea of the Wolfenden Report that not all sins are properly given the status of crimes…. If a line can reasonably be drawn anywhere, homosexual acts in private between consenting adults fall properly on the same side of the line as fornication.[28]

During this same period in various countries a growing number of theologians and church leaders, influenced by changing approaches in psychiatry, began to consider homosexuality to be a predisposition and even an alternate lifestyle, instead of disease or sin. At the same time, church statements from the 1960s also reflect a restatement of the classical approach to same-sex eroticism, coupled with a strengthened call to compassion for those involved. While trajectories were being set for a reversal of moral judgement in some quarters (in Canada, notably in the United Church), key voices continued to reflect the ongoing tradition of the church, while calling for discernment and care in the area of pastoral discipline. Amidst this group are theologians of such renown as Karl Barth in the first part of the twentieth century, and (more recently) Methodist New Testament exegete and ethicist Richard Hays. We might also cite the work of Joseph Cardinal Ratzinger, although many have vilified his efforts in a critique of ecclesial authority that goes far beyond our topic. Leaving such larger questions aside, it is important to note the same dual impulse in the 1986 "Letter to the Bishops," which he headed:

> An authentic pastoral programme will assist homosexual persons at all levels of the spiritual life: through the sacraments, and in particular through the frequent and sincere use of the sacrament of reconciliation, through prayer, witness, counsel, and individual care. In such a way, the entire Christian community can come to recognize its own call to assist its brothers and sisters, without deluding them or isolating them.... A homosexual person, as every human being, deeply needs to be nourished at many different levels simultaneously.[29]

The Current Situation

It is inevitable in a time of change such as we are now witnessing, that many of those who hold to a classical position will frame their writings argumentatively, that is, as a response to those who seek to change the church's understanding. We will sketch the current situation in three strokes: first, the work of Karl Barth, who wrote before the debate emerged in full force; then the responsive argument found in many current "conservative" treatments; finally, we will look to Richard Hays as a sensitive spokesperson for the classical approach. Barth and Hays are particularly helpful for two reasons: Barth offers a relatively "innocent" commentary, which because of his times did not need to refute in detail the revisionist position; Hays presents a well-informed and careful commentary that is all-too-aware of the debate. Moreover, these two works are complementary in their approaches, the first offering a theological context, and the second an exegetical one, for the classical response.

Karl Barth

Barth's treatment of this subject moves beyond a mechanical appeal to specific prohibitions in the scriptures and sets the issue of same-sex eroticism within an understanding of the creation and of humankind. Some have dismissed Barth's discussion on the basis of his thoroughgoing "theology of the Word," arguing that for Barth human reason can play no part in this discussion, so that we are simply to submit to an inscrutable divine will.[30] Others, such as Eugene F. Rogers[31] misread Barth's nuanced synthesis of scripture, and suppose that Barth's "abstractive categories" vitiate his "pronouncements" on the issue of homoeroticism. That is, Rogers suspects that Barth constructs a concept of "man" and "woman" that acts as a screen "resistant to the blowing of the Spirit."[32] So he opines that Barth's decision against same-sex eroticism is based mainly upon these constructed ideals, and not on a reading of the biblical text. In support of this, Rogers declares that Barth does not (and cannot) use Romans 1 to any great extent in his analysis of the issue. This may be true in Barth's Romans commentary, which is intent on other matters. It is astonishing, however, that Rogers misses the coherent connection made between idolatry and same-sex eroticism in *Church Dogmatics* III.4.

Such charges belittle Barth's treatment of this and other subjects. Revelation remains authoritative for this theologian, but he is well aware of the problem of abstraction, and appeals to reason in a patent manner as he works out the implications of the Word. Barth sets the questions of human sexuality within the framework of relationship, taking seriously the scriptural pattern of the human as turned "toward" God and the male as turned "toward" the female (and vice versa). Moreover, in his *Dogmatics* III.4.141ff., he takes full account of the dynamic of the biblical narrative. The first chapters of Genesis present marriage as the *telos* of the encounter between man and woman (Gen 2:24) but also hint toward the ultimate *telos* of humanity, that is, the union of humanity with God. He sees the Incarnation as the significant turning point. Before the Incarnation marriage was an absolute necessity for humankind, and afterward it is to be honoured as mirroring the great union of God and humanity. It remains a relative necessity, the normative way in which man and woman both realize their nature; yet celibacy comes into its own, too, as a witness to the penultimate nature of human sexual joy, and the ultimate *gamos*. Both his *Church Dogmatics* (III.4.166) and his *Commentary* on the Epistles treat sexuality as directly related to human self-understanding and response to God. Harmony and reciprocity are God's will and gift, both on the level of Creator-creature and on the human level of man-woman. So, in the same *Dogmatics* that stresses the tri-unity of the Godhead and humankind's mirror of that in the male-female relationship, Barth explains: "Humanity as fellow-humanity is to be understood in its root as the togetherness of man and woman." Marriage was intended in the ideal creation and is necessary still, as man and woman each are commanded to orient themselves toward each other: "to consider one another, to hear the question which each puts to the other, and to make responsible answer to one another."[33] The divine command regarding male-female unity is not arbitrary, but arises from their very nature. Barth echoes St. Paul: "Neither is the man without the woman, neither the woman without the man, in the Lord."

Barth explains that neither an uncommitted heterosexual relationship nor a same-sex union can ultimately fulfil this call to fellow-humanity, even though same-sex eroticism "in its early stages ... may have an appearance of particular beauty and spirituality." This is because both the uncommitted liaison and the attempt to find fulfilment in one of the same sex are expressions of autonomy, "trying to be human in the self as sovereign man or woman." The individual human, then, is never called to a *beata solitudo* ("a blessed solitude") because our nature is radically social. Our desire to be autonomous is expressed in a multitude of ways, of which *heterophobia* (expressed as homosexuality) is only one expression: we strive to know better than God, and so tend to idolatry. Again, in his *Commentary* on the epistles (both versions), Barth describes how once the "frontier" between God and man is not recognized (so that the Creator is no longer understood as over against and other than humanity), it is inevitable that the natural boundaries of life are also broken down. That is, inability to see the distinction between Creator and creation leads also to a confusion of distinctions in the natural realm: the role of male and female may be compromised (or even "despised"); the sanctity of the marriage bond between husband and wife may be ignored for spurious partners. Delight in the appetite, in *eros* itself, or in the self-sufficient relationship, then entraps those involved. The crossing of identity boundaries and the rejection of the created plan ends, as it began (Rom 1:25), in idolatry: "For in this supposed discovery of the genuinely human man and woman give themselves up to the worship of a false god."[34]

Barth's language has struck some as uncompromisingly harsh, but this is because of the theologian's consistently forthright approach toward God's sovereignty and human rebellion. What he has to say about homoeroticism "whether in its more refined or cruder forms"[35] is repeated about any human attitude or action that ignores God's will. Cheek on jowl with denunciation of the act and the mind-set, Barth as sinner also speaks of "God's forgiving grace" and calls upon the healing and corrective imperative given to doctor, psychotherapist-pastor, legislator, and judge. Where he might have waxed eloquent regarding the viciousness of some behaviour, he has been taught well by Paul regarding the ubiquity of human brokenness and the lavish love of a truthful God. Homoerotic desire, which may be tempting because it is experienced in the early stages as "redolent of sanctity," leads to the "tragedy of concrete homosexuality."[36] The individual caught up in this lifestyle needs to hear Paul's words about the complementarity of man and woman "in the Lord" (1 Cor 11:11), and respond both to God's word and God's love.[37]

Contemporary Critique of Revisionism (with Rogers as illustrative)

Barth's work on this issue is integrated thoroughly with his theology and is declarative rather than apologetic or confrontational. More frequently in the last thirty years, Christian scholars have found it necessary to frame their discussion of homosexuality in terms of the debate that is dealt to them, spending much time in the refutation of views that are a novelty in the church. In particular, they have responded to their "gay-positive" Christian interlocutors, who have sought to harmonize the scriptures with "the voices of experience and wisdom." Key names in this reactive debate are Richard Lovelace, D.F. Wright, Marion Soards, Richard Hays, and Robert Gagnon. Richard Lovelace, in *Homosexuality and the Church*, engages with the superficial grounds for polarization over this issue in the 1970s, and astutely examines and re-establishes the traditional position, while calling both the self-righteous conservative and those engaging in homoeroticism to repentance. D. F. Wright's entry on "Homosexuality" in *The Encyclopedia of Early Christianity* provides a masterful overview; his second entry (in *Dictionary of Paul and his Letters*) goes on to respond to those who have tried to read the Pauline letters against their grain. Marion Soards (*Scripture and Homosexuality*) exercises a pastoral concern regarding the questions of ordination and church membership in a deliberately popular book that probes intelligently the scriptures and the Reformed tradition. Richard Hays, in both his 1994 article "Awaiting the Redemption of Our Bodies" and his more recent book *The Moral Vision of the New Testament*, combines pastoral concern with careful exegesis and a convincing rebuttal of revisionist exegesis. Most recently, Robert Gagnon's *The Bible and Homosexual Practice* offers a thorough exegesis of the scriptural passages, a refutation of the revisionist arguments that is probably unparalleled, and a convincing *apologia* for the authority and on-going relevance of the biblical witness. Gagnon also provides a window by which to view the current debate in the church, making explicit the risks that attend anyone (especially the "traditionalist") who participates. Nonetheless, he is, he says, constrained to speak for the sake of the church and society, because of his judgement that the scriptural texts are routinely being distorted by *eisegesis*, and because he senses that "the window of opportunity for speaking out against homosexual behaviour is closing."[38]

Together, these authors provide a body of refutations and a credible critique of the revisionist position. Much of the debate necessarily rages around the Pauline texts, for these provide the most promising common ground. After all, Paul's letters are admittedly connected with praxis, whereas the gospels do not handle the matter *per se* and the Old Testament passages can be more easily excluded as relative to their time and place, through an appeal to "genre" or to a certain definition of the gospel. The most serious argument with which the classical writers engage is the following: frequently, revisionists plead that Paul's negative depiction of homoeroticism has only to do with certain types of sexuality, specifically, with those persons who are not truly homosexual, yet who act homoerotically "against [their] nature." Thus Paul, according to the revisionist, would not disapprove the practice by those who are by nature homosexual. Again, some writers suggest that Paul is speaking about those who sell their bodies for gain (and thus these writers would try to limit the meaning of either *malakoi* or *arsenokoitai* to male prostitution); or they say that Paul is referring to those who practise pederasty (and thus they would limit Paul's disapproval to the ancient Hellenistic practice of erotic behaviour with young males).

The classical responses to these two contextual arguments run as follows. The first qualification, that Paul is referring only to certain types of sexuality when he speaks of what is "against nature" in Romans 1, makes the mistake of thinking that Paul has in mind certain individuals or types. But in Romans, Paul's brush strokes are large, as is his canvas. He is speaking of humanity (Adam) and of Israel and Gentiles in general. He is not giving an account of the election of individuals, nor of the psychology of the individual "legalistic" Jew, nor a description of individuals who practise homoerotic behaviour. To introduce two categories, one of people who act homosexually according to nature, and one of those who do so against nature, is to introduce a distinction alien to Paul's point. For Paul, humankind has a single nature found in its relationship to God as creator.

On the second suggestion, that *malakoi* or *arsenokoitai* referred to prostitution in particular, there is simply no evidence whatsoever for it, notwithstanding the serpentine arguments of Boswell in *Christianity, Social Tolerance and Homosexuality* and L. William Countryman in *Dirt, Greed and Sex*.[39] Paul's problem with homoerotic behaviour in Romans 1 is its same-sex quality, whether male to male or female to female, not the economics of sexual trade. It is bizarre to think that *malakoi* and *arsenokoitai* are thematically linked to a few of the other weaknesses listed either in 1 Corinthians 6 or in 1 Timothy 1:9–10. (Countryman, for example, understands *arsenokoitai* as "associated" with other vices having to do with misuse of body and property, like "kidnapping" or "harlotry.") The vices in both lists, however, are conglomerates, introduced to show the reader the varied sins from which the Christian community has been or is being rescued (1 Cor) or to speak broadly about what is "contrary to sound teaching" (1 Tim).

Finally, on the hypothesis that Paul had only pederasty in mind: a historical clarification of Hellenistic "love of boys" needs to be made: the Graeco-Roman "ideal" did not entail erotic love of children, but of young (teenage) males, of the same age at which young women would be given in marriage. Frequently the more mature male was only slightly older than the partner. Had Paul intended to proscribe pederasty (as we understand pederasty today), he had recourse to many other more precise terms. In fact, the discussion in Romans, with its inclusion of female homoerotic behaviour, indicates that exploitation and victimization were not the issue. (Paul has a lot to say about the abuse of power elsewhere.)

Those holding to the classical approach insist that we cannot (dis)qualify Paul's discussion so that it appears "out of sync" with contemporary questions. Nor can we render what Paul said irrelevant, through an appeal to his theological or cultural limitations. It is not helpful to follow, for example, Eugene Rogers who argues in *Sexuality and the Christian Body* that God's grace is wider even than Paul himself suspected, embracing same-sex couples as well as Jew and Gentile. In mounting this argument, Rogers uses the phrase "against nature" in Romans 11 to neutralize Paul's disapproval of homoeroticism in Romans 1: God can also act "against nature." To see homoeroticism as blessed is to imitate God's inclusion of the "unclean" Gentiles. This, however, reads against the sense of both texts. Romans 1 speaks about what is contrary to nature in the context of the created order and its disruption by sin and corruption. Romans 11 offers a figure of speech to help the Roman Gentile Christians appreciate the wonder of God's inclusion of them, through Christ, in a covenant originally made with Israel. Thus Paul speaks of God "grafting" branches that do not "by nature" belong to the vine: his intent is to move Gentile Christians away from an attitude of superiority, as some had assumed God had no further concern for those who belonged to the Jewish nation. Paul goes on to speak of a wonderfully inclusive household of God, but all of this by way of what Jesus has done to "banish ungodliness" and to "take away … sins" (Rom 11:25). Never are the Gentiles included so as to continue in godless behaviour; never is the Jew who turns to Jesus confirmed in thinking that he is redeemed simply on the basis that Israel was given the Law. Rogers picks up on the theme of inclusivity in this passage (and in Gal 3:28) without taking account of God's plan for those within the new community. Of course the extent of grace is vast. But to be touched by God's grace means to have ungodliness banished, to move away from "disobedience" (a key word in Romans 11), to be enlightened by the Spirit and to "present the body as a living sacrifice" (Rom 12:1). It is precisely to be drawn out of the life against God and against nature, and into right relationship with both, in the new life of the body of Christ. God's purpose in including us within the household is to heal, not to tolerate or bless our fallen condition.

The strength of Rogers's argument is that he has taken seriously the entire sweep of the scriptural story, reading it as a whole, seeing ethical directives within the scriptures as orienting humanity toward her final goal — unity with God. However, at several turns he mis-steps. Key to this is his assumption that Paul was theologically limited. Similarly, he feels justified in misappropriating the profound treatment of Paul Evdokimov. In *The Sacrament of Love*, Evdokimov sets forward marriage alongside monasticism as two forms of one ascetic vocation, by which human beings in their bodies are made holy. Evdokimov's thesis is sound, Rogers says, but his work "dated" with regard to its emphasis on celibacy and marriage only. Evdokimov is correct that God uses the very bodies of Christians to sanctify them — but this applies to homoerotic couples as well! We know this, Rogers argues, because same-sex couples find in their union a means of grace. This appeal to experience is made by other apologists for homoerotic unions, who also admit that Paul disapproved of such activity, but think that he was hampered by an unscientific view of sexuality. Then it is claimed that the scriptures have nothing whatsoever to say about "homosexuality" as we understand it today. According to this line of argument, the biblical writers wrongly assumed that homoerotic behaviour is an avoidable choice; had they had the benefit of our psychological studies, they would have written differently on the issue.

Such an argument assumes that there is a scientific consensus about same-sex preference and behaviour, which is not the case.

The "common wisdom" about homosexuality is that it is innate, unchangeable, and not unhealthy. These views are not accepted by all specialists. David F. Greenberg, for example, argues on the basis of cross-cultural studies for a social rather than a genetic matrix for homosexuality.[40] A very recent study of twins concludes that "the pattern of concordance ... of same-sex preference for sibling pairs does not suggest genetic influences independant of social context."[41] In light of this study and others done by Bailey and Pillard,[42] the "genetic hypothesis" is still questioned and qualified in professional circles.[43] Moreover, some specialists have had success in the re-orientation of those who are seeking to leave the gay or lesbian lifestyle.[44] There is simply no monolithic agreement in this area. A helpful resource in sorting through the medical evidence is the new work by Stanton L. Jones and Mark A. Yarhouse, *Homosexuality: The Use of Scientific Research in the Church's Moral Debate* (2000).

Even if a true consensus were to emerge on these issues of cause and permanence, Rogers's approach remains seriously flawed, for it does not take full stock of Paul's discussion in Romans 1. Richard Hays[45] points out that when Paul treats homoerotic behaviour within the context of general disordering, he does not presuppose that sin occurs because we are free moral agents. On the contrary, Paul pictures a situation in which humanity is, in some sense, enslaved by sin (Rom 6:17), so that neither the will nor the passions fall into line with reason. We have a predisposition to corruption and sin: this does not render pathology healthy or sin "morally neutral." Alcoholism is now understood to have a genetic dimension, but this does not mean that drunkenness is morally neutral, nor that society "discriminates against" people who frequently drink too much if it attempts to limit the possible damage through laws about driving, and so forth.

Nor, of course, are statistics of frequency an indication of how homoerotic behaviour is to be assessed in ethical terms. The ten per cent figure for homosexuality in America (based dubiously on the Kinsey report) is strongly questioned,[46] and the actual proportion of male homosexuals is thought to be closer to two per cent. There are two points here. Even if the higher number were to be verified, or if the population of declared homosexuals were actually to rise to ten per cent or more, frequency does not settle the moral question in a world in thrall to corruption. Should the incidence of psychopathology or alcoholism increase, we would not therefore be justified in calling it good. Secondly, frequency does not settle the question of whether homosexuality is essential in nature to some persons. To note that homosexuality is a common practice among a given population does not in itself explain anything about how our bodies, minds, hearts, and spirits are related. The make-up of a human being remains mysterious, and is as much a matter for theological study as it is the proper subject of psychology and anthropology. No woman today wants to be defined wholly by her sexuality: why would we approach homosexuality as an all-encompassing category? The classical approach would likewise assert that it is dehumanizing to sum up any person by reference to sexuality. The hope put forward by both the gospels and the epistles is that God has done, and is continuing to do, something about the heart (i.e., the centre) of those who are in Christ, so that they will in the end fully mirror the glory of God, in every aspect of their being. For the traditionalist, then, the issue does not stand on its own, but is tied to the scriptural story of who we were created to be, what we have become, and what God intends for us.

Richard Hays

A sensitive and eloquent witness to this view is mediated to us through New Testament scholar Richard Hays,[47] who covenanted with a close friend of his, "Gary," to let his experience count for something in the church. Gary died of AIDS before the plan was completed, but Hays relates his compelling story and the hard thinking that both of them did together. His friend Gary had experienced his own homosexuality as a "compulsion and an affliction" for over twenty years, and had searched many current books affirming gay activity in the churches (by McNeill, Mollenkott, Boswell, etc.); he found in them only "wishful interpretation." Caught between gay rights activists in the church, and homophobic reactionaries, Gary turned to his friend. "In particular, Gary wanted to discuss the biblical passages that deal with homosexual acts. Among Gary's many gifts was his skill as a reader of texts. Though he was not trained as a biblical exegete, he was a careful and sensitive interpreter…. However much he wanted to believe that the Bible did not condemn homosexuality, he would not violate his own stubborn intellectual integrity by pretending to find their arguments [i.e., the revisionists'] persuasive.[48] So sensitive reader and biblical exegete, friend awaiting death and friend dreading the death of another, looked to the scriptures for truth and for comfort. They finally made this discovery: "The biblical witness against homosexual practices is univocal."[49]

"Are homosexuals [then] to be excluded from the community of faith? Certainly not. But anyone who joins such a community should know that it is a place of transformation, of discipline, of learning, and not merely a place to be comforted or indulged."[50] Hays's careful mapping of their search through the pertinent passages, his placement of these within the scriptures as a whole, his work of synthesis and interpretation, and his consideration of other authorities for the church, especially the role of experience, is sustained and clear. Especially prophetic is this warning: "in its rush to be inclusive, the church must not overlook the experience reported by those Christians who, like Gary, struggle with homosexual desires and find them a hindrance to living lives committed to the service of God."[51]

Gary was searching for a church that would be faithful enough to be truly inclusive: inclusive enough to call every member of her body to ongoing repentance and fullness of life, while all of us await the full redemption of our bodies. No doubt Gary would have dismissed as condescending those "half-way" strategies that admit homoerotic unions to be less than God's perfect will, but the best that some can manage, given their present condition. He held out for the hope that there was truly no male or female, no gay or straight in Christ: and this meant being brought into God's very own life of purity and health. However, life in Christ did not mean for Gary a reorientation toward heterosexual desire. Some Christians today do speak of this kind of healing in their sexuality; this was not Gary's experience, yet he was content with God's grace as he committed to abstinence. Professor Hays saw in his friend a powerful symbol of God's power made perfect in weakness, embodying our present situation "in between the times." God's Spirit is at work among us, yet full glory remains a future hope. Gary's integrity, and the faithfulness of others like him, reverse the symbol of disintegration featured by Paul in Romans 1. Both "Gary" and his academic friend Hays, who entered reluctantly into this raging and church-splitting controversy, witness redemptively to all of us about Christ's grace, love, and fidelity.

The Eastern Church

It is unfortunate that the perspective of the Orthodox Church must be dealt with here as a kind of afterthought, for the present writer (among many others) has found much wisdom in this tradition. Moreover, the writings of P. Evdokimov and Schmemann have made accessible to Western Christians strong biblical and Christian foundations for a profound understanding of creation and of sexuality. I lament that the brilliant and faithfully synthetic reading of Paul Evdokimov has been so wrested from its context in the current *apologia* for homosexuality in the church by Eugene Rogers. Rogers, making (ab)use of Evdokimov's thesis regarding two forms of asceticism, monasticism and marriage, employs statements by this Eastern theologian in a way that he would never have dreamed, nor approved. Rogers is pleased that Evdokimov conveniently removes procreation as absolutely essential to marriage, but takes no account of the theology of "icon" that permeates both *The Sacrament of Love* and also *Woman and the Salvation of the World*.

Evdokimov, in unlikely concert with Barth ("homosexuality is a sexual union which is not and cannot be genuine,"[52] *Dogmatics*, would surely respond to Rogers that homoerotic relationships are false icons, that one needs communion with *the other* in order to picture God's love for the church: man with woman demonstrates the self-emptying by which Christ loves the church and by which the church responds; the celibate in monastic orders perhaps more directly pictures this sanctifying union. Or again, the married play out in their bodies the sanctifying mystery to which we are called at the final consummation; celibates by their restraint play out the "not yet" quality of our communion with the Holy One. The married need the celibate so that they will not make marriage an idol; the celibate need the married to remind them that the body is important, that they and monastic soul-agony are not self-sufficient. Homoeroticism falls between the stools, and so cannot fulfill either role as sacramental: though in individual cases there may well be goodness found, the homoerotic union is by its nature prone to either "pleasuring" idolatry or same-sex solipsism, or both. Once we put aside God's twin gifts of marriage and celibacy, we cannot "re-envision" a sacrament that will be truly "eucharistic" — that is, which makes a priestly and joyful offering back to God of his primal gift. The work of Evdokimov is important to the Western church because it reminds us powerfully that ethical instructions in the Bible and in holy tradition fit in with the way things are, with their very natures: we are (personally and in communion with others) glorify-ers, windows of the One who Is. We are, by our nature, iconic beings who mirror various truths about the God of Life and Reality. That is to the end of our joy, not our suppression.

As a separate issue, however, homoeroticism has not been as thoroughly discussed in the contemporary Eastern communion as in the West — probably because there is no vigorous Eastern equivalent to the revisionist position. Despite the lack of centralized authority in this communion, Orthodox dioceses and parishes continue to take seriously the discussions of fathers such as Chrysostom, who remains a family name among communicants. Moreover, they continue to uphold the injunction of canon law that prohibits the priesting of those who engage in same-sex erotic activity.[53] Indeed, the consensus against homoerotic practice in the church is so strong that changing attitudes in the West played a major role in the withdrawal of the Orthodox from full membership in the World Council of Churches. At the same time, there is a strong pastoral tradition in the church that does not ignore the pain felt by those who are tempted to this lifestyle. Given its strong ascetic tradition, those who embrace homoeroticism are censured, but those who seek to live chastely are enjoined to engage in "agona, that is, spiritual and moral struggles against [such passions]."[54] In offering this counsel, the Eastern Church does not differentiate between this and any other temptation. It does take this issue seriously, however, because it follows Chrysostom in his reading of Romans and 1 Corinthians, and in his understanding this expression of human passions as particularly damaging to the family, and as contributing to the corruption of morals in society.[55]

The discussion within the Orthodox Church between two well-known clerics demonstrates a strong agreement about position and pastoral response, even while there is room for debate. The subject of discussion is Kallistos Ware's newest edition of *The Orthodox Church* (1996), which holds to the classical position, but also advocates that counsellors "show the utmost pastoral sensitivity and generous compassion … in all specific cases of homosexuality."[56] The reviewer of Ware's book, Hieromonk Patapios, evidently worried that Ware has capitulated to the spirit of the age, comments:

> His Grace is right in advocating pastoral sensitivity here, just as he is in maintaining that the Church cannot give Her approval to same-sex unions. Archbishop Chrysostomos, who was trained in psychology and taught this subject before becoming a monk, likewise observes that homosexuality is a cruel and

demonic disorder which merits precisely the kind of gentle pastoral approach that Bishop Kallistos recommends. But, as His Eminence emphasizes, such care applies to any kind of sin, sexual or otherwise, and we should not, because of political pressure from "gay rights groups," pretend that this particular sin deserves special leniency.[57]

This glimpse within the communion demonstrates clear differences in tone and in perspective. Yet both the eirenic Ware and his more pugnacious critic agree on the foundational matters of principle and pastoral care. The aplomb with which homoeroticism is handled is instructive for those polarized and passionate Christians in the West who have elevated the debate to the level of a shibboleth. On the other hand, it is unfortunate that there is so little written explicitly on the question, given its high profile today. In particular, it would be helpful to see more recent discussions of the issue in terms of its pastoral dimensions, along the lines of that produced twenty years ago by Elizabeth R. Moberley in *Homosexuality: A New Christian Ethic.*

Conclusions

So we come to the end of our long tour. It is clear from our investigation that the acceptance of same-sex erotic practice, along with the valorization (or acceptance) of a gay worldview, are novelties in the church. The principle that homoerotic sexual activity is contrary to the will of God has remained a constant until approximately the last forty years. How this position is reached, and its practical sequels are, however, different stories: the church has not been consistent in clarity of hermeneutic or in its pastoral wisdom. These three factors are significant desiderata: careful attention to method in the reading of scripture, a self-conscious approach to the question of tradition, and a faithful yet sensitive heart as we address those who we believe do not here follow the mind of Christ.

Moreover, the close investigation of homoerotic psychology in our century has offered a challenge for those counsellors in the church who are seeking healing and integration for those troubled by homoerotic tendencies. Typically revisionists have presented contemporary psychology as iconoclastic to the classical understanding of this issue. Such a presentation is as simplistic as pitting "science" against "Christianity" — the best science aids in the worship of the Creator of the Universe and is not to be ignored. As for psychology and psychiatry, it is clear that there remains a strong divergence of opinion, even considering the recent removal of homosexuality from the index of psychiatric illnesses. Human sexuality is a deep mystery, and the insights of all specialists should be welcome in helping us to plumb its depths. Especially where specialists do not depict homosexuality as a healthy life alternative, their findings should not alarm the ecclesial community, but be instrumental in deepening the pastoral response of a loving and discerning church. Christian professionals in psychology and psychiatry should be encouraged to specialize in this area, so that the church can become increasingly active and not simply conservative in its approach to homoeroticism. We are called in wisdom and compassion to a close walk with those who struggle personally and not simply cerebrally with this problem. It is hoped that even as the church remains faithful conceptually, its members will repent, where necessary, of their unwillingness to grapple with this pain, and their sometimes prudish neglect of those who so suffer. Orthodoxy and orthopraxy must work together, so that God's truth and God's love, which have embraced in Jesus, are mirrored in us.

The challenge to God's people in a time of turmoil is to act with the mind of Christ, and not simply to react or entrench. The issue that we have discussed must be seen for what it is — a particularly poignant "presenting cause" of deeper points of division over the authority, vitality, and continuity of the church. Our older siblings in the faith have seen similarly troubled moments. At her best, the church has emerged from internal conflict strengthened and with a deeper understanding of what she believes and how she should live. Dietrich Bonhoeffer, who also learned the depth of God's grace in a dark time, speaks powerfully to us about ethics, reality, and truth: "If one is to say how a thing really is, i.e., if one is to speak truthfully, one's gaze and one's thought must be directed towards the way in which the real exists in God and through God and for God."[58] Bonhoeffer thus sends us back to Romans 1, that we might see God's world and the creation as they really are. It is his prayer that God's people, bestowed with the vision of Christ, will learn to see, to give thanks, and to worship God as we see truly and speak truly. May it be so.

Notes

1   This five-act approach to scripture is sketched by N.T. Wright in *The New Testament and the People of God*.

2   Sherwin Bailey, *Homosexuality and the Western Christian Tradition*, pp. 2–4.

3   Careful exegesis of Ezekiel 16, however, shows that the prophet read the Sodom story in light of Levitical proscriptions against homoerotic acts. On this and the continuing tradition regarding homoeroticism in Sodom, reflected in Jude and 2 Peter, see R. Gagnon, *The Bible and Homosexual Practice*, pp. 79–90.

4   See, for example, the dictionaries of Liddell & Scott or Bauer-Arndt-Gingrich-Danker.

5   Here we have the primal sin, according to Alexander Schmemann; see *For the Life of the World: Sacraments and Orthodoxy*, pp. 15–18.

6   Larry Hurtado, "The Bible and Same-Sex Erotic Relations," p. 19.

7   See Richard B. Hays, "Awaiting the Redemption of Our Bodies," in ed. J.S. Siker, *Homosexuality in the Church: Both Sides of the Debate*, p. 9.

8   3 Maccabees 2:4-5, Charlesworth OTP II.

9. Sherwin Bailey, *Homosexuality and the Western Christian Tradition*, p. 91.

10 Chrysostom, *Homilies 3* and *4*, on Romans 1:26–27 and Romans 1:18–25, in *A Library of the Fathers of the Holy Catholic Church Anterior to the Division of the East and West*, vol. 7, pp. 33–43, 44–52.

11 Chrysostom, *Homily 5*, *A Library of the Fathers*, vol. 7, pp. 53–71.

12 *A Library of the Fathers*, vol. 12, pp. 320–321.

13 We refer here to his assumptions about concupiscence in his treatise on "Original Sin" and to his controversy regarding liberty in marital sexual concourse with Bishop Julian of Eclanum.

14 *Confessions* 3.8. Tr. Pine Coffin.

15 *Ibid.*

16 D.F. Wright, "Homosexuality." In ed. E. Ferguson, *Encyclopedia of Early Christianity*, 2nd ed., vol.1, p. 542.

17 On this see, for example, McNeill and Gamer, trs. and eds., *Medieval Handbooks of Penance.*

18 It is worth pointing out that Aquinas is not as rigorous — at least in practical terms — as some of the medieval Penitentials (late sixth through twelfth centuries), which forbade all physical contact, including touch and kissing; these latter, when performed with simple affection and not with the intent or effect of arousal, are approved by Aquinas. Evidently he is not intent to "build a hedge around the law," as were some other medieval ecclesial legislators; presumably he considers that reason can make its own convincing case.

19 John Boswell, *Same-Sex Unions in PreModern Europe*, pp. 350–353, tr. on pp. 312–315. Virginia Mollenkott, "Overcoming Heterosexism," in ed. J.S. Siker, *Homosexuality in the Church*, pp. 145–149, credits Boswell with the discovery of an early Greek liturgical document, perhaps from the fourth century or earlier, that he purports is a ceremony for same-sex union. Her reference to Boswell's research predated his 1994 publication of *Same-Sex Unions in PreModern Europe*, in which these rites are in fact dated to the twelfth and thirteenth centuries.

20 *Calvin's New Testament Commentaries: A New Translation, The First Epistle of the Apostle Paul to the Corinthians*, tr. John W. Fraser, p. 124.

21 Calvin, *Commentary on Romans*, tr. Ross MacKenzie, p. 35.

22 See for example, Richard F. Lovelace, *Homosexuality and the Church*, p. 21.

23 Calvin, *Commentary on Romans*, p. 36.

24 *Lectures on Genesis*, chs. 15–20, in *Luther's Works*, ed. J. Pelikan, vol. 3, p. 254.

25 *Lectures on Romans*, in *Luther's Works*, ed. H.C. Oswald, vol. 25, pp. 164ff.

26 See W. Blackstone, *Commentaries on the Laws of England*, 14th ed., ed. E. Christian, chapter 215, section 216.

27 See the words of Scott, a director of a hostel in Sudbury, Middlesex, cited in Coleman, *Christian Attitudes*, p. 157.

28 House of Lord Debates, 12 May 1965, vol. 166, cols. 71–72.

29 "Letter to the Bishops," in J. G. Melton, *The Churches Speak on Homosexuality*, p. 44.

30 See C. Curran, *Catholic and Moral Theology in Dialogue*, p. 190.

31 Eugene Rogers, *Sexuality and the Christian Body*, pp. 145–46.

32 *Ibid.*, p. 145.

33 Karl Barth, *Church Dogmatics* III. 4, p. 167

34 See *Dogmatics* III.4.166 but also *Commentary on Romans*, tr. E.C. Hoskyns.

35 *Church dogmatics* III. 4

36 *Ibid.*, p. 166.

37 A recent exchange in the Presbyterian Outlook (March 13 and May 17, 2002) speculates that the late Barth may have changed his view on same-sex eroticism. The exchange between George Hunsinger and Matthias Gockel takes its point of departure from Barth's indirect role in the 1969 change of the German penal code — a role effected through the mediation of Barth's assistant Eberhard Busch and the concerted efforts of the ethnologist Rolf Italiaander. Italiaander had requested that Barth write on this topic, but Barth indicated that he had more important subjects to address. Instead, Italiaander received indirect

word through Busch that Barth would not want his comments on homosexuality in CD III/4 (that homosexuality was by nature an "unfree form of fellowship") to be used to defame homosexuals or to legitimate their legal punishment. Busch goes on to say, "In light of changes and new insights that have occurred since the time of writing, Professor Barth is no longer quite satisfied with his previous passing utterances on this topic, and would certainly express himself somewhat differently today." Finally, he speculates that Barth "might come — in conversation with physicians and psychologists — to a new judgement and depiction of this phenomenon." (ed. Italiaander, *Offene Briefe* 1945 – 1968 [Zurich, 1984], 540–43). Busch's own speculation notwithstanding, any specific rewriting of Barth's position remains elusive. Nothing here indicates that "not-quite-satisfied" Barth had *reversed* his position. Indeed, he was not galvanized to correct his previous work, and, as Busch indicates, still considered heterosexual relations to be the "normative paradigm."

38 Robert Gagnon, *The Bible and Homosexual Practice*, p. 35.

39 For more on this see, among others, Robin Scroggs (*The New Testament and Homosexuality*) and Richard B. Hays ("Relations Natural and Unnatural" in *Journal of Religious Ethics* 14, pp. 184–215).

40 David Greenberg, *The Construction of Homosexuality*.

41 P.S. Bearman and H. Bruckner, "Opposite-Sex Twins and Adolescent Same-Sex Attraction," *American Journal of Sociology* 107 (2002), p. 1179.

42 Bailey and Pillard, "Heritable Factors," *Archives of General Psychiatry* 50 (1993), pp. 217–223.

43 For an excellent treatment of this hypothesis, see Jeffrey Satinover, *Homosexuality and the Politics of Truth*.

44 Cf. Elizabeth Moberley, *Homosexuality: A New Christian Ethic*, and J. Nicolosi, *Reparative Therapy of Male Homosexuality*.

45 Hays, "Awaiting the Redemption of Our Bodies," p. 10.

46 E.g., J. A. Reisman *et al.*, *Kinsey, Sex and Fraud.*

47 In "Awaiting the Redemption" and *The Moral Vision of the New Testament.*

48 Hays, *The Moral Vision of the New Testament*, p. 380.

49 *Ibid.*, p. 398.

50 Hays, "Awaiting the Redemption," pp. 14–15.

51 *Moral Vision*, p. 399.

52 Barth, *Church Dogmatics, III.* 4, p. 166.

53 Canon 19, John the Faster; Canon 4, Cyril of Alexandria.

54 S. Harakas, *Contemporary Moral Issues Facing the Orthodox Christian*, p. 94.

55 See both Harakas and the position of "The Greek Orthodox Diocese of North and South America," in J.G. Melton, *The Churches Speak on Homosexuality*, p. 133.

56 Ware, *The Orthodox Church*, p. 296.

57 http://orthodoxinfo.com/phronema/review_toc.htm

58 Bonhoeffer, *Ethics*, p. 365.

Works Cited

Ancient Texts (where actually quoted)

Augustine. 1946. *Literal Meaning of Genesis*. Tr. J. H. Taylor. New York: Newman.

————. 1961. *Confessions*. Tr. Pine Coffin. Penguin Books.

Calvin, John. 1960. *Commentary on Romans*. Tr. Ross MacKenzie. Grand Rapids, MI: Eerdmans.

Calvin, John. *Calvin's New Testament Commentaries: A New Translation. The first Epistle of the Apostle Paul to the Corinthians*. Tr. John W. Fraser. Grand Rapids, MI: Eerdmans.

Chrysostom. 1941. *Homilies 3 to 5 on Romans*. In *A Library of the Fathers of the Holy Catholic Church Anterior to the Division of the East and West*. Vol. 7. Oxford: Parker.

————. 1943. *Homily 5 on Titus*. In *A Library of the Fathers of the Holy Catholic Church Anterior to the Division of the East and West*. Vol. 12. Oxford: Parker.

Luther, Martin. 1961. *Lectures on Genesis*. In Luther's *Works*. Ed. J. Pelikan. Vol. 3. St. Louis: Concordia House.

————. 1972. *Lectures on Romans*. In Luther's *Works*. Ed. H. C. Oswald. Vol. 25. St. Louis: Concordia House.

Tertullian, n.d. *De Pudicitia*. London: T&T Clark.

Contemporary Authors

Bailey, Sherwin. 1955. *Homosexuality and the Western Christian Tradition*. London: Longmans.

Bailey and Pillard. 1993. "Heritable Factors." *Archives of General Psychiatry* 50: pp. 217–223.

Barth, Karl. 1933. *Commentary on Romans*. Tr. E. C. Hoskyns. Oxford: Oxford University Press.

————. 1957. *Church Dogmatics* III.4. Edinburgh: T&T Clark.

Bearman, B.S., and H. Bruckner. 2002. "Opposite-Sex Twins and Adolescent Same-Sex Attraction." *American Journal of Sociology* 107: pp. 1179–1205.

Blackstone, W. 1803. *Commentaries on the Laws of England*. 14th ed. Ed. E. Christian. London: Strahan.

Bonhoeffer, D. 1955. *Ethics*. Tr. Nevil Horton Smith. Ed. E. Bethge. London: SCM Press.

Boswell, John. 1981. *Christianity, Social Tolerance and Homosexuality*. Chicago: Chicago University Press.

_____. 1994. *Same-Sex Unions in PreModern Europe*. New York: Villard.

Coleman, Peter. 1980. *Christian Attitudes Towards Homosexuality*. London: SPCK.

Countryman, L. William. 1989, new ed. 2001. *Dirt, Greed and Sex: Sexual Ethics in the New Testament and Their Implications for Today*. London: SCM Press.

Burr, Chandler. 1993. "Homosexuality and Biology." *Atlantic Monthly* 271 (March): pp. 47–65.

Curran, C. 1971. *Catholic and Moral Theology in Dialogue*. Notre Dame: University of Notre Dame Press.

Evdokimov, Paul. French original 1952. Tr. 1985. *The Sacrament of Love: The Nuptial Mystery in the Light of the Orthodox Tradition*. Trs. P. Gythiel and F. Steadman. Crestwood, New York: St. Vladimir's Press.

_____. Tr. 1994. *Woman and the Salvation of the World: A Christian Anthropology on the Charisms of Woman*. Tr. A.P. Gythiel. Crestwood, New York: St. Vladimir's Press.

Gagnon, Robert A.J. 2001. *The Bible and Homosexual Practice: Texts and Hermeneutics*. Nashville, TN: Abingdon.

Gagnon, Robert A.J., and Dan O. Via. Forthcoming. *Homosexuality and the Bible: Two Views*. Minneapolis: Fortress Press.

Greenberg, David F. 1988. *The Construction of Homosexuality*. Chicago: University of Chicago Press.

Hansard, *House of Lord Debates*. 12 May 1965, vol. 166, cols. 71–172.

Harakas, S. 1982. *Contemporary Moral Issues Facing the Orthodox Christian*. Minneapolis: Light and Life.

Hays, Richard. 1986. "Relations Natural and Unnatural: A Response to John Boswell's Exegesis of Romans 1." *Journal of Religious Ethics* 14: pp. 184–215.

_____. 1994. "Awaiting the Redemption of Our Bodies." In ed. J. S. Siker, *Homosexuality in the Church: Both Sides of the Debate*. Louisville, Kentucky: Westminster/John Knox.

_____. 1996. *The Moral Vision of the New Testament: Community, Cross, New Creation: A Contemporary Introduction to NT Ethics*. San Francisco: HarperSanFrancisco.

Hurtado, Larry. 1996 "*The Bible and Same-Sex Erotic Relations*." *Crux* 32.

Jones, Stanton L., and Mark. A Yarhouse. 2002. *Homosexuality: The Use of Scientific Research in the Church's Moral Debate*. Downer's Grove, Illinois: Intervarsity Press.

Lovelace, Richard F. 1978. *Homosexuality and the Church*. Old Tappan, NJ: Revell.

McNeill, John T., and Helena Gamer, trs. and eds. 1938. *Medieval Handbooks of Penance*. New York: Columbia University.

Melton, J. G. 1991. *The Churches Speak on Homosexuality*. Detroit: Gale.

Moberley, Elizabeth. 1983. *Homosexuality: A New Christian Ethic*. Cambridge: James Clarke and Co.

Mollenkott, Virginia. 1994. "Overcoming Heterosexism. " In ed. J. S. Siker, *Homosexuality in the Church: Both Sides of the Debate*. Louisville, KY: Westminster/John Knox.

Nicolosi, J. 1991. *Reparative Therapy of Male Homosexuality: A New Clinical Approach*. Northvale, NJ: Jason Aronson, Inc.

O'Donovan, Oliver. 1997. "Homosexuality in the Church: Can there be a fruitful theological debate?" In ed. Timothy Bradshaw *The Way Forward*. London: Hoddert and Stoughton.

Reisman J.A., *et al*. 1990. *Kinsey, Sex and Fraud: The Indoctrination of a People*. Lafayette, LA: Lochinvar-Huntingdon House.

Rogers, Eugene. 1999. *Sexuality and the Christian Body: Their Way into the Triune God.* Oxford; Malden, MA: Blackwell.

Satinover, Jeffrey. 1996. *Homosexuality and the Politics of Truth,* Grand Rapids, MI: Baker.

Schmemann, Alexander. 1995. *For the Life of the World: Sacraments and Orthodoxy.* Crestwood, New York: St. Vladimir's Press.

Scroggs, Robin. 1983. *The New Testament and Homosexuality: Contextual Background for Contemporary Debate.* Philadelphia: Fortress Press.

Soards, Marion. 1995. *Scripture and Homosexuality; Biblical Authority and the Church Today.* Louisville, KY: Westminster/John Knox.

Ware, Kallistos. 1996. *The Orthodox Church.* Rev. ed. Baltimore: Penguin.

Wright, N.T. 1992. *The New Testament and the People of God.* Minneapolis: Fortress Press.

Wright, D.F. 1993. "Homosexuality." In eds. G.F. Hawthorne and R.P. Martin, *Dictionary of Paul and His Letters.* Downer's Grove, IL: Intervarsity Press.

_____. 1997. "Homosexuality." In ed. E. Ferguson, *Encyclopedia of Early Christianity.* New York: Garland Publishing. 2nd ed., vol. 1, p. 542.

Church and Culture

The Concept of Rights in Christian Moral Discourse[*]

Joan Lockwood O'Donovan

The entrenchment of rights language in contemporary discourse is beyond dispute. No less significantly, there are indications that the concept of rights is itself passing beyond dispute.

The concept of subjective rights, or rights ascribable to individuals and groups, has entered contemporary political and legal currency primarily through the liberal contractarian tradition. Consequently, the meanings of the term "rights" cannot be properly ascertained in detachment from this theoretical context. For these meanings are embedded in a constellation of political-legal, philosophical, and theological concepts with a complex history. Thus, to appraise the contemporary vocabulary of "rights" is to appraise the dynamic theoretical complex that has given rise to it. If such an appraisal seeks its standard of judgement in the Bible, then it is bound to proceed theologically.

---

[*]   This essay was originally published in the Irish publication *lion and lamb* 26 (Autumn 2000), pp. 20–25. It was abridged and edited by Alwyn Thomson, editor of *lion and lamb*, from an original published in *Studies in Christian Ethics* 9:2 (1996), pp. 52–65. It is reprinted here with the permission of Dr. O'Donovan and *lion and lamb*. (Issues of *lion and lamb* can be found at www.econi.org.)

My impression is that theologians often engage in a naive and facile appropriation of the language of rights. There is a quite predictable argument from the creation of humankind in God's image to the unique dignity of persons in community to their universal possession of rights. While different denominations bring important nuances to the argument, there nevertheless appears to be a consensus about the unproblematic nature of the move from human dignity to human rights once the theological "foundation" or "analogy" is prepared. "Rights" is accepted by all as adequately expressing the moral attributes of a theologically conceived humanity.

However, it is precisely the adequacy of "rights" as an element of theological-moral discourse that I wish to challenge, in the light of the pre-modern traditions of Christian natural law.

Two Orientations Toward Political Right

A close analysis of the history of the concept of subjective rights reveals a progressive antagonism between the older Christian tradition of political right and the newer voluntarist individualist and subjectivist orientation. Whereas in the older tradition, God's right established a matrix of divine, natural, and human laws or objective obligations that constituted the ordering justice of political community, in the newer tradition God's right established discrete rights, possessed by individuals originally and by communities derivatively, that determined civil order and justice.

In the older traditions, the central moral-political act on the part of ruler and ruled alike was to consent to the demands of justice, to the obligations inhering in communal life according to divine intention and rationally conceived as Laws.

In the newer orientation to political right that began to emerge in the fourteenth and fifteenth centuries, the active individual will occupied a central position. So, on the one hand, the Roman civil lawyers stressed the source of positive law in the commanding will of the ruler, and on the other hand, certain theologians attributed to individuals pre-political "natural" rights or powers that placed moral-legal constraints on the operation of political authority.

Not until the seventeenth and eighteenth centuries, however, did the subjective rights of individuals supersede the objective right of divinely revealed and natural laws as the primary or exclusive basis of political authority, justice, and law. These centuries dominated the transformation of the Western Christian tradition of natural law and natural right into a tradition of natural **rights.**

The theoretical elaborations of the concept of rights from the fifteenth to the eighteenth centuries have invested it with lasting intellectual content. For contemporary moral and political theorizing this content is in varying degrees inescapable, being woven into the fabric of politics in this century — the fabric of democratic, pluralistic, technological liberalism.

Christian political thought that is not wholly satisfied with this fabric recognizes the need to divest the concept of rights of its offensive theoretical material. But when it attempts to separate some conceptual threads from the fabric, the result inevitably falls short: either too much of the fabric adheres to the threads, or the threads lose their coherence.

To substantiate this judgement would require prior completion of two tasks: first to delineate the inherited theoretical content of the Western "rights" tradition, and second, to demonstrate the incompatibility of this content with the biblical theological doctrines that Christians regularly invoke to ground the concept of rights. I propose to undertake the first of these prior tasks, with the hope of helping readers judge for themselves the historical and theological plausibility of contemporary Christian appropriations of the language of rights. I will consider the central historical content of rights theories that is theologically problematic in three areas: the roles played by property rights, contract, and freedom of choice.

The Role of Property Rights

In the 1320s Pope John XXII attacked the Franciscan Order's vow of poverty, which entailed the renunciation of all legal rights of ownership of the material goods used by members of the order. The pope contended that all lawful consumption of material goods was inseparable from property right in them or dominion (*dominium*) over them. He reinforced his case with the assertion that *dominium*, in the legal sense of full property right over earthly goods, belonged to Adam in his created state and reflected the divine *dominium* over the earth. This argument anchored property right in an original created human power of disposal or control over temporal things.

In the fourteenth and fifteenth centuries, the idea of right (*ius*) as a power belonging to a subject was carried forward by Jean Gerson (1363–1429). Gerson extensively explicated the concept of *ius* as "a dispositional *facultas* or power, appropriate to someone and in accordance with the dictates of right reason." And he conceived "natural *dominium*" as the divinely bestowed *ius* of "every creature" to "take inferior things into its own use for its own preservation." Furthermore, Gerson joined to man's "natural *dominium*" the *dominium* or *facultas* of liberty.[1] He thus paralleled man's original power of using exterior things with his original freedom — his power of using himself, his body, and his actions.

Hobbes and Locke

The seventeenth-century proprietary concept of subjective right arrived at its zenith with the political writings of Hobbes and Locke. Its essence was an understanding of the individual as free inasmuch as he is the proprietor of his person and capacities, his freedom being conceived as both independence of the wills of others and a function of possession.[2]

Hobbes's chief contribution was his conception of "right of

nature" as the individual's unrestrained liberty "to use his own power" and to act for his self-preservation.[3] Against the earlier rights theory Hobbes asserted the radical priority of natural right to natural law and the radical separation of natural right from social obligation.

In their natural condition, Hobbes's individuals have unlimited right to use everything, including one another's bodies, unbounded by obligations of natural justice. Only the intolerable insecurity of right in this condition necessitates the prudential stratagems for peace known as "laws of nature," which include the "mutual [contractual] transferring of right" by individuals to a civil power recognized by them for the purpose of securing to them a sphere of limited rights. The one portion of individual right that is inalienable is the right to one's life and to the means of ending it, so that the citizen may by right forcibly resist violent assaults on this fundamental possession by the civil power itself.[4]

If Hobbes's emphasis gave rise to a model of social relationships as acquisitive, atomistic, and competitive, Locke's concentration on property right gave rise to a proto-Liberal economic or market model of social relationships.

Locke elaborated certain internal relationships among subjective rights as forms of property. The most important of these was the relationship between the individual's ownership of his capacity to labour and his ownership of the produce of his labour. By analogy with God's exclusive proprietary right over his creation, Locke's individual has exclusive proprietary right over the objects created by his work within the broad rational constraints of natural law. The individual's control of his labour is merely one aspect of his autonomous freedom — his right of unrestrained disposal of his actions apart from the obligations belonging to the natural law: hence, his acquisition of material property presumes a sphere of moral autonomy.

Exchanging Natural Right for Civil Right

The centrality of property in labour for Locke's theory of private property focused attention on the consequences of alienating one's labour by a wage contract, and so on the quality of labour as a transferable commodity. These considerations threw into sharp relief the question of what portion of natural right was alienable and what was inalienable.

A century later this question would occupy the forefront of American Revolutionary thought, and the answer proposed by Thomas Paine revealed the outer limit of libertarian individualism. According to Paine, each individual on entering into society retains those natural rights in which "the power to execute is as perfect in the individual as the right itself," and "deposits ... in the common stock of society" those in which, "though the right is perfect in the individual, the power to execute them is defective." In conceiving the exchange of natural right for civil right Paine draws on the analogy of a joint stock company: "Every man is proprietor in society, and draws on the capital as a matter of right."[5]

The continuing predominance of property right within the negative libertarian tradition is hardly surprising, for it sustains the concept of a right or freedom as a power of acting possessed by a subject that entails the obligation of non-interference on the part of all other subjects, and especially of government. The influence of property right on the more recent tradition of positive or welfare rights is less obvious. But if welfare rights constitute obligation-imposing demands on others made by subjects on the basis of their powers of action, then they remain within the ambit of property rights.

The logic of the connection is that individuals are impeded in fully using their personal property (their freedoms, powers, or capacities) because the necessary means are unavailable to them. Their property in these capacities implies their claim-right to these means. That claim-right is held against the government, which has, therefore, the duty to provide the relevant means. To understand why the claim-right is held against the government is to understand something of the evolving role of contract in Western political rights theory.

The Role of Contract

In all Western theories of individual natural rights, the idea of contract has proved indispensable to the theoretical transition from original right to civil and social rights. In the sixteenth and seventeenth centuries, both Protestant and Catholic theories of political covenant integrated individualist and naturalist ideas. For the most part, however, these ideas were set within a solid matrix of more traditional theo-political premises.

The Exchange of Rights

The crucially novel element introduced into social and political contract conceptions by the more radical English Puritans and Whigs in the mid-seventeenth century onward was the idea of an exchange of rights — of natural for civil rights. This idea resonated with commercial overtones. The basis of political society and rule was thereby brought into the sphere of economic transaction. One effect was to accentuate the superior bargaining position and adjudicating power of contracting individuals, or associations of individuals, and the dominant role of calculative rationality in setting the terms of the contract.

Another effect was to deprive the sphere of public welfare and public law of a moral basis independent from that of private welfare and private law. As the transcendent guidance of revealed and natural law, recognized by most seventeenth-century rights theories, has gone further into eclipse, it has become clearer that such independence of the public realm requires a basis beyond the mutual limiting of individual wills and a logic beyond prudential strategies for enhancing personal property. In contemporary contractarian liberalism, all communal obligations are derived from contract, and the only residual social right is the creation of free-market forces. It is hardly surprising in this theoretical climate that political authority and action should themselves succumb to the logic and principles of market economics. Politicians, as Ian Shapiro points out, "sell a commodity as entrepreneurs, employ agencies to 'package' their products for advertising, and gear those products to what they believe the market demands."[6]

Correspondingly, citizens in their dealings with the state are increasingly consumer-conscious: they seek the most advantageous political exchange, the best possible protection and provision for their indefinitely expanding range of personal rights in return for surrender of some freedom and material property. On the basis of their ever more explicit contractual relations with the state, as formalized in bills and charters of rights, citizens have growing incentives and opportunities to demand legal redress of the failures of governmental and public agencies to furnish the expected goods and services. Such political contractualism spells the most extreme reduction of public law and the common good it enforces to private law and private good.

Freedom of Choice: The Universal Right

In a society whose only coherent public moral language is that of subjective rights, the only universally respected right is that of freedom, understood as the sovereignty of the subject over his physical and moral world — that is, his emancipation from all externally imposed material and spiritual constraints on his freedom of choice and self-determination. A common thread throughout rights theories is the idea of the bearer of rights as a self-transcending will who uses the world around as well as his own body and capacities to achieve certain self-referential ends. Even if these ends and the means of realizing them are given in divine and natural law, the rights-bearer is still regarded as the primary source of political meaning, social worth, and positive law: when they are not so given, the rights-bearer is regarded as the exclusive source. The secularization of liberalism in the eighteenth and nineteenth centuries has meant that the self-positing, personal, creative will acknowledges fewer and fewer external obligations and objective goods.

It is precisely on account of the supposed sovereignty of the rights-bearing subject that the concept of rights is not simply co-ordinate with the concept of obligations. As Shapiro had demonstrated, the classical rights theories continue to confer "asymmetrical rights on the agent or maker" that impose obligations on others.[7] The resulting situation is a competition among sovereign subjects to maximize their freedom, that is, to maximize protection of and provision for their rights. General belief in the equality of subjects in respect of rights entails rights-bearers in honouring the claims of others, but only insofar as their legitimate prudential calculations allow. Conflicts among right-claims, therefore, can be resolved only by pragmatic compromises.

Resolving such conflicts within the contractarian tradition has been rendered even more difficult by the absorption of utilitarian interest theory, which presents individual judgements about utility as highly subjective, and as such incommensurable. The outcome of stressing incommensurability of "interest" or "utility" judgements is to focus public consensus on freedom of choice as the pivotal right.

Concluding Observations

Our task has been to examine the three dominant conceptual elements of the Western tradition of rights theory: property right, contract, and freedom of choice. Within this tradition the rights-bearing subject has been conceived as the exclusive proprietor both of his spiritual and physical being and capacities and also of those external objects necessary to their preservation and development.

His orientation to his environment has been portrayed as controlling, acquisitive, and competitive: he disposes, uses, exchanges, commands, and demands. His freedom as self-possession consists in independence from, or non-subjection to, other wills, externally imposed obligations, and natural limitations. The self-possessing subject forms social and political relationships through the formal mechanism of the contract, whose terms typically mirror those of an economic transaction undertaken from calculations of self-interest.

It may appear facile to argue the incompatibility of unadulterated secular liberalism with the Christian doctrines that are regularly invoked to support the generic concept of human rights. At a certain level this incompatibility is obvious to all current Christian apologists for rights. But the question that has yet to be satisfactorily answered is why Christian thinkers have been and are willing to adopt a child of such questionable parentage as the concept of human rights.

The answer, I suggest, lies in the affinities between some modern theological interpretations of these biblical doctrines and the classical liberal anthropological premises. The theological exercise I am recommending would at least indirectly clarify these affinities. It would present theological alternatives to, for instance, interpreting the *imago Dei* as human participation in God's rational, self-positing freedom, and interpreting the covenant as human partnership in God's sovereign, creative ordering of the world. Both of these interpretations, combined in the popular concept of "responsibility," are more open to the political-ethical language of subjective rights than to that of objective rights and obligations.

Amidst the universal political enthusiasm for rights in the civilized world, theologians with reservations about the concept are in an unenviable position. In attacking what has become a virtually unassailable datum of the Christian social conscience, we run the risk of being mistaken for complacent pietists or atavistic romantics. At the least we expose ourselves to the accusation of being unconcerned with the apologetic equipment of Christian evangelism.

However, there are enough signs about of social anomie, moral confusion, and ideological fatigue to suggest that the risk is worth taking. We may, after all, be witnessing the bitter historical irony that the revitalized striving in contemporary society for the substance of community, reciprocity, equity, and public trust is being undermined by its most trusted theoretical support.

Notes

1   Richard Tuck, *Natural Rights Theories: Their Origin and Development* (Cambridge: CUP, 1979), pp. 25–27

2   C.B. Macpherson, *The Political Theory of Possessive Individualism: Hobbes to Locke* (Oxford, Clarendon Press 1962), p. 142.

3   Thomas Hobbes, *Leviathan*, ed. M. Oakshott, (London: Collier-MacMillan, 1962) p. 103.

4   *Ibid.*, pp. 103–133.

5   Thomas Paine, *The Rights of Man* (NY, Dolphin Edition, 1961), p. 306.

6   Ian Shapiro, *The Evolution of Rights in Liberal Theory* (Cambridge: CUP, 1986), pp. 197–198.

7   *Ibid.*, p. 146

Evangelical Freedom

John Webster

I

We are schooled by cultural convention to believe that freedom is self-determination. The convention is long-standing and pervasive. Its origins, largely hidden from us within our everyday dealings with the world until retrieved by critical historical reflection, lie in some deep mutations in the West's traditions of religious, philosophical, and political thought and practice from the early modern period. Its presence is made known in a complex set of images of human selfhood that form our civic, economic, and moral accounts of ourselves. Among its most enduring and culturally successful corollaries is the assumption that the existence of God and human freedom are necessarily antithetical.

One of the primary tasks of a theology of evangelical freedom is to bring that cultural convention to consciousness, and to show that it is both contingent and inhumane. That is, a theology of evangelical freedom has to demonstrate that the conventional conception of freedom as self-government is precisely that — a *convention*, an intellectual and practical strategy for negotiating certain problems that arose in the course of the history of the West's religious and political life. And it has also to demonstrate that the convention's claim to promote human well-being is untruthful; that it is, in fact, destructive of the very reality of liberty that it seeks to uphold and defend.

But this critical or polemical task of Christian theology can only be a secondary undertaking. Its primary task in the matter is descriptive, indeed celebratory: that is, the task of loving and joyful depiction of evangelical freedom. It is the claim of the Christian faith that the understanding and experience of evangelical freedom alone can illuminate, chasten, and heal us of the convention that holds us in thrall and that is destructive of the peace and good order of our culture. What is evangelical freedom? Evangelical freedom is the freedom announced in the gospel. The gospel is the proclamation that in Jesus Christ, the risen one who is now present in the power of the Holy Spirit, God the Father's eternal decision to live in fellowship with his human creatures has been unshakably secured. In fellowship with this God, creator, reconciler, and perfecter, we have our freedom as the creatures of God's mercy. Evangelical freedom is the freedom that God bestows on the creatures who, in seeking freedom apart from God, have ruined themselves and fallen into slavery. Its origin lies in the Father's grace, in the omnipotent goodness of God in which he secures the creaturely freedom that he purposes. Its establishment is in the person and work of the Son of God, who is the embodied act of God's liberating of sinners from bondage to decay and death. Its end is in the Spirit's reconstitution of creaturely life and liberty in company with the triune God. In what follows, we offer, first, a sketch of some of the constitutive features of modern understandings and practices of freedom, and, second, the briefest of Christian dogmatics and ethics of freedom as the freedom for which we have been set free.

II

Modern understandings and practices of freedom are a central feature in one of the most important shifts in Western culture, which began before the Renaissance and Reformation in the rise of nominalist philosophy, and which continues to shape our socio-economic and political order as well as our reflective images of ourselves. The shift is one in which human selfhood comes to be morally, politically, and metaphysically fundamental. As part of this transition to an anthropocentric culture, freedom is radicalized; that is to say, freedom is turned into the very root of human authenticity and dignity. Freedom comes to be constitutive of that which is inalienably human; its inhibition comes to signal the destruction of the humane.

What we might call "fundamental freedom" — freedom as the basis and distinguishing property of humankind — consists in self-constitution or self-government. Freedom is first, the distinctively human capacity for self-constitution through action. A human person is human insofar as she is free; and she is free insofar as she can properly be identified as the originator of purposive action. For to be is to act, and to act is intentionally (voluntarily, without overwhelming external constraints) to realize oneself. Truly human action, that is, is a matter of the human agent's self-constitution. In free action, the human agent puts into effect her intentions and so makes herself in a way that is fundamental to her being. The agent's action is not merely to be conceived as the externalizing or "acting out" of what that agent finds herself to be. Authentically human action is not mere action in accordance with a pre-given human nature (such action is judged to be "mere" role playing, neither intentional nor free), but rather a making of the agent's nature by free action. Tucked inside this concept of freedom, then, is the notion that the human person is best understood, not as substance but as voluntary subject and agent. Being human is not a matter of having a certain nature or being placed within an ordered reality of which I am not the originator; rather, the distinguishing feature of humankind is, at last resort, the will. The agent is characterized, above all, not as a sort of substance, but as enacted intention. The subject is agent, and in her action is demonstrated her capacity for the self-determination that is freedom: in free action, the human subject is self-positing.

Making self-constitution humanly fundamental is, in the end, radically constructivist. Accordingly, freedom is inseparable from self-government. The freedom that the agent realizes in voluntary acts of self-constitution is to be understood as autonomy. The agent is free insofar as she is autonomous: literally, a law to herself. "Law" — that is to say, the norms by which we govern action, make discriminations between policies, and hold up practices for evaluation — is thus radically internalized. Classically conceived, law is the structure of given reality ("nature"), and the imperative force of that reality. To say that reality is law is to say that it presents itself to us as an order that requires me to be shaped by and to act in accordance with its given character. On a modern (and a postmodern) account of freedom, by contrast, "law" is not an externally derived norm, but rather a corollary of my most fundamental activity of self-projection or self-constitution. It bears upon me only as the object of my choice (political, economic, religious, sexual). And so only as a self-legislator can I be said to be free.

One centrally significant feature of this constructivist understanding of freedom as self-constitution and self-government is that freedom is often construed in oppositional terms. Freedom, that is, comes to be portrayed as an opposing of the self to forces that seek to inhibit, contain, or envelop the self and rob it of its authenticity, its self-constituted and self-legislated identity. The dynamic of freedom is thus one of acting against a countervailing force, whether that force be nature, custom, law, society, or God. Thus, for example, freedom may be set over against nature. To be free is precisely to stand apart from the supposedly given. The experience of freedom (like the self-consciousness to which it is closely allied) is only conceivable if there is a space between the free self and that which is given: the space of freedom. Nature — metaphysical, material, political, legal, moral — is always that to which freedom is opposed and that which may quickly become an object of resentment. By its very givenness, nature constitutes an order of reality that is an obstacle to free self-constitution, a blockage in the path of self-government that must be overcome or transcended. The goal of free selfhood is thus not self-fulfilment in accordance with the order of nature, but self-shaping, a making of the self by struggling free from nature.

Similarly, freedom is to be set over against situation. Freedom is antithetical to the particular sets of circumstances in which agents find themselves, which present themselves as an obligation to undertake certain tasks or a call to certain kinds of responsive (and therefore responsible) action. Like nature, situation is oppressive and must be cleared away by the assertion of liberty. In particular, freedom is real over against social situatedness — over against the way in which human existence is determined and limited by entanglements with others. For if freedom is fundamental to identity, and if identity is achieved by self-constitution and self-government, then other persons cannot be intrinsic to my freedom, but must — like nature — be that which I have to negotiate in order to be free. Society is heteronomy, and therefore erodes the autonomy in which my freedom consists.

A sketch like this cannot pretend to be anything other than a rough and ready portrayal of a cultural convention in which nearly all of us are implicated; a full account of the matter would require a massively ramified history of the intellectual and civic traditions by which freedom as autonomy is carried. From a theological point of view, one of the most indispensable components in an understanding of that history is the way in which modern conceptions and practices of human freedom both trade upon and reinforce misperceptions of divine freedom. Indeed, it is at least arguable that *the* determinative feature of the moral and spiritual landscape that had to be conquered and obliterated in the establishment of freedom as self-determination was the existence and freedom of God. It is often noted that modern conceptions of human autonomy assume a competitive understanding of divine and human freedom. That is, into the idea of freedom as self-determination is built a presumption that God's freedom is intrinsically a limitation upon human liberty, since our freedom and God's are inversely proportional. Insofar as God is free agent, his presence and activity will inevitably annex the space in which human freedom operates; that space must properly be retrieved for humankind if we are to be freely self-constituting agents. More simply: God's freedom will always interfere.

From the point of view of a theology of evangelical freedom, this misperception is a consequence of the retraction of a specifically Christian understanding of God and God's freedom, and the replacement of that specifically Christian understanding by something much more abstract, as well as much more threatening, namely, an idea of God as impersonal causal force, mere absolute power. The retraction of a Christian understanding of God is partly to be explained by the priority accorded to philosophical theism, in which a generic idea of God as transcendent ground of all things is deployed, first as a preliminary to Christian theology and then as a replacement for positive Christian trinitarian and incarnational teaching about the nature of God and of God's relation to the world. But the retraction is not without its theological roots; more than one strand of the history of theology in modernity has failed to appeal to positive Christian teaching in its response to philosophical criticism, at cost to the internal structure of Christian doctrine, and with the result that trinitarian teaching in particular drifted toward the margins of theology, with little real work to do.

Because of this, a theology of evangelical freedom will respond to conceptions of freedom as self-determination by returning to the inner structure and content of Christian teaching, seeking to show that the spectre of an absolutely free deity who is by definition the enemy of human freedom is just that: a *spectre*, and one that has to be exorcized by careful and loving attention to what the gospel announces concerning the nature and purposes of God. In making the character of God's freedom its first concern, theology will seek to exhibit that the construal of human freedom as self-determination is rooted in a misconception of God, one that issues in a misconception of human freedom. Indeed, theology will suggest that to think of the world as the kind of place where human freedom can only be maintained if we think of that freedom as self-governance is to think of the world untruthfully. Far from protecting human authenticity, freedom as self-governance is the expression of alienation from God, and therefore inhumane.

What is required of the church and its theology, therefore, is a dogmatics and an ethics of freedom. Dogmatics and ethics are the church's attempts to submit its mind to the gospel; they are part of the struggle by which the church's thinking and speaking are sanctified as they are taken into the service of the gospel. In its dogmatics, the church orders its thinking toward the gospel as an *indicative*, as a claim to truth. Part of the gospel's claim to truth is a claim about the nature of God's freedom and the nature of the freedom proper to the creatures of God. A dogmatics of freedom is thus an attempt to spell out the character of the free God in his directedness to his free creatures. In its ethics, the church orders its thinking toward the gospel as an *imperative*, as a call to action. For the gospel is not only the announcement of how we are to think aright about God and humankind. It is also a summons to freedom. And so a theology of evangelical freedom will include an ethics of freedom. Dogmatics and ethics are not speculative; they are part of the church's endeavour to orient its life by the truth about God and the human situation, and to discern the shape of truthful human action. Only on the basis of a Christian specification of the freedom of God in relation to the freedom of the creature can a theology of evangelical freedom proceed; and, moreover, only on such a basis can Christian faith offer any attempt to heal us of the hurtful axioms that have so deeply embedded themselves into modern practices of freedom, both inside and outside the church. If the church has been largely tongue-tied or concessionary in bearing witness over the matter of freedom, it is in part because of a reluctance to engage in the kind of theological clarifications by which the gospel shapes the church. What is required is a gospel-derived account of freedom as that which creatures discover in fellowship with the free, self-bestowing God made known in Christ and in the Spirit. Above all, we must set aside the bad habit of polarizing divine and human freedom, and must attempt to display how the gospel concerns their integration.

The task, then, in establishing a theology of evangelical freedom is that of letting our thinking be guided by the account of the nature of God and of God's creatures which is set before us in the history of God's fellowship with us. In that history are enacted the identities of the free God and of the creatures of his grace whom he reconciles and perfects. The theological thinking of the church must not be led by abstract conceptions of freedom (human or divine) taken over from its cultural settings, but rather by the gospel's answers to the questions: Who is God? and Who is the free creature whom God reconciles and perfects for fellowship with himself?

III

As with all matters concerning God, so in the matter of God's freedom: the primary question is not "What is God?" but "Who is God?" The former — abstract — question invites answers that determine God's essence in advance of any specific considerations of the mode or manner of God's existence. By contrast, the latter — concrete — question is answered by beginning from the given reality of God's self-manifesting existence and only on that basis moving on to determine the essence of God. Because a Christian theology of the freedom of God is a thinking in the wake of God's revelation, it addresses itself to this latter question. For revelation is of all things the most concrete and particular. It is the communicative presence of God, vouchsafed to us in God's works of creation, reconciliation, and perfection as Father, Son, and Holy Spirit. In those works God sets before us his identity as *this one*, the triune creator who has reconciled his fallen creature and is now bringing it to its final fulfilment. His freedom is the freedom of the one who does this work, and in so doing manifests that his freedom is freedom to be God for us and with us. In short: if we are to think truthfully of God's freedom, avoiding the abstract antitheses that have so ruined the modern conception of freedom, we must grasp that God's freedom is the freedom of the triune God.

God's freedom is his freedom as God the Father, creator of heaven and earth. God's freedom is not simple arbitrary power or unfocused will. Rather, because God's freedom is made known in the act of creation, it is a freedom that is actual in his purposive act of bringing into being another reality to exist alongside himself. God's freedom is not an infinite reserve of potency that could be actualized in ways other than those that he determines for himself as creator; it is rather the undeflected energy with which God follows the direction in which he determines to be himself. His freedom is thus freedom for fellowship with the creature. As creator, *God is free* — standing under no necessity, having no external claims upon himself, in no need of the creature; as free Lord, God the Father is and creates *ex nihilo*. But because God is free *as creator*, his freedom is not a merely empty or formal idea but a very definite direction and act of relation. And, moreover, as an act of relation, God's freedom is teleological — it involves not simply an initial act of making heaven and earth, but also the preservation and governance of the creaturely realm. As creator, that is, God's freedom is the grace in which he promises himself or commits himself to the creature. The free creator is the free Lord of the covenant, the origin and sustainer of fellowship with himself.

God's freedom is his freedom as God the Son, the reconciler of all things. God's freedom as Father involves the grace with which he pledges to maintain fellowship. That pledge is enacted in God the Son, who restores the covenant between God and his creatures after it has been broken by the creature's wicked and false attempt to be free from God. The creature seeks to be apart from God; only in that way, the creature believes, can real freedom be exercised. This attempt to master its own destiny becomes the creature's ruin and misery, because it strikes at the root of the fellowship with God in which alone the creature has its being. In this situation of the absolute jeopardy of the creature, God's freedom demonstrates itself, not as freedom to withdraw from fellowship, but precisely as an utter determination to maintain fellowship. (Whatever else it may mean, this is part of what is set before us in the story of Noah.) And God's maintenance of fellowship culminates in the person and work of the Son who, as God in the flesh, is reconciliation embodied and effective. He *is* Emmanuel, the fulfilment of the free divine resolve and promise: I will be your God, you will be my people. The fulfilment of this resolve is, of course, entirely gratuitous — God fulfils his freedom in that "the Word *became* flesh." But, as in the Father's work of creation, so here in the Son's work of reconciliation: God's freedom is freedom for and with, not freedom apart from or against.

God's freedom is his freedom as God the Holy Spirit, who brings all things to their perfection. In the work of the Holy Spirit, the reconciliation of the creature that has been willed by the Father and accomplished in the person and work of the Son becomes real as the creature's own history. By the power of the free Spirit, God sanctifies the creature, completing his purpose for it and so finally establishing the work begun in creation and maintained in reconciliation. It is the Spirit who thus consummates the purpose of God, not the creature itself. Creation and reconciliation are not brought to fulfilment by the creature itself. The perfecting of the creature by the Spirit is no less a free work of divine sovereignty than any other of God's works. But the Spirit's freedom is known in the work of making real the relation to God in which the creature has life. The Spirit is Lord, sovereignly free, majestic and unfettered; but as Lord, the Spirit is also the life-giver, bestowing upon the creature the life (and therefore the freedom) forfeited in the creature's betrayal of the covenant. As free Spirit, God directs his ways to the final realization of fellowship with those whom he has created and redeemed for life with himself.

What may we draw from this trinitarian sketch of the freedom of God? Two things. First, God's freedom is his "aseity," his being from himself. God is the sovereign originator and accomplisher of all that he is and does. Second, we can only grasp what it is for God to be thus eternally and majestically self-moved when we attend to the direction of the divine movement, which is toward us in his work as Father, Son, and Spirit. God's freedom is the glorious spontaneity, reliability, and effectiveness in which he is the Holy One in our midst.

IV

What of the freedom of the creature? For Christian theology, that question can only rightly be answered after the question of God's identity as the free creator, reconciler, and perfecter has received an answer. To begin by determining the conditions of creaturely freedom in advance of an understanding of God, and then inquiring into the compatibility of human freedom with God's freedom is simply to remain captive to the destructive convention of human freedom as self-government. A theology of evangelical freedom will work from an understanding of God's freedom toward an anthropology of freedom. God's triune freedom, we have seen, is the sovereign purposiveness with which he establishes fellowship. Human history is the "space" — arena, setting — in which that fellowship is realized. For the Christian gospel, moreover, the history of God with us is definitive of what it means to be human. It is not a mere modulation or particular form of a more general human history, but is ontologically definitive: to be human is to be the reconciled creature of God pointed by God to perfection. Our freedom, therefore, is the capacity bestowed on us by God to take an active part in the history of fellowship with our creator, reconciler, and perfecter.

To understand this, we need to lay aside the assumption around which so much of our economic, political, and sexual identity is organized, namely the assumption that freedom is autonomy. Freedom is, rather, the capacity to realize what one is. What we are is reconciled creatures, those set free for true humanness by the work of the triune God. To be free is not to exercise the false freedom to invent myself by my actions, or to be creator, reconciler, and perfecter to myself. Nor is it mere unrestricted will. It is, rather, to be what I have been made to be, to fulfill my vocation as creature of God, and so (and only so) to exist in authenticity. Two things flow from this.

First, human freedom is *given*. Because it is the freedom of creatures, it cannot be wholly self-originating. But the contingency of human freedom, its dependence upon the agency of another, is not a restriction but a specification, a way of characterizing its particular nature. In the same way that our life is no less life for being the gift of God, so our freedom is no less freedom for its dependence upon the free grace of God. Or, we might say, given freedom only seems a lesser reality if we cling to the decision that only absolute freedom is real freedom, and that nothing but autonomy can guarantee our authenticity.

Second, therefore, human freedom is freedom within situations, and not sheerly transcendent. The modern ideal of freedom idealizes freedom as independence, thereby mirroring the degenerate idea of divine freedom that it was designed to negate. But evangelical freedom is not my removal from the realm of contingency and relation; it is, rather, the character of my relations with that which is other than me. Freedom emerges in my occupancy of the space of the material and social world and, above all, in my relation to God as my origin and end. I am not free in abstraction from these relations, nor simply when those relations are a function of my will and exist solely by my sovereign choice. Rather, I become free when I become myself in the space of relations in which I exist. Those relations are the occasions of my freedom when they quicken me to fulfil my nature as creature of God and fellow-creature with others. Freedom is thus not some property or potency that I have in myself anterior to all relations and to the givenness of nature and situation; nor is it something that is necessarily constricted or compromised by relations and situations.

Freedom is that which I come to exercise as I exist in freedom-granting fellowship.

Evangelical freedom cannot therefore be conceived or practised as a single spasm, an act of defiance or protest against the fact that I find myself within an order of reality that is not of my invention. Such accounts of freedom, however deeply ingrained they may be, are too thin to furnish a persuasive account of free human selfhood, above all because they reduce all relations to hostile and oppressive determinations. It is certainly true that not all aspects of our situation do quicken freedom: some relations can be life-denying, robbing us of authenticity. But these diminutions of freedom are overcome, not by abstracting selfhood from the dependencies that are fundamental to what it means to be human, but by the restoration of the human self to the space in which freedom can be received and acted out.

Human freedom is, in short, that which we are given as we live in the space of fellowship that is made by God's free acts of setting us free. In that space we are met by God as the maker, rescuer, and preserver of our freedom, and by those others to whom we have been bound as fellow recipients of grace. What is the form of this freedom for which, according to the gospel, we have been set free?

Evangelical freedom is a form of life that acts out of the fact that I have been set free from "the law of sin and death" (Rom 8:2). Sin tyrannizes and limits God's creatures as they act out the falsehood that in order to be human they must make themselves. Such self-making is self-destruction, because it breaks the human side of fellowship with God. Since it is only in fellowship with the creator that we can have life, sin and death are inseparable; together they form the despotic principle ("law") that enslaves humankind; for the gospel, however, that tyranny has been overcome by "the law of the Spirit of life in Christ Jesus" (Rom 8:3): in what "God has done" (Rom 8:3) in Christ and in the effective presence of that achievement in the Holy Spirit, sin and its entailments — death and bondage — have been condemned (Rom 8:3), and life and freedom have been irreversibly established as the condition by which we are governed.

Evangelical freedom, emerging from our being put to death and made alive in Christ and the Spirit, is thus freedom from the *care of self* that so harasses and afflicts the lost creatures of God. My freedom is in part my freedom from final responsibility for maintaining myself, a freedom that is the fruit of my having been liberated from the anxious toil of having to be my own creator and preserver. Evangelical freedom is rooted in a security given to me — not dreamed, imagined, or effected by stringent acts of self-realization. That security is such that in Christ I am inviolable, and so free from concern for my own preservation. Such inviolability is not expressed as self-defensive closure of myself against all transgression from without, but as a profound lack of self-preoccupation, a confidence that has its roots in the sheer objectivity of my condition as one set free by God. The compromise of my liberty that I have made by seeking to be my own liberator has been overcome; because by the Spirit I am in Christ, having my centre not in myself and my own acts but in Jesus Christ who has set me free, then all other bonds are set aside. I no longer need to cultivate my freedom; and so I am free. A particular mode of this freedom is the freedom to pray. Prayer is an act of evangelical freedom because in it is expressed our liberation from anxiety and self-responsibility, and our freedom to live from the fellowship with God in which we trust in the divine promise. Prayer thus expresses the fact that, as we have been set free by God, so we have had taken from us the evil custody of ourselves which we thought ensured our safety but which in fact fastened us to sin and death. Prayer, indeed, is at the centre of the fellowship with God that is determinative of whatever is authentically humane.

Free for fellowship with God, I am thus free also for human fellowship. If freedom is self-governance, it is the end of love; if, however, freedom is the restoration of my identity in company with my fellows, then I am free to act in support of my neighbour's cause. "Let no-one seek his own ends, but the ends of his neighbour"

(1 Cor 10:24). Far from being a compromise of freedom, such a rule guides us toward the practice of freedom. To "seek one's own ends" is not to realize one's true nature but to mobilize all one's forces in living out of oneself, making oneself by choices; and so it is to place oneself in the hands of death. To seek that which is one's neighbour's is, by contrast, to be free for life. Looking to the neighbour's cause is not mere self-abandonment; it is rather to exist in the human fellowship by which, precisely by not striving to realize ourselves, we attain to the liberty of the children of God.

Such, then, is a sketch of evangelical freedom, for which we have been set free by the gloriously free God, our maker, redeemer, and end. Whether such an account of freedom can commend itself to modern culture is not easy to know. Its persuasiveness depends on many factors: on a willingness to stand apart from dominant conventions; on the existence of forms of Christian common life that exemplify the practice of a freedom that is beyond autonomy or heteronomy; but above all on the coming of the Holy Spirit, who is the agent of all persuasion in the matter of the gospel. To understand and practise freedom we need to become different people. It is the office of the Spirit to make us such; the office of the church to bear witness in word and action to the Spirit's convincing work; and the office of the church's theology to assist that witness by trying to speak the gospel well.

The Authority of Experience

Among Anglicans in Moral Debate*

Christopher Lind

A nglicans familiar with the religious debates of the sixteenth century will often discuss the issue of authority in terms of scripture, tradition, and reason. However, they do not necessarily attribute equal authority to each. Those who find themselves following Martin Luther will give priority to scripture (*sola scriptura*). Those who are comfortable identifying themselves as Catholic will give priority to historical witness as identified by the tradition of the early church. Those who have been carried along by the wave of the Enlightenment give priority to reason as clarifying authoritative judgements.

Increasingly, experience is considered a source of authority in conjunction with scripture, tradition, and reason. Some people resist the authority of experience because they consider it unbiblical. Yet one could argue that experience is the foundation for one of the major forms of scripture, namely the Wisdom tradition (Proverbs, Psalms, Ecclesiastes, Job, and other books). What is the

---

* Portions of this essay were published in different articles in the first two volumes of *Wrestling with God: Longing for God* (vol. 1) and *Turning to God* (vol. 2), The Primate's Theological Commission (Toronto: ABC Publishing, 2001/2002).

Wisdom tradition if not distilled experience — distilled by many communities from many places? It does not represent a single, coherent narrative and biblical scholars can trace fragments of the tradition to a variety of other ancient near-eastern cultures.[1]

Four Meanings of Experience

At the turn of the twenty-first century, it is also common for people to rely upon their own experience as a part of the fourth authority in religious affairs. However, in citing experience, they can mean very different things.

Some will place themselves in continuity with the eighteenth-century Anglican, John Wesley, who founded the Methodist Movement. Wesley found his faith re-oriented and his life changed by a personal experience of God's presence — the "heart strangely warmed." The experience to which he referred and which he considered decisive, was the experience of the Holy. It became for him a test of faith. Today, we would describe this as a charismatic experience and we might talk about the various gifts (or charisms) the Holy Spirit brings.

A closely related type of authoritative religious experience is the mystical experience. Since it may not be experienced as the presence of the Holy Spirit, it would be inaccurate to describe it as charismatic. It may be an experience of the Holy, the Divine, the Other, or of awe, majesty, or power. One of the characteristics of such an experience is that words fail to do it justice. It clearly has authority in the lives of those who experience it for it can move people to action or life decision.

A third meaning of the authority of experience uses different language entirely. In this case people talk about the authority of conscience. Conscience is thought of as personal experience; however, it is not experience of the world but personal experience of the Divine. It has its roots in St. Paul's injunction that the divine law is written on the human heart. It also has roots in the ancient theory of natural law: the will of God is available not only through special revelation, but also through the general revelation of nature. Significantly, this access to the divine will requires mediation neither by a priest nor by the church. Conscience has been very important in the life of the Christian church because it has been used as a countervailing authority and an instrument of resistance to established powers. It is familiar to us in the pacifist tradition of those who seek exemption from military service because they are conscientious objectors to war, and of those who oppose political moves on the grounds of conscience. Their numbers have included many Anglicans. In a very different context, when the Anglican Church of Canada decided to ordain women for the first time in 1976, no one was required to receive communion from women priests if their consciences required them to abstain. From this point of view we can say that the authority of experience is already well established among Anglicans.

Each of the first three forms of experience is individual and personal. The fourth is communal experience, and it may be the most important because it runs counter to the individualistic trend of modern culture. In contemporary theological movements such as liberation theology and feminist theology, attention is focused on collective experiences of oppression and suffering as privileged moments of divine action. This is where the God who suffers cries out the loudest. This is where the God who liberates is most energetic. This is where God's mission is most compelling. Collective experiences of suffering give us access to God. In this way they are authoritative for faith and give us a lens through which we can examine it. They provide us with an interpretive key to both scripture and tradition. In Central America and in South Africa, people ask themselves what interpretation of scripture makes the most sense of their suffering — what reading of the historic teaching of the church would be the most liberating for them?

In the internal procedures of the Anglican Church, when we also give priority to collective experience over individual experience, we call it discernment. When candidates present themselves for ordination, we do not simply accept their word that they have experienced a call from God to serve the church. We send the candidates to a committee charged with a collective discernment of this call. We seek the authority of communal experience. Similarly, when we make major decisions in the church, we gather the wisdom of the church community in diocesan or general synods. We tend to privilege the wisdom of the community over the experience of the individual except in rare cases of conscience. The authority of tradition can also be thought of as the authority of communal experience, only the experience is witnessed to by the historic, not the contemporary, community.

However, many people who proclaim the authority of experience today are referring neither to a charismatic or mystical experience, nor to an experience of the divine law through conscience. Some are reflecting a general mistrust of external authorities that is typical of Western culture at the beginning of the twenty-first century. Today, many people want to judge for themselves, and they rely on the authority of their personal experience to do so. Nowhere is this more prevalent than in the field of Christian ethics, where all authorities are under a cloud of suspicion and all moral norms seem to be under review. I have not described this as a different meaning of experience because it is so highly individualized that it has no claim on others. There is only my experience and your experience, not experience *per se*. It is different from charismatic and mystical experience and also from the experience of conscience because it requires no external validation whatsoever. It is not so much a form of authority derived from experience as a questioning of all authority. It is apt to assert, "The authority of my interpretation has precedence over all others."

Different Moral Languages

Have you ever been in an argument with someone about an ethical issue and felt that the two of you were speaking different languages? In the field of ethics, there are many moral languages and there are Christian versions of most of them. Each language carries with it a certain worldview. The metaphor of language is helpful because no one would presume to say that French is right and Spanish is wrong. Rather, people are more likely to say that when you are in Mexico, Spanish is more appropriate than French if you want to make yourself understood. In any discussion of experience, we need to take account of the moral language we are speaking. The various forms of experience carry different weights in these different moral languages. Let me describe three of the largest language families, recognizing that there are many dialects within each of them.

The first is the language of obligation, the language of duty. The technical term for this language is "deontological." The emphasis here is on paying back or giving what is owed. If God created the world and gave us life, these are gifts we can never repay, though we try mightily. The great Genevan Reformer John Calvin spoke this language. In this worldview, God is the primary actor and we are the respondents. Our task is to fulfill our duty toward God. We also have obligations toward our neighbour, which imply that our neighbours have a claim on us. Our neighbours, in other words, have rights, which we have an obligation to honour. So the language of rights, even human rights, is a variant on the deontological language of duty and obligation. In philosophy, the primary exponent of this view was Immanuel Kant.

The second moral language is the language of intention. The technical term for this way of speaking about moral issues is "teleological." Anyone who tries to defend themselves from moral criticism by saying "I didn't mean to do it!" is speaking this language and drawing attention to the difference between intention and actual result or consequence. Our legal system also speaks this language; the Criminal Code has harsher penalties for crimes that were intended than for those that were unintended. The Roman Catholic Church speaks this language primarily, though not exclusively, because it was the language used by the great Dominican theologian, St. Thomas Aquinas. In this worldview, we all come from God and our intention should be to return to God. All of us have a destiny in God to be fulfilled. This destiny can be fulfilled if our end is viewed with clarity and our intention is sure. In philosophy, the primary exponent of this view was Aristotle.

The third moral language is simultaneously the most powerful and also the most problematic for Christianity. This is the language of consequences. Here the moral value of an action depends upon the action's results. People who judge the morality of an action primarily by the actual results are using the language of the dominant Western secular culture. This is also the language of the market. It doesn't matter why someone is selling a product or why someone else is buying it. If they are both willing and they agree on a price, society judges this to be a fair transaction and a moral act. Its goodness consists in its having served the interests of both parties. The language of consequences is important to us because consequences are apprehended by experience. The technical term for this language is "utilitarian." While this moral language is an ancient one, it acquires its name from the work of the nineteenth-century philosopher John Stuart Mill.

As churches become minorities in Western societies, they are being forced to speak the language of the majority. When Canadian churches try to persuade Canadian politicians not to bankrupt the churches with lawsuits over residential schools, the churches are forced to argue that the consequences of such a strategy will be harmful to both society and the government. The churches may believe that the government has an obligation to protect the churches from harm (language #1), or they may believe that Canadian society cannot become what it was meant to be by these actions (language #2). However, the language that is most likely to be heard and understood is the language of consequences and utility (language #3). This language is problematic for Christians because it is the most recent and unfamiliar. It is not prominent in scripture or in the teachings of the church. It is still a minor language even in the documents of the Reformation. However, it is the language of commerce and it dominates today's world.

In terms of debates about sexual orientation and practice, some people argue that homosexual activity is immoral because of God's commands against it in scripture (language #1: deontological). Others argue that sexual orientation is a matter of nature not choice, so in order to become their most fully human selves, they must give expression to the sexual orientation given them by God (language #2: teleological). Still others argue that changing or not changing our social customs and church practices will have good or bad consequences for society or the church (language #3: utilitarian).

Experience can play a role in the deontological language, but in moral decision-making based on obligation it is not how we feel, nor how others experience our actions, that matters, but our experienced sense of duty toward God, our neighbour, or our own conscience. When, according to legend, Martin Luther hammered his Ninety-five Theses to the door of the castle church in Wittenberg, he indicated he was indifferent to how others experienced his actions. "Here I stand," he said later to the imperial council. "I can do no other, for to go against conscience is neither good nor right."

Experience traditionally played a large role in the teleological approach, but this moral language was suppressed for hundreds of years, largely through the efforts of the seventeenth-century French philosopher and Christian reformer Blaise Pascal, who launched a campaign against the excesses of "casuistry."[2] Priests at the time were charged with adjudicating the appropriate penance for sins heard in confession. Casuistry was the art of bringing general moral principles to bear on particular cases; that is, of deciding how what ought to be, might be realized in each person's unique and complex circumstances. In other words, the person's experience helped shape what was fitting. Pascal's campaign brought casuistry, or the art of interpreting the ideal in terms of the actual, into disrepute.

It has re-emerged at the end of the twentieth century as the dominant approach in bio-ethics because of the large number of variables involved in particular health care issues.

Obviously, experience plays the most significant role in consequentialist or utilitarian discourse. The consequence of one person's actions enter another person's experience, and experience is the painful check against the prideful assumption that all consequences can be anticipated.

All the moral languages are found wanting by contemporary reformers, however. The most prominent movement for reform comes from feminist voices, Christian and otherwise. As Paul Lauritzen put it, "feminist insistence that women's moral experiences be taken seriously has dramatically changed the field of ethics...."[3]

The Feminist Critique

There are three ways feminist critics appeal to experience in ethical discourse. They are the appeal to the unseen, the unthought, and the unheard.

The Unseen

Because the tradition of moral theology (the Roman Catholic term) or Christian ethics (the Protestant term) has been created almost exclusively by men, the moral experience of women has been either suppressed, diminished, or ignored. Feminist theologians and ethicists have legitimated a turn to experience as a way to make visible the otherwise unseen moral concerns of women. For example, contemporary concerns about sexual harassment and abuse in the church and society are a direct result of women sharing their experiences and making them visible. We can now see what was unseen before.

The Unthought

The second way in which feminist critics appeal to experience in ethical discourse has to do with how we think about issues as well as what issues we think about. For example, feminists have criticized the theological tradition as reflecting a distorting series of dualisms, which are also reflected in our culture.[4]

We tend to value reason as separate from and superior to emotion, and in a related way we value the masculine as separate from and superior to the feminine. If we were to take women's experience seriously, then the way we engage in theological and ethical reflection would be different. We would think in ways we haven't thought before. "To acknowledge experience as a legitimate source of moral knowledge means that one does not immediately dismiss what one knows or feels experientially simply because it conflicts with conventional wisdom or because traditional categories of analysis leave little room for experience."[5]

The Unheard

The third way in which feminist critics appeal to experience has to do with the unheard moral experience of women. The most oft-quoted exponent of this view is the American educational theorist Carol Gilligan, who criticized the experiments of Lawrence Kohlberg because all his research subjects were boys. When she repeated his experiments with girls, her results were different. When she analyzed her results more carefully, she discovered that the majority of girls had a different form of moral reasoning, one that gave priority to interpersonal relationships.[6]

This form of reasoning was not exclusive to girls but was a dominant mode in girls and a subordinate mode in boys. She had to train herself differently in order to hear the moral experience of girls. "If a moral theory requires that we act in a particular way in a particular situation, but when we are in that situation we do not think and feel that what the theory requires is the right thing to do, then the theory will be put in doubt by the experience. Thus if we would only attend to and value it, personal experience could be an important source of insight when deliberating morally. But we must listen in order to hear."[7]

Conclusion

So the appeal to experience is critical, especially with regard to moral issues. Experience in one form or another is almost always involved in our moral decision-making. The type of experience we privilege, and the moral languages we use, can affect what we see as important, how we think about the world and our place in it, as well as how and to whom we listen. However, acknowledging the importance and authority of experience does not end debate on controverted issues. It may only increase it. In the same way that we are prepared to be critical of church leaders or of certain forms of biblical interpretation, so we must apply our critical skills to the category of experience. We cannot acknowledge the moral significance of human experience without acknowledging the need for adjudicating among competing claims based on it. "Experience is not unmediated; it is not transparent.... In appealing to experience, we do not just appeal to a kind of brute fact about the world; rather, we engage in an interpretation of reality. So the appeal to experience can never be the last word."[8]

As I hope the foregoing has made clear, it is simply inaccurate to claim that experience has no authority for Christians in the Anglican tradition. So, if we are to debate the relative priority of experience as an authority, we need to be clear about what we are describing. Experience can be personal or communal, contemporary or historical, divine or worldly. Once we are clear on what we mean by experience, we must be prepared to be as critical in our attitude toward it as we are to any other authority. Then we can focus on what criteria will be helpful in adjudicating conflicting claims based on experience. Within the Anglican tradition we can clearly see examples where the church already uses the wisdom of the community as a criterion to adjudicate individual claims to the experience of God's call to ordination. We can also see examples where the church has legitimized the appeal to the experience of conscience in the implementation of the decision to permit the ordination of women.

As Christians debate moral questions, whether they are related to issues of sexual orientation or residential schools or other questions, they should not be surprised to encounter disagreement. In addition to differences of fact and moral value, we are also speaking different moral languages. This should not take away from the desire of all people of faith to love God and love our neighbours as ourselves. The task of working out what this means in practice has never been easy, but it has always been necessary.

Notes

1   A good introduction to the Wisdom tradition continues to
    be *The Way of Wisdom in the Old Testament* by the Canadian
    biblical scholar R.B.Y. Scott (New York: Macmillan, 1971).
2   See Jonsen, A., and S. Toulmin, *The Abuse of Casuistry*
    (Berkeley: University of California Press, 1988).
3   Paul Lauritzen, "Hear No Evil, See No Evil, Think No
    Evil: Ethics and the Appeal to Experience," HYPATIA, vol.
    12, no. 2 (Spring 1997), p. 85. I rely extensively on
    Lauritzen's analysis in what follows.
4   See Beverly Harrison, *Making the Connections* (Boston:
    Beacon Press, 1985).
5   Lauritzen, p. 91.
6   Carol Gilligan, *In A Different Voice* (Cambridge: Harvard
    University Press, 1982, 1993).
7   Lauritzen, p. 93.
8   Lauritzen, p. 97.

The "Appeal to Experience"

Biblical Roots and Critical Developments

Carroll Guen Hart

One of our most familiar human activities is trying to name a new thing that has happened to us. For me, this happens when I am unwell and cannot yet identify the problem. I woke up one night with numbness in my arms and legs and, in the absence of a definitive diagnosis, was open to terrifying possibilities. After consulting with my doctor, I was able to name that experience: repetitive stress injury to the neck, caused by too much work at the computer. While that naming did not of itself remove the pain and the numbness, it did locate that frightening experience within a larger pattern of causes, symptoms, underlying problems, and therapeutic actions. Naming provided recognizable meaning. That in turn enabled me to channel all of that energy from paralyzing fear into fruitful and healing action.

This struggle to "name" has also happened in my difficult history with gay and lesbian friends.

I grew up in a socially conservative, fundamentalist household in the American west, and was formed into an unquestioning and (at that time) largely tacit condemnation of gay sexuality. As I moved on in life and away from fundamentalism, I sought help from a counsellor who was extremely helpful and supportive at a difficult time in my life. But when I suddenly discovered that he was gay, all my reflex hatred poured out. I remember saying over and over, "At least adultery would have been normal." What I meant was that being gay went beyond the bounds of ordinarily recognizable sinfulness into the terrain of ontological, structural, boundary-crossing wrongness. It was wrong, you might say, in a much more fundamentally abnormal way.

And yet as I poured out my condemnation, I was troubled by the awareness that this person had been so good to me. He had, in effect, modelled for me a new image of God. He had had faith in my future when I could not have it for myself. And so I found myself stuck in a hard place. This person was structurally evil, a blot on the good creation, and yet had been an instrument of God's redemptive work in my life. A lesbian friend of mine once put it very well. When a friend expressed his inherited condemnation of gay sexuality, she said, "Look me in the eyes and say that to me." He tried and failed, and that upset him so much that he embarked on a long and painful process of self-examination, as well as examination of his faith. That is what I experienced.

And as I looked into the eyes of that counsellor, and into the eyes of gay friends and acquaintances since, I have seen the good in their lives. I found that I could no longer simply condemn them as structurally evil. I had to listen to what they wanted and needed to say. What they had to say was that in their own faith journey they had reached a desperate point at which they could no longer believe that God had created them wrong or evil because of a sexuality that they had not chosen and which many had tried to change. Out of desperation they had come to believe that God had created them good. This recognition had come to them as an authentic experience of God's affirmation and redemption. They had concluded that theirs was a different form of human sexuality, one which, because it was unrelated to procreation and socially distinct from the economic and property relations of marriage, could more clearly focus on the divine purpose of sexuality as a source of intimacy, pleasure, and joy. And they must believe that God, having created them with the desire for a person of the same sex, would not forever forbid them to satisfy that desire, within the boundaries proper to right human relationships.

As I have listened to these friends I have found a need to return to scripture with a slightly changed awareness. I can no longer assume uncritically that heterosexual relationships are normative whereas homosexual ones are not; rather, I find myself looking at what makes a sexual relationship *of any sort* normative, or not. I find myself looking at the network of social meanings that structure the notion of marriage and that support or pressure it in certain directions. I find myself looking anew at the meaning of sexuality and what it might say about the way we are created. I am still in the midst of that journey.

This has been a deeply unsettling but enriching process. I believe it has been a God-sent one. At the same time I am told by fellow-believers that this is disrespectful of scripture and tradition, a modernist "revisionism" that turns away from the difficult calling of the church. That is not how it has felt to me. But how do I begin to name it in a way that enables the church community to recognize it? Rowan Williams has helpfully identified the task:

> … If I am serious about making a gift of what I do to the Body as a whole, I have to struggle to make sense of my decision in terms of the common language of the faith, to demonstrate why this might be a way of speaking the language of the historic schema of Christian belief.[1]

When I went through the complex diagnostic process of identifying my repetitive stress injury, I had at my disposal an entire medical community and a vast body of research and medical experience. But in naming my experience of the wholeness of gay and lesbian friends, it has been infinitely more difficult to find a shared vocabulary, since it has involved the critical questioning of some of the Christian tradition's normative categories. In what follows I will describe some ways in which I have tried to articulate my experience in the common language of the faith.

The process by which my understanding of homosexuality — and indeed sexuality in general — was changed was rooted in human experience, both my own and that of others. So it seemed natural to turn to what we all routinely call the "appeal to experience" in an attempt to name it. Here experience takes *its* place, along with scripture, tradition, and reason, as one of the four authorities on which Anglican faith rests.

The notion of "fourfold authority" actually comes from John Wesley, the Anglican priest who founded the Methodist movement. In fact, he added a fifth authority — the Church of England.[2] Scott Jones says:

> For Wesley the elements are defined in such a way that they constitute one locus of authority with five aspects. Christian faith and practice are governed by scripture, which is reasonable in its claims, exemplified in antiquity, vivified in personal experience, and most fully institutionalized in the Church of England.[3]

For Wesley as for the empiricist philosopher John Locke, the source of descriptions of both the physical and spiritual worlds is experience; it is "the only authority that can supply evidence for the state of one's soul." Experience also provides the "testimony" or "inward proof" of the working of the Spirit in each of us that makes us God's children. Finally, experience functions as the goal of the Christian life.[4] Wesley would only make the gentlest movement toward what we straightforwardly call an "appeal to experience" that authorizes us to explore new articulations of Christian norms in response to different forms of life and practice.

But the notion of "fourfold authority" has its own pitfalls. Too often it mistakenly posits "experience" as a separate authority over against scripture, tradition, and reason. An uncritical acceptance of what we loosely call "contemporary experience" opens the door to letting go of scripture and Christian patterns of thought and discernment. For example, women's real experiences of masochism, when picked up by some versions of feminist theory, become the basis for a wholesale rejection by feminist theology of the "sacrificial suffering" motif in scripture. Also, a generalized appeal to the human rights of the individual can be a way of bypassing complex processes of discerning Christian norms.[5] My colleagues in dialogue have pressed me to see that these appeals to experience have not been received by the church as expressing the common language of the faith, but as departures from it.

For the purposes of this essay, I will continue to use the formulation of a fourfold appeal to scripture, tradition, reason, and experience, because in their common usage they suggest different angles on our faith that are useful and important for Christian discernment and argumentation. I will try to hold them lightly, not as platonic ideas but as flawed but possibly useful reminders of important considerations. More specifically, I will try to suggest ways in which we might name an appeal to experience in the common language of the faith. I will try to make a case for the notion that our own experience of God's working in the world and in human life presses us to return to scripture and tradition, yet to challenge traditional and current formulations of faith and to explore new ones in response to that new experience. So the issue is: How do we understand this process — experience changing the formulation of faith — in authentic and recognizable Christian terms?

In proposing an answer, let us consider the working of God's Spirit. I shall suggest that the Spirit works on us in a variety of ways to illuminate for us God's complex and novel work in our contemporary world, thereby requiring us, as a matter of course, to confront and rework our traditional formulations. I will examine some scholarly reflections on the working of the Spirit of God and the ways in which the community of faith needs to remain open to what God is saying. The three texts I will use primarily are Michael Welker's *God the Spirit*,[6] James Dunn's *Jesus and the Spirit*,[7] and John V. Taylor's *The Go-Between God*.[8] Because of the very brief compass of this essay, I cannot recapitulate all of their scriptural grounding, but can only pull out some of their summary reflections and point briefly to what that might mean for my topic.

Spirit in Creation, Torah, and Prophets

What is Spirit?

Let me begin with John V. Taylor's observation that "spirit" is in fact a metaphor. The Hebrew word *ruach*, like the Greek *pneuma* and the Latin *spiritus*, all mean "wind" or "breath":

> Something in the physical world — the fierce wind of the desert, the breath of a living creature — is used as an image of an incorporeal element in man [*sic*] which cannot easily be named in any other way; and then this human "spirit" is itself used as an image of another ineffable force which man feels working upon him and believes to be divine.[9]

Spirit moves in and through beings, animating and enlivening. On the human level, "spirit" tries to name that intangible personhood or identity that animates us and makes us recognizable in all that we do. Whenever we come face to face with another being's spirit, that meeting has the quality of an "annunciation." The spirit of the other announces itself to us and catches our attention in a profound way.[10] "Spirit" thus images an ordinary but mysterious dimension of reality — a dynamic interconnectedness among creatures that makes them dramatically present to each other.

God's Spirit, the Holy Spirit, is a certain manifestation of spirit, one that draws us and all creation, in the spirit of Jesus, toward the realization of God's kingdom. God's Spirit works as the "go-between God," connecting human spirits and the beings of all God's creatures "anonymously and on the inside"[11] in a way that cannot, for the most part, even be perceived, much less controlled. God's

Spirit works in and through all creatures, drawing the whole of creation toward "greater complexity, sensitiveness and personhood,"[12] and calling us all to awareness, choice, and sacrifice. Our lives are transformed through encounters with others in whom the Spirit is working.

Furthermore, the prophet Joel says that the Spirit will be poured out on *all* flesh; it will fall on all, crossing over "national, cultural and other humanly erected boundaries."[13] This pouring out of the Spirit has the powerful effect of "releas[ing] the experience of God's presence from a domain defined and definable only by cultic law."[14] Michael Welker says that

> ... when the Spirit of God is poured out, the different persons and groups of people will open God's presence with each other and for each other. With each other and for each other, they will make it possible to know the reality intended by God. They will enrich and strengthen each other through their differentiated prophetic knowledge. From various perspectives and trajectories of experience, they will direct each other's attention to the agent responsible for their deliverance.[15]

This means that every person who has become a participant in the pouring out of the Spirit can "receive and mediate prophetic knowledge," and can see and enable others to see "what God is doing in and on the ruptured members of God's people not only to heal them for themselves, but to bind them together for each other and to revitalize them." It means that God's presence becomes known through the "specific abundance and diversity" of the differentiated community, and cannot be contained in a single group. And it means that God's presence is not grasped with "reductionist, abstract distortions," but is experienced in the "complexity of diverse, concrete, mutually challenging and mutually enriching attestations to the reality intended by God."[16] Finally, this outpouring of the Spirit brings about an "ungovernable interaction that cannot be one-sidedly initiated and controlled from individual sides and regions."[17]

At the beginning of his ministry, Jesus read Isaiah 61:1–2: "The Spirit of the Lord is upon me, because he has anointed me to bring good news to the poor. He has sent me to proclaim release to the captives and recovery of sight to the blind, to let the oppressed go free, to proclaim the year of the Lord's favour" (Luke 4:18). He then sat down and said, "Today this has been fulfilled." In so doing, he identified himself as the Suffering Servant who is God's anointed one. Jesus as Messiah will usher in that new time of the Spirit that has been long foretold by the prophets. This is one of those "annunciations" that are the clear work of the Spirit, but it is also a sign of the invisible permeation of the Spirit that is the hallmark of the new creation. For Jesus is characterized throughout the gospels as a person who is completely open to God's Spirit in any given situation.

In John's gospel, as Jesus prepares for his death, he promises the sending of the Spirit to be our Comforter (John 14:26 and 16:12ff). James Dunn says:

> Notice the balance achieved in these verses between the continuing revelatory work of the Spirit and the revelation already given. 14.26: "he will teach you everything" — this must include teaching which Jesus had not been able to give his disciples while on earth (cf. 16.12); "and will keep you in mind of all that I said to you" (cf. 15.15) — the new revelation has the continual check of the original revelation. 16.12ff.: "he will guide you into or in all truth (new revelation — v. 12), which is balanced by, "he will not speak on his own authority…" (*Jesus is the truth* — 14.6). Again, "he will declare (*anaggelei*) to you the things that are coming," which is balanced by, "he will glorify me, for he will take what is mine and declare it (*anaggelei*) to you." The dialectic of the Johannine concept of revelation is summed up in that one word, *anaggelei*. For it can have the force of "*re*-announce," "*re*-proclaim"; but in 16.13 as in 4.25 it must include some idea of new information, new revelation

(cf. Isa.42.9; 44.7; 46.10), even if that new revelation is in effect drawn out of the old by way of reinterpretation. In this
word, as in these passages as a whole, both present inspiration
and interpretation of the past are bound up together in *the
dynamic of creative religious experience.*[18]

This is why we can say that "each generation is as close to Jesus as
the last — and the first — because the Paraclete is the immediate
link between Jesus and the disciples in every generation," and why
we have the freedom to "reinterpret and remould" the original
formulations of faith, using them as a "check and restraint."[19] This
recalls the description of the new covenant in Jeremiah 31:31–34,
in which the law will be written on our hearts.

The experience of the church at Pentecost is the fulfillment of
the "pouring out" of the Spirit foretold by Joel and Isaiah. The
Spirit falls upon members of all nations and peoples, crossing
boundaries of ethnicity and social level and cultic status to form
them into the body of Christ. The Spirit is poured out freely, forming the body of Christ out of many who were afar off. And the
Spirit dwells in us permanently, permeating our lives, rather than
coming for a time and then departing. This is the time of the new
covenant. Here Luke brings out the "vitality" and the "sense of
immediacy of divine direction through Spirit and vision" which
characterized the early church.[20] Again, this outpouring of the Spirit
forms and reforms the church and hence cannot be controlled by
the church; like the wind, it blows where it will and the church can
only prepare itself to keep recognizing unanticipated movements
of the Spirit.

In this time of the new covenant, the apostle Paul adjures us to
live in the freedom of the Spirit. Since all of us have the Spirit within
us, testifying to our spirits, leading us into all truth, and reminding us
of Jesus, we no longer need rules and laws. Taylor says that

> being the new mankind [*sic*] means living towards one another
> without rules in the same gloriously responsible freedom and

truth as we see in Jesus himself. However often the church seems to make a mess of it, as various congregations in the New Testament obviously did, and however risky and open to misunderstanding such a way of life may be in a missionary situation, the Christian community must persevere in this freedom of the Spirit, learning through its mistakes and drawing endlessly upon the forgiveness of God.[21]

Thus life in the Spirit is intended to be "a ceaseless personal response to the call and claim of Jesus in each new situation by the individual disciple from within the Christ-centred fellowship."[22]

A concrete example of the church acting in the freedom of the Spirit is found in Luke's account of the Jerusalem Council, which deliberated on the normative implications of Peter's dream of the sheet coming down from heaven. Several features are striking here. The first is that this action is based on a dream, though the Council clearly connects Peter's experience of the Spirit falling on Cornelius with the dream. As Taylor reminds us, Spirit works in and through "the elemental world of our dreams, the raw emotion of our fears and angers, the illogical certainties of our intuitions, the uncharted gropings of our agnosticism, the compulsive tides of our history."[23] Secondly, this dream, conjoined with their experience of Cornelius himself, persuades the Council to disrupt tradition in an amazing way — to admit the Gentiles into the circle of the clean. As Dunn concludes:

> What we have here, then, is a — possibly even the — classic confrontation between old revelation, confirmed by centuries of history, and a new insight, given not through Jesus himself but in the course of an expanding, developing mission. It would have to take clear indication of divine approval and tremendous confidence in the agreed judgment of the leadership for such an epochal step and breach with unbroken tradition to be taken. With the Christian mission continuing to develop today, the church cannot avoid being confronted with similar

hard questions in the resolution of which not all will be satisfied.[24]

Dunn finds that Luke is very open to the newness of the Spirit, and shows very clearly how this openness was crucial to the growth and development of the early church. However, Dunn also says that, in his enthusiasm, Luke sometimes "leaves many obvious questions and problems unanswered."[25] In some of his writings, he tends to assume the rightness of such manifestations of the Spirit, and does not really consider the possibility that such apparent manifestations may actually lead us away from God's intent. Hence, while the early church clearly constituted itself as open to that "volcanic inferno"[26] of the newness of the Spirit, the wider counsel reminds us that it is also incumbent upon us to test the spirits.

Discerning the spirits

Paul, of all the New Testament writers, is the one who is most concerned with the discernment and testing of spirits. According to Dunn, Paul picks up on the emergent newness of the Spirit as described by Luke and locates it within a complex "ongoing dialectic"

> ... between the more formal authority of apostle as apostle and the kerygmatic tradition on the one hand, and the charismatic authority of all ministry within the community and of the community itself on the other; between the individual with its word or act containing its authority within itself as charisma, and the community with its responsibility to test and evaluate all charismata; between the decisive salvation-history events of the past (resurrection appearance commissioning and kerygmatic tradition) and the new situations, problems and demands requiring new revelations and fresh interpretation of the tradition.[27]

Paul's criteria for discerning the Spirit are communal, says Dunn, and they are threefold: 1) the test of kerygmatic tradition — God's Spirit will conform to the gospel confession that "Jesus is Lord" (Rom 10:9), which brought us into grace and liberty and brought the church into existence; 2) the test of love, that humble and self-less manifestation of grace that makes an action beneficial to both individual and community; and 3) the test of building up the body — acting not for one's own aggrandizement but for the building up of the whole body into the fullness of Christ. Dunn says that "whatever does not build up, whatever word or action destroys the congregation's unity or causes hurt to its members or leaves the outsider merely bewildered, that word or action fails the test of *oikodomé*, and should be ignored or rejected, no matter how in-spired, how charismatic it seems to be."[28] Paul, he says, describes the distinctive character of genuinely Spirit-led Christian freedom by stressing "its integral relation both with the wider community of believers in the present and with the revelation of Christ in the past."[29] Hence this is not religious experience understood as an "autonomous authority," but the Spirit's legitimate volcanic fer-ment subjected to the "check of community evaluation and to the test of kerygmatic tradition."[30]

Taylor too reminds us that in opening ourselves to God's Spirit, we may also be opening ourselves to the demonic and to the el-emental tides in our inner lives. But God's Spirit is the Spirit of Truth, and throughout scripture "spirit" and "word" are linked: "The Spirit of the Lord speaks through me, his word is upon my tongue" (2 Sam 23:2) and "And as for me, this is my covenant with them, says the Lord: my spirit that is upon you, and my words that I have put in your mouth, shall not depart out of your mouth, or out of the mouths of your children, or out of the mouths of your children's children, says the Lord, from now on and forever" (Is 59:21). Taylor suggests that we think of "spirit" as signifying "the undifferentiated, all-pervading power of awareness and mutual-ity," while "word" signifies "particularity and form, meaning and purpose."[31] Since Jesus is the Word by whom our awareness is informed, it is through him that we discriminate the work of God's

Spirit from that of other spirits. Spirit and Word exist in mutual interrelation; for if our life in the Spirit needs "the clarity and the particularity of the Word made flesh to give it discrimination," our life in Christ also needs "the Spirit's gift of awareness to ensure that it is indeed the *living* Word we are responding to."[32]

All three writers remind us that, when life is open and responsive to the Spirit, it will be characterized by paradox and conflict, as it always has been. All three use the term "religious experience" in reference to the life in the Spirit, to signify the contemporary, felt, existential quality of this life. And they remind us that it is much more difficult to understand or clearly identify what we are currently experiencing than it is to understand and clearly identify what has gone before. In our contemporary experience we do not have the benefit of hindsight but must act anyway. Moreover contemporary experience is always contested by a variety of spirits clamouring for our allegiance. Dunn says that authentic religious experience is characterized by the "paradox of life and death," and the "conflict of Spirit and flesh."[33] The community of faith is called to enter the turbulent realm of Spirit, which challenges us to recognize God's ever-new ways of acting in the world. So we must test the spirits, but also take the risk of acting in the Spirit. This is not easy. As Taylor points out, the genuine exercise of our freedom in Christ means that we will make mistakes and will need to repent and learn from them.[34] We will also experience conflict. Dunn insists that conflict is an essential element of genuinely religious experience; hence

> ... the Christian who takes Paul seriously should never be
> alarmed at the paradox and conflict of his religious experience.
> Nor should he be depressed at defeat, or conclude that grace
> has lost the struggle. On the contrary, spiritual conflict is the
> sign of life — a sign that the Spirit is having his say in the
> shaping of character. Suffering means hope (Rom. 5.3ff.). Death
> is part of the present experience of life (2 Cor. 4.10ff.). Since
> life now must be life in this body, the Spirit can only be present

as paradox and conflict. It is this paradox and conflict which is the mark of healthy religious experience — not its absence. The Spirit is absent when we stop fighting, not when we lose.[35]

Perhaps this is why Taylor suggests that, whereas mission is often envisioned as "the planned extension of an old building" (as it may look in hindsight), it is actually more like an "unexpected explosion,"[36] and we need to accustom ourselves to this unsettling reality.

Spirit as difficult gift

It is all too clear that continuously experienced life in the Spirit can, for the church, become a gift of which we are reluctant to avail ourselves. This was as true of the early churches as it is of our own time. Religious experience is a frightening thing, with the possibility always there that we will make the wrong decision. Hence we continually find ways of controlling the unsettling quality of the Spirit's working in and among us.

First we look for rules beyond the checks of communal evaluation and kerygmatic tradition. Dunn, following Paul in Romans and Galatians, warns us against turning these fluid criteria into "legal-type rules and formulae," and against allowing community evaluation to become "authoritarian church," or kerygmatic tradition to become "ecclesiastical dogma." We may not walk by rule or law, but must live in the freedom of the Spirit, open and sensitive to the changing texture of life in God's world, flexible and able to adapt to the Spirit, which blows where it will.

Second, we try to shut down the Spirit by refusing to acknowledge the Spirit's work. Michael Welker interprets the difficult notion of "blaspheming against the Holy Spirit" in these words:

The saying about the impossibility of forgiving blasphemy against God's Spirit is directed against those who disregard the undeniable experience of diverse deliverance out of distress from which there is, by human standards, no escape. It is directed against those who do not want to recognize the demonstration of God's power in God's selfless help to those who are suffering without prospect of deliverance. It is directed against those who take the last hope away from others and who obstruct their own access to a last hope. The saying about "blaspheming the Spirit" contemplates nothing less than the "impossible possibility" that people might go against the obvious experience of liberation and deliverance and might block, both for themselves and for others, the view of God's delivering power.[37]

Blaspheming the Spirit is, thus, refusing to recognize or to open ourselves to the Spirit's working. Although the Spirit's working will be unsettling to us and will create tension and perhaps even conflict, we are warned not to close ourselves off from it or to try to shut down or discredit another's experience of the Spirit. This is not to deny the need for discernment; but we are not allowed to short-circuit the process by discrediting at the beginning another believer's experience of the Spirit.

In these scholars' analyses of New Testament views of the Spirit, it becomes increasingly clear that the Spirit speaks particularly of the necessary and fruitful tension between the new and the old. Dunn points to a passage from Johannes Weiss:

An "origin" in the sense of an entirely new creation never occurs.... The "new" is always in the broad sense a re-grouping of older elements according to a new principle, based upon stronger forces and unique experience of actuality.[38]

Dunn comments that "using Weiss's terms, the danger is that the 'new' of Christianity will be regarded *solely* in terms of 'a regrouping of older elements' without due regard to the 'unique experience of actuality.'"[39] Rowan Williams echoes this concern in somewhat different terms. In his discussion of the faith as an expanding network of narratives, he warns that the more such narratives are seen as illustrations subordinate to a governing theoretical structure, the more the tradition closes in on itself, offering self-justifying projections rather than the risks of incarnation. The more these stories are seen as fresh statements (new metaphors?) in a common tongue, the more the tradition shows itself to be a living — and therefore an incomplete — thing.[40]

Contemporary experience can never become simply an "illustration" of something already finished and complete, but must be a genuinely fresh statement that retains the possibility of challenging and expanding what has gone before. Similarly, Dunn insists that we must strive to preserve

> ... the living dialectic between the religious experience of the present and the definitive revelation of the past (the Christ event), with neither being permitted to dictate to the other, and neither being allowed to escape from the searching questions posed by the other — an unceasing process of interpretation and reinterpretation.[41]

As communities of faith, we must retain that freshness of "religious experience" whose dynamic interaction with the original witness to the Christ event continually keeps our faith alive and growing.

Dunn may speak for all three scholars when he concludes his book *Jesus and the Spirit* with this striking challenge to the church:

> Perhaps the biggest challenge to twentieth-century Christianity is to take the Pauline exposition seriously, and to start not from what now is by way of tradition and institution, but instead to be open to that experience of God which first launched Christianity and to let that experience, properly safeguarded as Paul insisted, create new expressions of faith, worship, and mission at both individual and corporate level. One thing we may be sure of: the life of the Christian church

can go forward only when each generation is able creatively to reinterpret its gospel and its common life out of its own experience of the Spirit and word which first called Christianity into existence.[42]

So although the diverse manifestations of Spirit highlight the need for discernment of the spirits in accordance with criteria for Christian community — kerygma, sacrificial love, upbuilding of the body — this need for discernment may never be taken as an excuse for closing down the genuine newness of the Spirit in our own experience and in our own time.

Experience within Scripture and Tradition

What I have said proposes that we can understand religious experience as an experience of the realm of spirit, within which we may discern movements of the Spirit. In religious experience, the felt experience of "annunciations," of possible new moves by God, exists in tension with the tradition, challenging and being challenged by it; such contemporary, felt experience is the instrument by which the inherited faith becomes new and true in our own time. This tension, and the Spirit's movement, have been part of the whole history of God's people.

The biblical story provides us with a set of basic normative categories — creation, sin, redemption, righteousness, justice, shalom, among others — and a story in which the people of God struggle in every generation to realize God's gifts. The dynamic is always one of a history of redemption that creates a people called to be a light to the nations. In the time of the new covenant, the people of God are brought together by the Spirit out of all nations and peoples, without regard for boundaries, by the outpouring of the Spirit that forms the body of Christ. The story includes a formative tradition that identifies and anchors the people in their redemptive history and calling. It includes a necessary element of newness as God's Spirit works in ever-new ways. In every age, from the beginning until now, God's people have responded when God called them into a new life, into a new land, into a new body. The risks remain the same in their very newness and uncertainty, from the time God called Abraham to leave his home and venture into an unknown land. God's people have been through this many times before.

The written scriptures have their own claim on us, telling the story that shapes our identity and preserving the testimony of those who knew Jesus in the flesh. But it is not helpful to view the scriptures as an undifferentiated lump that requires unquestioning obedience. Nor are the scriptures the whole of God's work in the world. The scriptures point beyond themselves to God's manifold creation and to the Spirit who will dwell in us and who will lead us into all truth. Calvin insisted that the written scriptures are "spectacles" through which we look at the world,[43] and which enable us to see God and God's Spirit at work in our world. To use a slightly different image, scripture is a light to our path; hence we ought not to stare into the light but to walk by it. The written scriptures are not God's only and final word to us, but rather a "canon"[44] or measure by which we discern God's continuing actions in our own world.

I have provided this brief overview because it is essential to remember that the attempt to acknowledge the raw, risky edge of our experience of God is not some "revisionist" poisoned fruit of modernity, but lies at the heart of scripture and of Christian tradition. Thus scripture is not a static set of rules and principles, but rather an ongoing, varied story that gives context to rules and principles and that preserves the multiple tensions between the old and the new. We need to see this plurality not as undermining the normative force of God's Word to us, but rather as encouraging us to continue the conversation by opening ourselves to the possibility of the Spirit's new and unsettling working in our own times and in our own communities and lives. "Experience" in this sense cannot be placed outside of "scripture" as an extraneous "modern" authority that challenges and overturns "scripture," but should rather be understood as an essential part of scripture itself. Experience is part of the continuously unsettling and reconfiguring dynamic that is appropriate to the life of a baptismal community. The "appeal to experience" is best taken as a reminder to be open to something that always makes us uncomfortable and that, as a result, we prefer to disregard — the variedness of God's moving in and among creatures, and the newness and uniqueness of the concrete contemporary experience. That experience will require us to re-engage with our scripture and our tradition, and will require a new formulation that integrates old and new.

If "experience" in this sense is an essential part of the full dynamic of Jewish and Christian tradition, then we need to understand that tradition itself is not a static "pronouncement." Rather, it is an ongoing process of discernment that always lives in the dynamic tension between the old and the new. What has become settled tradition for us was, in its own time, a risky response to the Spirit. We can think of examples: the early church struggled to acknowledge the unclean as part of the body of Christ; the evangelical churches struggled with slavery; the confessing churches grappled with the problem of the Third Reich; Charles Gore and others tried to meet the challenge of Darwinian science. The choices made in those times were no less risky than choices we must make in our own time.

We even make a choice when we appeal to "tradition" as having normative value for current decisions. In this sense "tradition" is that which we intentionally decide to "hand over" to meet the needs of a new situation.[45] This "handing over" keeps the future in continuity with our past, even as it makes the resources of the past available for a new future. We always, if only tacitly, make decisions about what is worth "handing over" and what ought to be left in the cupboard of our own time as something we found useful or even necessary but which perhaps ought not to bind a new generation. On the other hand, if what we "hand over" is not sufficient, often a new generation will go behind the immediately preceding generations and explore the much larger scope of Christian tradition to find resources that were not "handed over" to them and consequently seem new. In any case, as Rowan Williams points out, tradition itself is normative or "orthodox" only in the sense that "its present life and experience is always liable to be brought into question by the abiding possibility of retrieving the original points of novelty, distinctiveness, and discrimination which brought it to birth."[46] Thus genuinely normative Christian tradition must remain open to the continuing movements of the Spirit in our time and every time.

"Experience" is part and parcel of both scripture and tradition; the same complex dynamic is at work wherever we find the people of God in all ages. And the question of when to let go of something, when to question something, when to move forward in a risky situation, when to reject a new proposal as not consonant with our tradition of faith, and how to resolve conflicts and disagreements about all of the above — this is just the normal texture of our faith. It is our attempt to live life in the Spirit, even as we struggle with the new and the old within us. This is the life of faith in all ages; it would be inaccurate to portray the past as life within a settled tradition, disrupted all at once by modernist "revisionists" intent on destroying the tradition.

A normative appeal to experience

But if this complex dynamic has existed throughout scripture and tradition, what might we mean by the notion of an "appeal to" experience, scripture, tradition, or reason? In fact these "appeals" are abstracted out of the complex whole. Each reminds us of considerations that must enter all adequate reflections on Christian faith and witness.

The appeal to scripture is to the original stories and proclamations that establish our identity as people of God. As Christians we have a particular interest in the testimony of those who knew

Jesus, for these testimonies articulate the identity and calling of the church within the larger history of salvation. They tell us who we are and they describe that to which we are called.

The appeal to reason is to our capacity for consistent and penetrating thinking. It recognizes that we remain true to scripture not by treating it as a medium of divination that we blindly obey, but by asking probing questions about consistency, grounds, rationale, and presuppositions. This is not to deny that reason itself can become a kind of rival god. But reason relates faith to ordinary life and thus prevents the discourse of faith from becoming completely self-enclosed.

The appeal to tradition is to our cumulative communal story shaped by a long-lasting pattern of decisions, choices, and practices. Tradition is always accountable to scripture in that it carries forward the authentic gospel of God's redemption. Its development requires that each Christian community be accountable to all others, both supporting and challenging all to live up to the same difficult calling.

Finally, the appeal to experience is to the contemporary working of the Spirit in God's creatures and in creaturely situations. As Rowan Williams says, "I cannot escape the obligation of looking and listening for Christ in the acts of another Christian who is manifestly engaged, self-critically engaged, with the data of common belief and worship."[47] Spirit makes it possible for us to meet God in the depths of our own spirits and in the connections we feel with other beings. Spirit enables us to act freely and gracefully because we are surrounded by and in touch with God's own Spirit. Honouring experience as the manifestation of Spirit keeps us open to human life as it is lived.

The challenge for the Christian community is to maintain a balance among all four appeals to authority. Very likely each individual or community will find one more congenial than the rest, perhaps because it most readily names a powerful experience of God's redemption. However, a preference must not be turned into an exclusive ideological position. If we think of the four bases of authority as four points on a circle, then adequate theological reflection requires us to continue around the whole circle, stopping at each point before returning enriched to the point from which we began. Perhaps, as so often, Rowan Williams catches it best when he says that

> ... what we are looking for in each other is the grammar of obedience: we watch to see if our partners take the same kind of time, sense that they are under the same sort of judgment or scrutiny, and approach the issue with the same attempt to be dispossessed by the truth with which they are engaging.[48]

What I intend is that we can recognize in each other a "grammar of obedience" even when we come to different conclusions. Then we can engage in thoughtful discernment of any one appeal to scripture, or tradition, or reason, or experience, without assuming that one should trump another.

Questions for experience

I will conclude by trying to articulate some of the questions that emerge for me when I try to be critically open to the reported workings of the Spirit in my gay and lesbian friends.

First, I need to ask where my experience of my gay and lesbian friends is named in this account. While the abstract issue of homosexuality had been something that I could dismiss, the lived experience of gay or lesbian believers caught my attention in a new way. I have heard what it feels like to be told that you, among all humans, are structurally evil, because of "disordered" sexual desire. This is quite different from the condemnation of a specific sexual desire toward a specific person because no attempt to act rightly in sexual relations can make any difference, because one's sexual nature is structurally wrong in its very existence. Heart-rending stories of people trying unsuccessfully to change the direction of their sexual desires have made many of us ask whether we know as much as we thought we knew about sexual desire generally. In a situation like this, the confession of God's acceptance rings hollow because it excludes so important a part of being human that it cannot sound like acceptance. It is always acceptance with a reservation toward gay and lesbian people. I have also heard, and seen, what a difference it has made for these people to recognize that their sexuality is "created good." It has helped them to believe that they are full members of the body of Christ. It has also liberated them to deal with the brokenness of wrong sexual acts, and to live their sexual lives in covenanted, intimate faithfulness.

Recognizing these experiences as true may well be an instance of the continuing outpouring of the Spirit, one that will call us to contemplate reformulating the familiar. However, it is appropriate to keep some open space here for reflection and discernment and to ask tough questions. We need to investigate all that science can tell us about how sexual desire develops and is formed, but we also need to listen carefully to first-person reports. For a phenomenon like sexual desire works at the intersection of physiological functioning and subjective feeling and consciousness, and it is unthinkable to investigate it without taking "experience" seriously. We should be eager to understand how God's creatures function, how Spirit connects creatures in many ways, including sexual desire, and we should be open to scientific investigation even as we critically question the assumptions that might shape a particular scientific investigation.

If we test a putative experience of Spirit by the Word, what might this process look like? We begin by assuming that our purpose is to affirm neither the complete independence of the individual to go his or her own way nor a legalism that betrays our freedom in Christ. The Word is Jesus and the good news of the kingdom that Jesus preached: one in which the lame walk, the lepers are cleansed, the eunuch has a portion, and the unclean ones are given an honoured place at the banquet. The good news also calls us back to our responsibility for shalom: justice, peace, and right relationship, caring for widows and orphans and strangers.

In terms of Dunn's test (following Paul) — kerygmatic tradition, love, and building up the body — I think we can make a strong case that accepting a different sexual orientation can actually help us all to bring our sexual lives more fully into the orbit of Christian formation, to develop the fruits of the Spirit, and to focus more intently on our baptismal ministry of service. None of us can rule out the possibility of difficult discipline in the service of shalom. However, I would be cautious about imposing special disciplines on gay sexuality until we have honestly listened to our gay and lesbian friends about their own experience of a form of sexuality that is alien to many of us. In addition, we ought to remember that asking these questions of our gay and lesbian friends will inevitably mean that the same questions will be directed at those of us who are straight.

As we test experience against the good news, we might also ask which precedent in the history of the church's reflections is relevant here? Would sexual orientation be like left-handedness or having black skin, which were once viewed as morally culpable violations of the created order, but are now viewed as morally neutral "variants"? Or is it more akin to the question of women's ordination, in which the church began to emphasize broad principles that allowed us to turn exceptional instances into normal practice? Or is it more like the widespread cultural prohibitions regarding consanguinity, prohibitions that have been upheld by the Christian tradition? Or is it like the inclusion of the Gentiles, the ones "far off," in whom the manifest pouring out of the Spirit "just as on us" necessitated a monumental revision to the religious tradition? What are the various options here, and what effects would they have as precedents?

The people of God have always been asked to step out in faith, not knowing where they were going. Abraham left the security of his own land, called to venture out to a new land. Israel, freed from Egypt, was sent then into the wilderness. The dispersed ones tried to sing the Lord's song in a strange land. The early Christians confronted a dream that transgressed important boundaries.

Later Christians struggled against slavery, Nazism, apartheid, and the subjection of women when they seemed like lonely voices crying in the wilderness. There are times when we are called to act, even when we do not have all the information that we might like. I believe that there are worse things that the church might do than try to act in the Spirit at the risk of making a mistake. Far worse is to risk quenching the Spirit out of fear or uncertainty.

But is it Anglican?

Anglican history is a four-centuries-long record of risking change in response to the Spirit, beginning with the Reformation itself. The translation of the liturgy and Bible into a language understood by the people placed them in the hands of those who could read. These, though a still small elite, were thereby enabled to interpret scripture and tradition in ways little intended by the ecclesiastical authorities who made them available in English. The bitter disagreements that soon arose among the heirs of the Reformers about scripture, tradition, and reason led to a ruthless and bloody civil war in the seventeenth century. The eventual result of this religious violence was the restoration in 1660 of a church that ejected dissenters and consistently avoided difficult issues. In all of this, is it possible to see with hindsight where the Spirit was at work and leading?

Late in the eighteenth century the evangelical revival met stiff resistance from those who stood firm by tradition. The Methodists found that they could no longer be contained by the established church. When, in the next century, the Tractarians made their self-conscious appeal to Catholic tradition, they were almost universally rejected by the church, which considered them to be in opposition to the certain word of scripture, the weight of Reformation tradition, and the clear light of reason. If we can see in the evangelical and Tractarian movements the work of the Spirit leading the church community into fuller realization of gospel, what do we see in the questions posed in the nineteenth century by the new sciences — history, geology, and biology? The fact is that evangelicals, Tractarians, and scientists have all had their way, and the church has accommodated them all, not by abandoning its commitment to the gospel, but by understanding that gospel is open to new formulations tested against the old.

In the twentieth century the Anglican churches have had to deal with issues that take them back again and again to scripture and tradition, using reason as a means of understanding both in response to new experience. It is no longer possible to argue as a matter of faith, provable by reference to scripture and tradition, that black people or Native people or women are, by their God-given nature, required to be subject to white Christian men. After the long history of the church's persecution of the Jews, conceived as those who had rendered themselves despicable by breaking covenant with God, the whole church, including the Anglican Church, was forced to revisit scripture and tradition in the light of the terrible experience of the holocaust.

The Anglican churches have considered other questions directly related to sexuality: remarriage after divorce, birth control, and abortion. In all cases the church listened compassionately to those who suffered most from an outright prohibition derived from tradition and supported with reference to scripture, and it discerned the Spirit prompting a deeper probing. By a slow, cautious process it found the way to greater openness. Now at the beginning of the twenty-first century, the same Spirit is leading us Anglican Christians into new territory once again as we listen to gay and lesbian believers seeking full accommodation of their sexuality in the body of Christ.

So the question "But is it Anglican?" is a very interesting one. It can bring with it a sense that Anglicanism respects tradition above all, to the point of treating all contemporary questions as "mischief." As the British series *Yes, Minister* puts it, "Many things may be done, but nothing may be done for the first time." This too is part of our sense of ourselves as Anglicans. And it can indeed lead us to privilege what is comfortably in the past and fear what is uncomfortably all too present. Perhaps this is the dark side of the Anglican Communion. But if it is, it has never yet stopped Anglicanism from facing up to the difficult and complex questions of the day. In fact our respect for tradition sooner or later leads us back to the growing edge of tradition that lies at the very heart of Anglicanism.

As I said at the beginning, an encounter with the Spirit has the quality of an annunciation. The Spirit speaks through human voices. I have finally been able to name my experience of hearing the voices of gay and lesbian friends as just such an annunciation. I continue to struggle to hear what scripture says; I continue to struggle with the way in which the church slowly discerns Spirit from alien spirits; I continue to struggle with the task of remaining open to other answers, other ways of making sense of all of this, other challenges to my own emerging convictions. Nevertheless I do increasingly believe that what I have felt and heard in the stories of my gay and lesbian friends, what I have seen in their lives, represents a genuine movement of the Spirit in our time. And I am confident that the faith of the church is so vigorous that it can embrace this development as one prompted by the Spirit, who now yet again requires us to explore our scripture and tradition in new, unsettling, and invigorating ways.

Notes

1   Rowan Williams, "On Making Moral Decisions," *Sewanee Theological Review* 42:2 (1999), pp. 156–157.

2   Scott J. Jones, *John Wesley's Conception and Use of Scripture* (Nashville: Kingswood Books, 1995), p. 64. Jones says that Albert Outler was the first to use the term "quadrilateral" in this connection, in "The Wesleyan Quadrilateral in John Wesley," in ed. Thomas A. Langford, *Doctrine and Theology in the United Methodist Church* (Nashville: Kingswood Books, 1991), p. 86.

3   Jones, *John Wesley's Conception and Use*, p. 64.

4   Jones, *John Wesley's Conception and Use*, pp. 95–103.

5   I am not suggesting here that "human rights" language has no validity. Indeed, I suggest that the notion of a "human right" is rooted in the Christian tradition's reverence for all individual persons as God's creatures, as persons for whom Christ died. A "human right" is something granted by God, and hence constitutes an absolute claim on us. I think a "human right" is properly understood as a fundamental limit to popular sovereignty; there are some things that we are not free to choose because they contravene what we owe to each person simply because he or she is a person, one of God's creatures. So there is clearly room for an appeal to human rights. However, I would also suggest that this notion has force primarily because it appeals to absolutely basic moral claims and convictions. It is a tool that is excellently designed for specific situations. But if we begin to use it to identify a large group of desirable goods, particularly those that are contested, we run the risk of evacuating the notion of "human rights" of all meaning. We also risk pushing more and more contested goods into the realm of the absolute and thereby taking them out of the sphere

of popular sovereignty. In that case, there is great danger that the whole notion of "human rights" will be perceived as no more than a power play, and will lose its moral credibility. That would be tragic. But it would also be tragic to take all contested issues out of the sphere of public deliberation, which would in turn eviscerate public life and our capacity for public deliberation about contested goods. In this case, I think the push for an ever-expanding category of human rights is a short-term fix with very bad long-term effects.

6   Michael Welker, *God the Spirit*, tr. John F. Hoffmeyer of *Gottes Geist: Theologie des Heiligen Geistes* (Minneapolis, MN: Augsburg Fortress, 1994).

7   James D. G. Dunn, *Jesus and the Spirit* (London: SCM, 1975).

8   John V. Taylor, *The Go-Between God: The Holy Spirit and the Christian Mission* (London: SCM, 1972).

9   Taylor, *Go-Between God*, p. 7.

10   Taylor, *Go-Between God*, p. 10.

11   Taylor, *Go-Between God*, pp. 5, 25–27.

12   Taylor, *Go-Between God*, p. 107.

13   Welker, *God the Spirit*, p. 127.

14   Welker, *God the Spirit*, p. 154.

15   Welker, *God the Spirit*, p. 151.

16   Welker, *God the Spirit*, p. 155.

17   Welker, *God the Spirit*, p. 142.

18   Dunn, *Jesus and the Spirit*, pp. 351, 352.

19   Dunn, *Jesus and the Spirit*, pp. 351, 352.

20   Dunn, *Jesus and the Spirit*, p. 357.

21   Taylor, *Go-Between God*, p. 163.

22   Taylor, *Go-Between God*, p. 177.

23   Taylor, *Go-Between God*, p. 51.

24   Dunn, *The Acts of the Apostles*, p. 199.

25   Dunn, *Jesus and the Spirit*, p. 357.

26   Taylor, *Go-Between God*, p. 45.

27 Dunn, *Jesus and the Spirit*, p. 298.

28 Dunn, *Jesus and the Spirit*, pp. 293–296.

29 Dunn, *Jesus and the Spirit*, p. 368.

30 Dunn, *Jesus and the Spirit*, p. 361.

31 Taylor, *Go-Between God*, p. 58.

32 Taylor, *Go-Between God*, p. 62.

33 Dunn, *Jesus and the Spirit*, p. 338.

34 Taylor, *Go-Between God*, p. 163.

35 Dunn, *Jesus and the Spirit*, p. 339.

36 Taylor, *Go-Between God*, p. 53.

37 Welker, *God the Spirit*, p. 218.

38 Johannes Weiss, "Das Problem der Entstehung des Christentums," *Archiv für Religionswissenschaft* 16 (1913), pp. 426ff. Quoted in Dunn, *Jesus and the Spirit*, p. 4.

39 Dunn, *Jesus and the Spirit*, p. 4.

40 Rowan Williams, "What is Catholic Orthodoxy?" In *Essays Catholic and Radical*, eds. Kenneth Leech and Rowan Williams (London: Bowerdean, 1983), p. 17.

41 Dunn, *Jesus and the Spirit*, p. 361.

42 Dunn, *Jesus and the Spirit*, p. 360.

43 Calvin writes that "For as the aged, or those whose sight is defective, when any book, however fair, is set before them, though they perceive that there is something written, are scarcely able to make out two consecutive words, but, when aided by glasses, begin to read distinctly, so Scripture, gathering together the impressions of Deity, which, till then, lay confused in their minds, dissipates the darkness, and shows us the true God clearly"(John Calvin, *Institutes of the Christian Religion*, 2 vols., tr. Henry Beveridge [Grand Rapids, MI: Eerdmans, 1973], p. 184, Book I, ch. 6, sect. 1, par. 64.). As a long-time wearer of glasses, it seems self-evident to me that we wear glasses not to look at the glasses, but to look at the world.

44 Here I am using "canon" in the sense defined by Charles M. Wood, to mean scripture's function as judge or measure

of "the Christianness of any putative Christian witness" (Charles M. Wood, *The Formation of Christian Understanding: Theological Hermeneutics* [Valley Forge, PA: Trinity Press International, 1981, 1993], p. 83). "Canon" here refers not simply to the words of scripture in themselves, but to scripture's ability to point to the story of Jesus as redeemer, and to our identity-shaping position in that story, in such a way as helps us to discern whether something that is proposed genuinely manifests the "Christianness" of genuine Christian witness.

45   Kathryn Tanner points out that traditional materials are always "products of human decision in a significant sense." She says that "The materials that are passed down and over to one time and place from some other time and place are always more numerous than those labeled 'tradition.' 'Tradition' is always a selection from the wide array of materials that could be so designated in virtue of their transmission from before and elsewhere. And even more generally, tradition is always a matter of human attribution; nothing about the materials themselves requires that designation. Even ongoing customary forms of action and belief do not constitute a tradition until they are marked as such and thereby assigned a normative status." Tanner goes on to say that "Which materials are designated 'tradition' is a matter for human judgment, a judgment hinging on a contestable claim for their centrality or importance to Christian life. In order to sustain the identity of this tradition across differences of time and place, the interpreter is not called so much to approximate the already given shape of those materials as to organize them in a way that makes clear what else might have a place within them" (Kathryn Tanner, *Theories of Culture: A New Agenda for Theology* [Minneapolis, MN: Augsburg Fortress Press, 1997], pp. 133, 134). I take this to mean that "tradition" can have

significantly different meaning in different contexts. It is not just "what we have always done" but a normative judgement about exactly what aspect of past practice ought to exert a normative claim on present and future actions. Thus tradition is not a thing but a judgement, and as such needs to be explained and justified in its own context. And a tradition that would be defended as Christian must always seek to make gospel present in terms appropriate to a new situation. In so doing, it is always possible that the tradition may be reconfigured under the pressure of a new experience — for example, the new awareness that slaves are persons for whom Christ died. Thus while tradition continues to be assigned normative force, its exact content has changed before and after the abolitionist movement.

46 Williams, "Catholic Orthodoxy," p. 14. This distinction is also made by Charles Wood when he distinguishes between scripture as "source" of Christian tradition and scripture as "canon" or "measure" of Christian tradition. Wood insists that scripture as canon is "the standard by which the 'traditioning' activity of the Christian community is to be critically assessed and directed" (Wood, *Formation of Christian Understanding*, p. 91). He goes on to say that "... with regard to any given element of biblical tradition, we are not only permitted but obliged to give it careful scrutiny, measuring it by the canon, before we permit it any constitutive role in the contemporary understanding of Christian witness. That each such element is part of the Christian heritage cannot be denied; that each is 'truly Christian' in the normative sense must not be so easily granted" (p. 115). It is my own sense that Christian "experience" of creatures and world is partly what prompts this healthy canonical questioning of tradition, even as the experience which prompts it is itself questioned canonically. If this sounds a little like rebuilding the boat while we're floating in it, that

seems to me to be a very accurate reflection of the healthy upheaval that is important to the serious Christian life.

47 Williams, "Moral Decisions," p. 157.
48 Williams, "Moral Decisions," p. 155.

Church Polity

Our Differences Need Not Destroy Us[*]

Rowan Williams

Some people wanted to know why Anglican Primates should be gathering in Portugal, which is not a great historic centre of Anglican activity, it has to be admitted. The answer is not simply that pleasant scenery takes your mind off the worst bits of ecclesiastical wrestling, but that the tiny Lusitanian Church — a product, like the German and Swiss Old Catholics, of nineteenth-century protest against the First Vatican Council — is celebrating its one hundred and twentieth anniversary and, as it is in full communion with the Anglicans, it seemed a good moment for a visit that honoured that church's history and distinctive witness.

But it could be seen as a focus of sorts for the major issue underlying the meeting. The Lusitanian Church came into being as a protest against one kind of clarity about central authority; how far can the Anglican Communion survive without some mechanism of authority more robust than currently exists? The

---

[*] This essay was originally written after the Meeting of Primates in Porto, Portugal, in February 2000. That meeting occurred on the heels of the irregular consecration in Singapore of "missionary" bishops for the Episcopal Church in the U.S. Thus it asked the question that has become pivotal: What is the nature of the unity of the church? In what way does the structure of the Anglican Church serve that unity? The essay is used here with permission. (*Ed.*)

consecration in February this year of two bishops in Singapore, who were supposed to be deployed for the pastoral care of traditionalist Anglicans in the United States, was an unprecedented breach in the received order of the Communion, since no attention was paid either to the views of the official Anglican leadership in the United States or to the counsel of the Archbishop of Canterbury. Many obviously expected the meeting to deliver a firm condemnation of this action.

But others expected a condemnation of a different kind. The main driving force behind the Singapore consecrations was the extraordinary bitterness of feeling in some quarters of the United States about the Episcopal Church's lack of unity over the issues around homosexuality. It has been, for a vocal minority, the last straw in a long process that is seen as the uncritical adoption by Episcopalians of a liberal, multi-cultural, relativist agenda. The theological fireworks of Bishop John Spong, formerly of Newark, New Jersey, who has been cutting long swathes through pretty well every received doctrine and ethical conviction of classical Christianity, have done a lot to sharpen up this discontent. Has North American Anglicanism no means at all, people ask, of reining in pluralism? And if it hasn't, are its structures at all trustworthy?

These tensions precipitated the Singapore crisis, and some traditionalists have been arguing that a canonical irregularity is far less significant than what they call the apostasy of North America. Their appeal has been to the Lambeth Conference resolution declaring homosexual practice incompatible with scripture, a resolution won largely by the overwhelming support of bishops from the growing and powerful Third World Churches, especially in Africa. There was undoubtedly some hope that the Primates' meeting, numerically dominated by the African and Asian archbishops, could deliver a "final warning" at the very least to the Episcopal Church in the United States. There was a visible penumbra in Porto of American conservatives, aiming to strengthen the resolve of traditionalist Primates, hanging around in doorways and lobbies.

But what emerged was — perhaps predictably — a less dramatic outcome, which some will undoubtedly see as a typical bit of Anglican evasiveness. The truth is that many Primates, especially the Africans, while they are uncompromisingly traditional about sexual ethics, can see the risks of the Communion either becoming completely mired in this question for years or breaking up over it. It was very clear that they wanted neither. One influential African archbishop declared forcefully that a lot of the discussion had been a waste of time for him, faced as he was with civil war, the effects of the AIDS pandemic and the debt crisis: "Some of us," he said, poker-faced, "are tired of sex ...." Of course the homosexual question is not one that affects the United States alone. But some impatience was palpable by the last few days of the meeting. The result was a carefully worded reminder to the United States that actions taken there had repercussions elsewhere, weakening the Anglican Church in the eyes of other Christians and — a more sinister matter — giving ammunition to the hostility of militant Muslims. The meeting seemed to have no appetite for denunciation, or even direct appeal to the United States for a moratorium on gay ordinations; the seriousness of the concern was registered, and the presiding bishop of the Episcopal Church was left to work out with his House of Bishops what the implications might be.

Similar restraint was in evidence over the Singapore affair. Here, while some more liberal Primates pressed for strong words, the consensus was that the Archbishop of Canterbury's initial response had said most of what needed to be said: that this was an action damaging to the Communion and, in its haste and secrecy, sending some very unhelpful messages about the proper processes of scrutiny and discernment for episcopal appointment. Judging from the conversation at the meeting it is unlikely that there will be any attempt to repeat such a step. America and the provinces involved in the consecrations (South-East Asia and Rwanda) will now have to work together to sort out the canonical mess created. Central to much of this was the clear statement that a province only excludes itself from the Anglican Communion by public and formal rejection of any aspect of what is familiarly called the "Lambeth Quadrilateral" — namely the supremacy of scripture in doctrinal matters, the two sacraments instituted by Christ, the creeds of the first four centuries, and the historic episcopate. Obviously there can be dispute as to whether some development constitutes a *de facto* breach of the Quadrilateral (would lay presidency of the Eucharist, as proposed by the extremely Protestant Diocese of Sydney, conflict with the second or fourth? Does the ordination of a practising homosexual overturn the first?); but the stress was laid on formal abandoning of this "grammar" of Anglicanism, in full recognition of the difficulties of deciding what constituted a merely implicit rejection. On this basis, the debate on sexuality is clearly seen as one that may divide provinces from one another (South-East Asia has already declared that it will not consider itself to be in communion with any diocese that repudiates the Lambeth resolution on sexuality), but does not necessitate decisions about whether a local church is or is not in communion with the Archbishop of Canterbury, and so formally part of the Anglican family.

It is a precarious balance, but leaves the emphasis on the solidity of sacramental practice and theological method as criteria for mutual recognition. This at least allows the assumption of a common agenda on most issues of mission and of justice, where the most deeply felt concerns of practically all the Primates actually cluster. It was sad that only on the last full day (which included a splendidly inflammatory, even visionary, address from the Secretary of State for International Development, Clare Short) did we note the achievement of the conference in Nairobi earlier this March, organized by the Coalition against Poverty in Africa (CAPA), a network largely Anglican in inspiration and leadership. On this occasion, several African Primates invited representatives of the World Bank for a face-to-face consultation about what was needed not only in the sphere of debt relief but also in respect of the construction of civil society in Africa in a way that will attack the problems of endemic corruption and militarism that aggravate the debt crisis. A superb report emerged from this meeting.

This is the kind of thing that a worldwide Communion can nurture, both practically and theologically; it evidently wasn't obvious to the Primates that it depended on unanimity over sexual ethics. In the last analysis, Anglicanism has always been wary of a central executive power. It has worked on the assumption that a common ecclesial language and theological method take you a long way, and its authority has been a mixture of authoritative texts and a process of rather untidy corporate interpretation of them. The Primates' meeting showed no signs of wanting to become a ruling synod. Its one plea was for more frequent meeting, and this is likely to happen: the present strains on the Communion are severe enough for personal contact and consultation to be imperative, so that actions are not taken without awareness of the wider context. The next few years will undoubtedly be increasingly painful and difficult for many Anglicans; but this particular meeting suggested that the classical Anglican method was not dead yet — and that the sheer experience of sustained biblical reflection (wonderfully led by David Ford of Cambridge) and uninhibited theological conversation may yet save Anglicanism from its own variety of the Vatican I debacle.

Conflict and Communion

Homosexuality and Church Practice in Anglicanism

Eric B. Beresford

Introduction

It is usually the case that ethical arguments for and against particular ways of living out the gospel in the life of the church are
presented as formal arguments whose conclusions should be true
for all times and in all places. While there are certainly some truths
that could not be challenged in any intelligible way whilst remaining within the Christian tradition, most assertions about how we
should live our lives are unlikely to be so obviously fixed. In part,
this is because the church is rarely able to ascribe meanings to
particular behaviours that are completely independent of how the
surrounding culture sees those behaviours. Only the most stead-
fastly sectarian of churches could remain indifferent to changes in
cultural understandings. So whether the response of the church is
to critique or to embrace cultural shifts, the church's own positions on particular moral issues, and the language it uses to speak
of them, will be affected by changes in the surrounding culture.
This is reflected in the widely recognized need of the church to
preach the gospel afresh in every age.

However, it raises some very difficult questions for Anglicanism,
which exists as a worldwide communion of churches. Anglicans
understand themselves as members of a single family, parts of a

single community but governed locally in accord with local needs. Anglicans seek to embrace both universality and particularity in a very intentional way. This means that we are always open to the possibility of divergences in practice that will be difficult to reconcile with our unity, but which cannot be solved by any sort of magisterial pronouncement that will restore unity, at least on the surface, or at the level of policy. Nowhere is this clearer than in the history of the conversations concerning homosexuality that have been a part of the life of Anglicanism for the past quarter century.

In what follows I will seek to contribute to the conversation about the church's pastoral relationship to gay and lesbian people, not by arguing for or against any particular position, but by seeking to describe some of the history of this debate as it has taken place within the Anglican Communion, with a view to trying to identify any clues that might emerge as to how we might continue to live together with such diversity of conviction where practices are evolving and seem likely to continue to evolve. At the centre of this conversation will be the events that unfolded at the Lambeth Conference 1998. My interest lies not so much in the details of the debates around motion I.10, nor in the particular conclusions reached, as in trying to describe as accurately as possible where those events left the church and how the church has sought to come to terms with itself since then.[1] It is my hope that by exploring the ways we have arrived at the current situation with regard to the question of homosexual relationships we might be better able to plan for the future. For the Anglican Church of Canada, this need has become all the more urgent since the decision of the New Westminster Diocesan Synod to proceed with liturgies for the blessing of same-sex relationships.

It is also my hope that one of the things that will become clear in what follows is the difference between debate and dialogue. That the history I shall recount has been characterized by debate is clear. Indeed, that debate has often been acrimonious. It has also been unproductive. It has been characterized by seemingly endless repetitions of well-established positions that become more and more intransigent with every repetition. More recently there has been the hopeful emergence of some more careful approaches to these debates in which the positions being opposed have been treated with greater care and seriousness than had been the case until recently.[2] However, by their very nature, debates are cast in oppositional terms. The purpose of debate is to clarify the truth and separate it from positions that are erroneous or incomplete. It may indeed turn out that neither side is in possession of the whole truth, but debate focuses its attention on the arguments being deployed and proceeds by eliminating options that prove to be untrue or inadequate.

By contrast, dialogue begins in a recognition of the community of dialogue partners. We belong together as members of a single community. As such, we share interests and concerns that often go unnoticed, but which, from time to time, bring us into conflict. Dialogue is not in the first place about winners and losers; it is about relationship and mutual responsibility. To understand a debate it is enough to explain the basic premises at stake for each side, and the arguments used. To understand a dialogue it is important to tell the story of how the community arrived at the place it finds itself in. That is what I hope to do in what follows.

The Situation Before 1998

The debates concerning same-sex relationships did not erupt from nowhere in 1998. Before the issue ever came to Lambeth, provinces had been dealing with challenges to the church's pastoral practices with regard to gay and lesbian people. This was particularly true in Europe and North America, where changes in social attitudes to gay and lesbian people allowed them to be far more visible than they had ever been before, first outside the church, then increasingly within it. As the wider society became more accepting of the lives of gay and lesbian people, some in the church began to feel that the church was being left in an untenable position, defending an outdated morality whose effect was to exclude people in a way that was simply incomprehensible in the wider society. Others believed that the move to change the discipline of the church represented a significant departure from fidelity to biblical teaching and had wide-ranging ramifications for central Christian teachings. They argued against what they saw as an uncritical acceptance of the social mores of the wider society and in favour of a distinctive Christian witness that, whilst difficult, would in the end prove to be the true expression of love for gay and lesbian people within the wider society. While the debates that followed have brought some changes in the life of the churches, it is simply not the case that any church has yet moved to complete and full acceptance of the intimate relationships of gay and lesbian people. The picture is still a picture of institutions in transition.

The Church of England

In the Church of England there is essentially a two-tiered approach to the issue in which gay and lesbian relationships are tolerated on the grounds of freedom of conscience for gay and lesbian laity.

> It is ... only right that there should be an open and welcoming place in the Christian community both for those homophiles who follow the way of abstinence, giving themselves to friendship for many rather than to intimacy with one, and also for those who are conscientiously convinced that a faithful, sexually active relationship with one other person, aimed at helping both partners to grow in discipleship, is the way of life God wills for them.[3]

The situation for clergy is more stringent, although the report of the House of Bishops advises against interrogating individuals on their sexual lives unless there is a strong reason to do so — namely the possibility of public scandal.[4] Nonetheless, the bishops were clear that the liberty extended to laity did not extend to clergy.

We have, therefore, to say that in our considered judgement the clergy cannot claim the liberty to enter into sexually active homophile relationships. Because of the distinctive nature of their calling, status, and consecration, to allow such a claim on their part would be seen as placing that way of life in all respects on a par with heterosexual marriage as a reflection of God's purposes in creation.[5]

In other words, whilst the toleration of homosexual relationships between lay people could be construed, at least according to the bishops, as a reflection of the ongoing debate in the life of the church, the toleration of such relationships between clergy would be the admission that change was appropriate and necessary.

North American Developments

In North America we have to be careful to distinguish clearly between the US context and Canada. The conversations have taken quite different directions in the two jurisdictions.

Episcopal Church USA

In the United States, although many would agree with the Church of England bishops in their view that change prior to agreement has the effect of pre-empting debate and prejudging outcome, in practice changes have taken place in particular parts of the country and the debate continues. Changes in the effective discipline in the church began in the Episcopal Church USA in the late 1970s. At that time the Diocese of Rochester (in New York) produced a liturgy for the blessing of same-sex relationships. This was neither requested nor authorized by an act of the diocesan convention, but was authorized by the bishop acting in his capacity as chief liturgical officer. A number of dioceses now have such liturgies generally also authorized by the bishop acting alone. Possible exceptions might be the Diocese of Maryland and the Diocese of

New Hampshire. In both of these contexts the liturgies used appear to have a more "official status."

The approach taken in the Episcopal Church has caused some frustrations on both sides of the debate. For those seeking change in the church's position it has seemed unsatisfactorily half-hearted. It allows same-sex relationships to receive *de facto* blessing in Episcopal churches, but no change of policy is stated and the position may seem tenuous. For those who believe that such developments would be inappropriate, the unofficial nature of such arrangements makes them difficult to control. Further, while the church has not yet changed its position, the existence and use of such liturgies over significant periods of time might make the debate seem less and less relevant to the actual life of the church. Not surprisingly, such arrangements have been controversial. Nonetheless, neither General Convention nor the relevant diocesan conventions have been particularly keen to interfere in these arrangements.

The ecclesiastical courts have proved equally unwilling to decide the issues for the church. In January of 1995 a presentment was filed against Bishop Righter charging him with heresy based on his ordination of Barry Stopfel, a homosexual man living in relationship at the time of his ordination. The charges were eventually dismissed as the court found that neither the doctrine nor the discipline of the church currently prohibit the ordination of a non-celibate homosexual person living in a committed relationship. Clearly, this decision did not satisfy those who brought the presentment or their supporters. On the issue of changed doctrine, they argued that a rite of blessing for same-sex relationships was indistinguishable from marriage and, as such, changed the way we understood marriage since it no longer applied to the union of one man with one woman. The court found that there were not sufficient grounds to conclude that such a change in the understanding of marriage was intended. Clearly, whether or not there is a change of "doctrine" depends both on our doctrine of marriage and on our understanding of the relationship of same-sex unions to married relationships. Anglicans are notoriously diverse in their view of both. Some Anglicans have wished to see marriage in sacramental terms following Catholic thought and others have seen marriage in covenantal terms following more Reformed theological approaches. Some Anglicans wish to extend marriage to same-sex couples, and others have argued that we are not dealing with marriage but simply with an analogous state of life. These differences have made the conversation much more complex.

One of the oddities of the Episcopal context has been that conversations at the level of General Convention have taken place through the offices of the Standing Commission on Liturgy and Music. This has meant that the commission has functioned as a doctrine commission in this area for some years. The anomaly arose because the first approaches to the General Convention concerned the development of liturgies. However, that surely reflects precisely the sort of initiative that is going to appear to pre-empt the debate. It may be that it would be more productive if this conversation were housed elsewhere.

Anglican Church of Canada

In Canada the conversation has tended to be much less acrimonious until recently. The issue first received attention in the mid-1970s and resulted in a pastoral statement issued by the bishops at that time. The discussions that led to the 1979 statement date back in the House of Bishops to 1976, when events in a number of dioceses forced the issue onto the agenda of the House of Bishops. The 1979 statement itself was thus the outcome of a long study process, and it is perhaps worth remembering that, while for many that statement has stood over recent years as a bulwark of orthodoxy, when it was produced it was considered to be extraordinarily radical. The bishop in the Diocese of Kootenay was censored, and in Huron the diocesan newspaper fulminated against the "revisionist stance taken by the bishops." Lost in many of the discussions was the claim of the bishops, articulated by the then Primate Ted Scott, that the guidelines set out in 1979 were intended primarily to be a pastoral document, guiding practice rather than bringing new legislation into existence.

> Our statement is not meant to be, in any way, legislation or a final doctrinal statement. It is a pastoral statement, and we intend it to assist us in the exercise of our pastoral ministry within the Church.[6]

The pastoral intent of the 1979 document could be seen in its opening phrases that stated:

> We believe as Christians, that homosexual persons, as children of God, have a full and equal claim with all other persons, upon the love, acceptance, concern, and pastoral care of the Church.

For many gay and lesbian Christians this pastoral intent did not seem to translate into pastoral action. In the first place, there was the actual content of the guidelines, the practical consequences of which were that homosexual unions could not be blessed and homosexual persons could not be ordained unless they first made a commitment to their bishop "to abstain from sexual acts with persons of the same sex as a requirement for ordination." A number of commentators argued that this set up a dual standard. Heterosexual persons were not required similarly to commit themselves to abstain from sexual relations outside of marriage. If such a commitment were simply deemed unnecessary, that assumption at the very least would seem oddly naïve. It also meant that gay men and lesbians were unable to speak of their relationships in any way that would contribute to understanding in the life of the church for fear of reprisal.

Still, many gays and lesbians were pleased to see their equality before God affirmed and were pleased with the suggestion, still to be followed through, that homosexuality be discussed within the framework of a broader discussion of sexuality. They were also pleased to see some expression of concern about the quality of their relationships. The bishops said,

We are aware that some homosexuals develop for themselves relationships of mutual support, help and comfort, about which the church must show an appropriate concern.

Nonetheless, gay and lesbian Christians saw little in the years that followed to indicate what that "appropriate concern" might consist of. The only thing that seemed to be clear was that such relationships should not be confused with marriage. Fair enough, but people on both sides of this issue were interested to know what the bishops thought such relationships might be.

If the reaction of the gay and lesbian community was initially one of an optimism that faded as time went on, the reaction of those who sought to uphold "the traditional teaching of the church" on this issue moved from one of suspicion to a widespread acceptance of the 1979 position. A distinction between homosexual orientation and homosexual activity allowed more conservative Christians to see here a document that allowed them to "love the sinner" while at the same time continuing to denounce the sin. This is nowhere clearer than in the then Bishop of Montreal's reflections on this document in the diocesan newspaper, *The Montreal Churchman*. Bishop Reginald Hollis pointed out there that the basic position of the church had on his view been affirmed. The acceptance of homosexual persons was tied to a rejection of homosexual activity.

Clearly many found this position incoherent. How can you accept someone, it might be asked, if you do not accept something as central to their identity as their sexual orientation? Once again the response of Bishop Hollis was to point out that the scriptural and traditional basis for accepting that sexual orientation was central to personal identity is to say the least rather thin. Still, this is a two-edged sword. By admitting to the gap between the Bible's understanding of sexuality and those things that we seem to learn from contemporary psychological and social theories, we open up the space in which the assumptions of scripture come into dialogue with contemporary learning. The claim that scripture seems to know nothing of "sexual orientation" can become a reason to question the adequacy or relevance of the scriptural critique of particular sexual acts. Sure enough, the debate that followed reflected this.

The bishops were not the only ones discussing these issues. Conversations took place at all levels of the church, and at the General Synod of 1992 a major block of time was devoted to an open forum on the topic. As a result of this forum the synod mandated a group to produce study materials to facilitate the broadest possible conversation throughout the church. By 1995 approximately 170 groups and 2500 people had used the study guide *Hearing Diverse Voices, Seeking Common Ground.* The results of this initiative were discussed at the 1995 General Synod. Hearings were held that led to a motion being presented and strongly supported that:

> affirmed the presence and contributions of gay men and lesbians in the life of the church and condemned bigotry, violence, and hatred directed toward any due to their sexual orientation.

Now it is important to note that the support for this motion was bipartisan. In other words, many who rejected the idea that same-sex sexual intimacy could be a legitimate option for Christians still supported this motion.

The report recommended, among other things, that the process of dialogue continue; that all of us should "learn and reflect more about our sexuality as a whole," and that the dialogue should be extended so that the "whole church family has an opportunity to be involved." The newly created Faith, Worship and Ministry Committee was given a mandate to provide leadership to the church to ensure the continuation of the dialogue. What the report played down was the degree of controversy that was generated by the study guide. For many, the guide failed to allow the church to hear diverse voices because it cut off the voices of those who did not believe that the church should move toward a change of its stance. This has been recognized by Faith, Worship and Ministry, which has promoted a number of consultations and begun to develop supplemental materials to broaden the range of perspectives that are heard in the discussions. Having said this, it is also true that the committee quickly discovered how difficult it was to broaden inclusion. Many of the problems faced by the committee that produced *Hearing Diverse Voices* have continued to affect the work of the Faith, Worship and Ministry Committee. If we are committed not only to speaking about gay and lesbian relationships, but also to speaking with gay and lesbian persons, such voices need to be made available for those contexts where they would not otherwise be heard, even though this can easily seem like advocacy for one point of view. Also, some of the "missing" voices — such as those who have experienced healing ministries directed toward gay people — proved easy enough to name but difficult to find.

Whatever the strengths and weaknesses of *Hearing Diverse Voices*, it has, I believe, contributed to a more respectful pattern of discussion. This needs to be further developed if we are to make any progress. If we wish to be heard, then we must find ways of speaking that will allow us to be heard by those with whom we disagree. We have found it too easy to address ourselves to those who are already converted to our point of view.

That attitudes were changing could be seen in developments taking place in the House of Bishops. Following the debate in 1995 they began an intentional process of deepening their listening and understanding. In preparation for their meeting in April of 1997, the bishops conducted a survey to assess what the will of the House might be at that point. Then something quite extraordinary happened that will, I believe, continue to build trust and further open and honest discussion. For the first time the House of Bishops decided not to go *in camera* as they discussed the issue of homosexuality. This was particularly striking because the survey they were discussing revealed that the bishops were divided in much the same way as the church at large. There were a small number of bishops wanting to see change soon, a few quite happy with the status quo, and some who believed that the principles that underlie the status quo still are serving us well, but who believed that the pastoral context within which those principles needed to be expressed and applied had changed. A new statement was therefore requested and a small group struck to prepare it. The group reported back in October of 1997, and once again the bishops continued to meet in open session as they discussed the statement.

The statement suggested that theological reflection and pastoral action in the church since 1979 had focused on four key areas: the place of gay and lesbian persons in society, the place of gay and lesbian persons in the church, the significance of committed sexually active relationships between people of the same sex, and the significance of such relationships for ordination of gay and lesbian persons. In brief, the statement pointed out that the church had spoken repeatedly and clearly in favour of the civil rights of homosexual persons and had opposed discrimination, for example in its support for Bill C-33, which made sexual orientation a prohibited ground for discrimination under the Canadian Charter of Rights and Freedoms. They called upon the church and all its members to continue to work to safeguard the freedom, dignity, and responsibility of every person and to seek an end to discrimination. They went on to recognize that the church's awareness of the presence of gay and lesbian people in the life of the church was growing and changing. The language of 1979 treated homosexual persons as "needy objects for pastoral care," and this was replaced by the recognition that we are all "partners, celebrating together the dignity of every human being, and reaching out together for the wholeness offered to us in the Gospel." From this perspective the bishops committed the church to "open and respectful dialogue with those who sincerely believe that sexuality expressed within a committed homosexual relationship is God's call to them" and to "affirm our common desire to seek together the fullness of life revealed in Christ." While the statement continued to affirm that only heterosexual marriage could be affirmed and receive liturgical blessing in the life and ministry of the church, the bishops acknowledged the need for continued conversation, and also for a deeper understanding of the way homosexual relationships are understood and valued by gay and lesbian persons. The good faith of the bishops in this attempt to reach out toward a better understanding of the experience of gay and lesbian persons was reflected in their recognition "that relationships of mutual support, help and comfort between homosexual persons exist and are to be preferred to relationships that are anonymous and transient." Finally, in a manner similar to that espoused by the English bishops, the Canadians made it clear that, in their view, the need for clergy to live exemplary lives meant that they could not be in a sexually intimate relationship unless it is recognized by the church. It follows that, until and unless the church is able to recognize same-sex relationships, such relationships would not be open to clergy.

It is perhaps to be expected that the 1997 statement pleased nobody. Conservatives saw a dangerous lack of clarity here that seemed to fudge the key biblical and doctrinal issues. Gays, lesbians, and their supporters believed that it reflected little if any progress after nearly twenty years of work. Still there was a reluctance to see the matter come to a resolution at the synods in 1998 or 2001. This is all the more surprising given developments that had taken place in the Diocese of New Westminster.

In May of 1998, months before the Lambeth Conference, a motion, later referred to as Motion 9, was brought to the diocesan synod in New Westminster, sponsored by three parishes. The motion that appeared was a compromise motion drawn from the three initiatives. It asked the bishop to authorize the blessing of same-sex unions in those parishes that request the opportunity to celebrate such liturgies subject to whatever conditions the bishop should choose. To the surprise of almost everybody the motion passed by a slim margin (51 per cent – 9 votes). The bishop, Michael Ingham, withheld his consent on the grounds that the margin was too narrow for a change of this significance. He further stated that he wished to consult with the House of Bishops and to see what happened at Lambeth. In the meantime, he called together a Council of Advice consisting of clergy from the parishes that proposed the motion, clergy from the parishes most opposed to the motion, two representatives of the House of Bishops, and some outside consultants. Although Lambeth could hardly have been read as an encouraging sign, it did mandate continued conversation and dialogue, and Bishop Ingham began such a process in the diocese, committing the synod to reconsider the issue in 2001. I will return to this process as I look at the situation after Lambeth. At this point I want to return to the events that marked the movement toward the Lambeth conference. Two other meetings are of significance: the consultations that took place in Kuala Lumpur and the Dallas consultation.

Kuala Lumpur 1997

The Kuala Lumpur meeting is significant for a number of reasons; not least, the meeting reflected a growing consciousness of the global significance of the churches of the South. In the statement issued from this consultation, the participants drew attention to the demographic shift that is taking place in the Anglican Communion, as a result of which most Anglicans are to be found in the global South. These regions of the world, although diverse in many ways, shared "a common experience of life overshadowed by ethnic hatred, political instability and neo-colonialism, social injustice and marginalization, crippling international debt and spiralling inflation, environmental damage and pollution, religious strife and intolerance, unbridled materialism and pervasive corruption." In the face of these challenges they joined the call for the year 2000 to be proclaimed as a Year of Jubilee centred on the remission of the unpayable burden of debt born by the two-thirds world.

Although many who gathered at Kuala Lumpur would see these issues as the critical issues, they were also concerned with what they saw as another form of colonialism, in which the agenda of the Communion was co-opted by the concerns of the global North, especially in the area of human sexuality. They affirmed that the only legitimate place for sexual expression was in heterosexual marriage. While many in the West wondered how this fitted with the toleration of polygamy that was granted to facilitate the mission of the church in certain parts of Africa by Lambeth in 1988, the target was clearly the growing toleration of homosexual relationships by the "liberal" churches of the global North. "The Holy Scriptures are clear in teaching that all sexual promiscuity is sin. We are convinced that this includes homosexual practices...." Whilst acknowledging that no province had, at that point, authorized the blessing of same-sex relationships or the ordination of those in such relationships, they were concerned at the toleration of such relationships and the refusal to prohibit ordination of those in such relationships or to discipline bishops who ordained them. The statement called for action from the whole Anglican Communion, thus raising the question that I shall have to deal with later. Within the Communion as it currently exists, what could such action consist of?

Dallas 1997

Later in the same year, about fifty conservative bishops from around the communion met in Dallas. This was taken as an opportunity to reaffirm the Kuala Lumpur statement and also to allow conservatives from the global South to strategize with conservatives from the Episcopal Church USA on how they might work together both at Lambeth and within ECUSA to promote the concerns of Kuala Lumpur. Once again Dallas tied together concern for global debt with human sexuality. While some saw this as a trade-off, others were struck by the way in which conservatives, who were normally far more concerned about biblical norms for sexual relationships than they were about biblical norms for economic relationships, were beginning to handle biblical materials in much more consistent ways around these two areas.

The Dallas statement provoked a flurry of statements and counter-statements from all sides in the period immediately before the Lambeth Conference. It quickly became clear that, whatever the best intentions of the organizers of the conference, sexuality was going to be a high profile topic for debate. One of the more quixotic interventions came in the form of a series of twelve theses published by Bishop Spong of Newark. In these, Bishop Spong tied his support for gay and lesbian people to his rejection of the traditional tenets of theism and of the resurrection and sacrificial death of Jesus. Reading the theses, one can think of almost nothing more calculated to confirm the views of those who saw the blessing of same-sex relationships as a departure from biblical Christianity. This, tied to the incipient racism of Bishop Spong's claims in a later interview that the African Church was in the grip of a theology that reflected its pre-modern social situation and modes of thought, made it clear that a confrontation was in the offing.

Lambeth 1998

The conversations about human sexuality took place as part of section 1 of the Lambeth conference. Under the overall chairmanship of Njongonkulu Ndungane, the section entitled "Called to Full Humanity" included sections on Human Rights and Human Dignity, The Environment, Human Sexuality, Modern Technology, Euthanasia, and International Debt and Economic Justice. The sexuality subsection was under the chairmanship of Bishop Duncan Buchanan of Johannesburg. It did not begin well. Delegates arrived to find an agenda which included listening to the experiences of gay and lesbian people. Some delegates were disturbed that these voices had been singled out for special attention. Although the chair and several other bishops sought to argue that this was a step in understanding the lives of those they were to speak about, in the end the bishops declined to listen to these voices.

From this point on, progress was difficult, and at first it seemed unlikely that any progress would be possible. The draft statement received by the bishops when they arrived was clearly unacceptable. Then several bishops were commissioned to try to start again with a new statement. The statement that they produced, which relied heavily on the Canadian House of Bishops' statement from 1997, provided the framework for renewed engagement in the group. Almost running out of time, they produced a statement that won the consensus of the group. Then the second bombshell hit. The bishops working in the subsection had such difficulty working on the statement that they agreed that a motion would be unwise. At the end of the last session, the chair announced that they were being told they had to produce a motion, and he proposed a draft that had already been tentatively submitted on behalf of the whole group. Once again the meeting almost fell apart, and once again the small working group was sent off to try to produce something overnight that would be more acceptable.

This is not the place to trace the details of the debate on the motion that was produced. Suffice it to say that the debate was far less temperate than the motion itself, although it was amended repeatedly, always in a more restrictive direction in terms of its attitude to gay and lesbian people. The amendments received varying degrees of support. One amendment, to strengthen the statement about scripture's opposition to homosexuality was, perhaps surprisingly, defeated. Several other motions that the bishops would have to deal with if the motion from the subsection was defeated also overshadowed the debate. In the end the motion was passed overwhelmingly. The motion commended the report of the subsection, acknowledged the presence of gay and lesbian people in the life of the church, and committed the church to listening to their experience and to assuring them of the love of God and full inclusion in the life of the church. The motion further spoke against discrimination and condemned "irrational fear of homosexuality." At the same time it said that the conference could not "advise the legitimizing or blessing of same-sex unions nor ordaining those involved in same gender unions." It expressed the view that scripture teaches that only the faithful union of a man and woman in lifelong marriage is the appropriate context for sexual intimacy and called all others to abstinence. This claim is particularly interesting in that, while in the context of the motion it was intended as a critique of same-sex unions, it in fact implies a rejection of re-marriage after divorce, a position not accepted by the majority of provinces within the Communion, and implies a rejection of the tolerance of polygamy that was passed at Lambeth 1988, a rejection that would not be supported by many who voted for this motion.

Not surprisingly, North American liberals were unhappy with the debate and its outcome. Surprisingly, they did not all vote against the motion. Their concern was that, if the motion was not allowed through, the motions that would follow were even worse, and it was clear that the conference was of a mind to pass a motion on this subject now that one had reached the floor. The reaction of North American conservatives to this debate has been interesting. Several Canadian conservatives expressed dismay at the tone of the debate. There seemed to be little concern about the pastoral impact of some bishops' strongly worded condemnations of homosexuality and barely disguised expressions of disgust and even hate. They were disturbed at the refusal even to hear the voices of those whose lives and loves were so harshly judged by the conference. Still, many conservatives, while regretting the tone of this particular debate, saw the conference as a watershed in the history of the Communion and a wake-up call to the churches of the global North. The balance of power had clearly shifted, and the debate on same-sex relationships had become symbolic of that fact.

In assessing what follows from the events in Lambeth we need to remember both the actual status of the conference and the hopes and expectations that were invested in it. On the one hand, there has been a growing desire in the Communion to see a more effective way of addressing the problems that threaten to tear us apart. In this respect, debates about human sexuality did not present new

problems. We had seen similarly fractious debates about the ordination of women and then about their consecration as bishops. At
Lambeth 1988 it had been suggested that, if any province admitted women to the episcopate, the unity of the Communion would
be severed. In fact, there were twelve women bishops at Lambeth
in 1998, and although they did signal the presence of ongoing
questions about authority and communion, the atmosphere was
generally courteous and collegial. What was new about the sexuality debate was its intensity. Certainly, the intensity was fuelled in
part by a sense that this was the issue around which biblical orthodoxy had to take its stand in the face of the "liberal drift" of the
churches of the global North. Whether this issue can bear the
freight that is thereby placed on it has yet to be seen. The difficulty is that there are other issues that might be construed as
presenting challenges to scriptural orthodoxy that simply could
not command the support that the critique of same-sex relationships received. For example, scripture is clear that the lending of
money at interest is bad, and this was the universal teaching of the
church for nearly 1600 years. The call for a return to the "plain
meaning" of scripture has attracted some support in those parts of
the Communion burdened by unrepayable debt, but despite shared
concerns over international debt, it clearly would not give rise to
the sort of North-South coalition that we saw around human
sexuality.

What has been clear is that the hope that a victory at Lambeth
would secure the unity of the Communion has not been realized.
From a historical perspective, it is odd that such a thought would
have been entertained. Lambeth has only ever succeeded in articulating consensus after it has emerged. It has never been able to
define and enforce consensus. In fact there is no structure for doing any such thing in the Communion. The only way in which a
Lambeth motion becomes effective in the life of a particular province is by being received by that province. This is rarely done.
The most obvious example would be the formation of the Anglican

Consultative Council. This body was not formed by Lambeth, as some have mistakenly said; it was formed by the provinces at the request of Lambeth, as each province passed enabling legislation to allow the Council to come into being. The Anglican Communion currently is organized as a series of self-governing churches, called provinces, each of which has its own history, canons, and constitutions. Although there is a family resemblance in the way we order our lives and conduct our worship (we are episcopally led, but governed by synods that include laity and clergy as well as bishops), there are also significant differences. It seems unlikely that provinces are going to be willing to let go of the autonomy they possess in any general way. The calls for central discipline, in the end, all relate to the desire to impose discipline over other provinces whose activities are troubling to us. At the same time there is a commonly shared unwillingness to have discipline imposed.

Divisions in the Order of the Church

The failure to find a mechanism to resolve disagreements and impose discipline on provinces that disagreed with the advice of Lambeth gave rise to significant levels of frustration in the period that followed. Conservatives in the global South accused ECUSA of "disobeying" the resolutions of Lambeth. ECUSA responded that it had not acted as a province in any way contrary to the resolution and was trying to address its own internal disputes as best it could. The Archbishop of Canterbury was asked to intervene but made it clear that he could not do so beyond the support and encouragement he was already giving.

Then, on 29 January 2000, shortly before the Primates met in Portugal, and on the last day of Moses Tay's tenure as Archbishop of South-East Asia and Bishop of Singapore, he and Immanuel Kolini of Rwanda consecrated two Episcopal priests, Charles Murphy III, of Pawley's Island, South Carolina, and John Rodgers, of Trinity Episcopal Divinity School, as bishops with the mandate to "re-establish the unity that has been violated by the unrebuked ridicule and denial of basic Christian teaching" in the Episcopal Church. The consecrations, which took place in a secretive liturgy in the cathedral in Singapore, sparked a storm of protest not only from ECUSA, but also from the Anglican Church of Canada and the Archbishop of Canterbury. A statement released from Lambeth Palace said, "It has come as a grave disappointment to the Archbishop, as it is his view that such consecrations are irresponsible and irregular and only harm the unity of the communion." Michael Peers, Primate of the Canadian church, was even more blunt. "Bishops are not intercontinental ballistic missiles, manufactured on one continent and fired into another as an act of aggression." He called the consecrations "an open and premeditated assault on Anglican tradition, catholic order and Christian charity."[7]

The questions that were now opened up included questions of how the order of the church could be maintained in the face of such a fundamental assault. Further, what was the authority of an archbishop, especially when acting outside the canons and constitutions of his own church as Moses Tay most certainly had done? Could a church authorize interventions outside its own jurisdictional region as the church in Rwanda did? Who calls a person to episcopacy, and, if there is no diocese with the order and authority to recognize and accept a new bishop, can a consecration take place? Whatever the answers to these questions, clearly the complications introduced when we bypass the lines of authority and accountability in this way make any disagreement, including those around same-sex relationships, much more difficult to disentangle.

The Meetings of the Primates

Of all the bodies within the Communion that meet regularly, the body that has given the most attention to the issues raised by human sexuality has been the meeting of the Primates of the Anglican Communion. Historically the Primates meet every three years. As they had met during Lambeth, they did not meet again between Lambeth and the Singapore consecrations. A great deal of pressure was therefore placed on the meeting in Porto, Portugal. In the event, the Primates chose not to focus on sexuality as such, but to explore "dimensions of the mystery of the church, and the holiness of our vocation and ministry." In other words the questions discussed were primarily about the nature of the church and the question of unity, and about the nature and role of primatial authority. In the light of this, the Primates acknowledged disagreement on matters of human sexuality. At the same time they came to the recognition that this disagreement was not to be construed in terms of who was, and who was not, faithful to scripture. "We recognize the seriousness and sincerity behind both concerns, and the shared desire to be faithful to scripture and to strengthen our unity in Christ." What then was to be the basis of that unity? To answer that question the Primates appealed to the Chicago-Lambeth Quadrilateral. Originally designed to articulate the basis for Anglican approaches to ecumenical dialogue, it was pressed into service as a statement of what holds us together.

> We believe that the unity of the Communion as a whole still rests on the Lambeth Quadrilateral: the holy scriptures as the rule and standard of faith; the creeds of the undivided church; the two sacraments ordained by Christ himself and the historic episcopate. Only a formal and public repudiation of this would place a diocese or province outside the Anglican Communion.

On the basis of this the Primates went on to say,

> We believe that the disagreement over sexual ethics and differences in the reception of Lambeth Resolution I.10 that clearly exists within and among the provinces does not necessarily amount to a complete and definitive rupture of communion.[8]

This certainly should not be taken as diminishing the seriousness of the situation we face. Indeed the Primates went on to make clear the divisive impact of decisions to continue to act in opposition to the recommendations of Lambeth I.10. At the same time the Primates reminded others that a part of Lambeth I.10 was a commitment to ongoing dialogue, and they called on the church to engage in that with greater seriousness and openness without prejudging the outcome of the debate. Finally, they made clear that any such process was fundamentally compromised by decisions to breach the catholic order and discipline of the church.

The conversation begun at Porto was continued at their next meeting, which took place just one year later at the Kanuga Conference Centre, in South Carolina. By this time, the Archbishop of the Southern Cone, Maurice Sinclair, and the Archbishop of the West Indies, Drexel Gomes, had produced a proposal to move forward to a more centralized expression of authority in their book, *To Mend the Net*. They wished to get this work discussed at the meeting, but the Archbishop declined, noting that it had not been produced either by or at the request of any Communion body. Instead he suggested that it be referred as a submission to the Inter-Anglican Doctrinal Commission, and informal discussion was allowed on the first evening as the Primates gathered. The focus of the meeting was once again the role of Primates. In particular, attention was paid to the canon law context and to the identifiable ways in which the canon law traditions of the Communion have been shaped and developed. The mood of the Primates at that meeting is well reflected in the fact that sexuality was far from being the sole or even principal focus of attention. They were concerned to remind the church that it faced many pressing issues and suggested that, while division around issues of human sexuality was real and painful, it should not be exaggerated out of proportion in a way that would eclipse other pressing issues. The Primates emphasized this concern when they adopted an action plan that outlined proposed steps to be taken to address a range of issues.

With regard to the developing realities around the blessing of same-sex relationships, the Primates took a step away from trying to resolve the debate. Instead, they recognized the concerns of those who felt alienated by changes taking place in certain provinces of the Communion and committed themselves "to seek for ways to secure sustained pastoral care for all in our Communion. We also resolved, as we did at our meeting last year in Porto, to show responsibility toward each other, and to seek to avoid actions that might damage the credibility of our mission in the world." At the same time they committed themselves to a process of study that they articulated as follows:

> to explore the common principles by which our churches are organized, beginning with the way we ourselves meet as primates;
>
> to enlarge and deepen our theological vision; and
>
> to collaborate and share our resources in theological education.
>
> Work will be done on these issues, so that God's people will be more and more able to read the Bible with wisdom, seeking to be formed in the truth and holiness of God.[9]

Once again the Primates acknowledged their divisions but refused to see them as necessarily dividing the church. Interestingly, the process of study they committed themselves to was not an exploration of the issues of human sexuality. This was ground that had been traversed quite frequently, and the Primates seem to have felt that little was to be gained by going over it one more time. Rather, they committed themselves to a study of the nature of the life of the church as experienced by Anglicans, and of theology as it shapes that common life and forms those called to exercise ministry in the church at all levels.

In comparison with the meetings at Porto and Kanuga, the 2001 meeting of the Primates held in Canterbury, England, paid far less attention to issues of human sexuality. Two elements of the meeting are, however, significant for this discussion. First, was the report of the work of the legal officers of the Anglican Communion and the proposal that they pay some attention to the canon law traditions and practices around the Communion as they impinge on Order in the Church, Ecclesiastical Government, Ministry, Doctrine, Liturgy and Rites, Church Property, and Inter-Anglican Relations. Once again we see the Primates focusing on the structures within which our disagreements are being expressed and that might be threatened by our divisions. The other item of interest was the statement on the doctrine of God. This statement caused something of a media flurry as some speculated that it had been drafted in order to curb more liberal provinces. However, it was written by a quite representative drafting group and, in fact, represents a return to a theme present already in Porto. The statement seeks to articulate the broad agreement on fundamental doctrine that is the basis for the communion we share and is the context for the disagreements we experience. The statement functions to make it clear that the issues that divide the Communion are not about whether we accept orthodox, creedal Christianity — but rather, reflect differing understandings of how that orthodox, historic faith is to be lived in the differing contexts of contemporary Anglicanism.

International Anglican Conversations on Human Sexuality

Following the Lambeth Conference the Archbishop of Canterbury gathered twelve bishops of a variety of theological perspectives and from different parts of the world to engage in a series of conversations that concluded with a report issued in the spring of 2002. Although the group was established by Lambeth, it did not report until after the Primates had met in Canterbury, so I am including it here. Commending the report of the conversations, the Archbishop of Canterbury acknowledged that many would find it disappointing, but noted that it was not intended to resolve the disagreements but to deepen the dialogue. While the bishops did not underestimate the gravity of the situation we are facing, it is interesting that they chose to open their observations with the note that

> As we arrive at the conclusion of our third and final consultation we have come more profoundly to treasure and respect, through one another's presence, the Anglican Communion as God's gift … grounded in our shared creedal faith, in word and sacrament, and in our common prayer.[10]

In addition to agreeing on the foundational role of scripture in all our conversations, the report also acknowledged that there were problems that needed to be addressed because of the complexity of homosexuality as a phenomenon and the need for a great deal more study. They also acknowledged that part of the problem lay in differences in the role and authority of bishops and in the understanding and function of collegiality in different parts of the Communion. What is particularly interesting is the repeated reference to the experience of the dialogue group as a community that generated a sense of mutual affection, concern, and responsibility. These feelings were reflected in their willingness to remain in community with each other despite significant disagreement, and in their generation of covenants that shaped their conversation in a way that reflected the mutual respect and affection they experienced. The dialogue group obviously benefited from their time together, and their recommendations reflect the fact that they found face-to-face conversation and the opportunity for deeper understanding of each other beneficial. They seemed to recognize that changes in discipline around same-sex relationships have implications for the wider Communion, and that they are likely to happen. Clearly, their hope is that better communication and stronger relationships will help the Communion to deal with the significant tensions that we will continue to face.

Anglican Consultative Council

The Anglican Consultative Council has met twice since Lambeth 1998. In Dundee in 1999, ACC-11 declined to address the issue of same-sex relationships directly, although a hearing was held that a number of members attended. The primary concern seemed to be that the tone of the debate at Lambeth had been unhelpful, and the members did not wish to be drawn into a similarly acrimonious exchange. By contrast, ACC-12, meeting in Hong Kong in September of 2002, had no choice but to address the issue head on. The Archbishop of Canterbury spoke of the matter in his presidential address.

> In short, my concern is that our Communion is being steadily undermined by dioceses and individual bishops taking unilateral action, usually (but not always) in matters to do with sexuality; and as a result steadily driving us towards serious fragmentation and the real possibility of two (or, more likely, many more) distinct Anglican bodies emerging. This erosion of communion through the adoption of "local options" has been going on for some thirty years but in my opinion is reaching crisis proportions today.

Although the Archbishop said that his target was not simply "matters related to human sexuality," he went on to name the Bishop and Diocese of New Westminster in what was taken by many present to be a personal attack, not only on Bishop Ingham, but also on Bishop Bennison from ECUSA, on the Archbishops of Rwanda and South-East Asia, and on the Diocese of Sidney. While one of those present believed that the Archbishop had misrepresented the facts, most were more concerned about the appropriateness of making direct criticisms of the acts and motives of individuals in a speech to which there is traditionally no reply. The Archbishop said,

> It is not my intention to address now the issue that has led some clergy in the Diocese of New Westminster to rebel against their own bishop and their diocesan synod. I respect the sincerity of Bishop Michael Ingham and his diocesan synod, and I do not doubt that they believe that they are acting in the best interests of all, as they see it.
>
> But I deeply regret that Michael and his synod, and other bishops and dioceses in similar situations in North America, seem to be making such decisions without regard to the rest of us and against the clear statements of Lambeth '98. And on the other hand, as I have said, it is disappointing to note the steps that have been taken in reaction by a number of clergy, bishops, and even archbishops in our Communion, equally in disregard of carefully thought-out Lambeth Conference resolutions.

Later I will address the motion introduced by the Archbishop, and passed by the Council. At this point I wish to focus on the impact of the address. Clearly, the Archbishop believed that it was necessary to speak directly to the situation. However, he did so in a way that raised considerable anger not only in the Canadian delegation, but also amongst other delegates who found themselves caught between their feelings of discomfort with the actions of the Diocese of New Westminster and their discomfort at having to deal with these issues in an environment that was now experienced as hostile and confrontational. Bishop Ingham, who was part of the Canadian delegation, pointed out that the synod and bishop had acted carefully over a period of time in which there had been a great deal of consultation. He expressed the view that the Archbishop's remarks were one-sided, focusing only on the concerns of those parishes who have chosen to seek the support of structures other than those offered by the diocese and failing to mention the arrangements offered, in line with the pastoral letter from Kanuga, to those who felt in good conscience that they could not agree with or be identified with the decisions made by the diocesan synod. With regard to the legality and constitutionality of the action he said,

> It remains to be seen what the Council wishes to do with the Archbishop's resolution on "deference to superior synods." The subordination of synods to higher bodies is, in fact, a matter for provincial authorities to determine. In any case, New Westminster has acted consistently within the legal and canonical authority of a diocese within the Canadian church and in deliberate consultation with its national House of Bishops and General Synod.

The diocese sponsored an information session attended by most of the delegates to the ACC, which attempted to explain the processes adopted by the diocese, and give some accounting of the history of the debate. What became immediately clear is that some of the questions that were addressed at this session related to the particular structures of the Canadian Church and its dioceses. The problem that faced the Council in attempting to respond to the motion placed before them was that they realized that they had little or no understanding of the actual structures of the church they were speaking about and of what types of decision and action might be possible given those structures. In the event, the motion proposed by the Archbishop of Canterbury was passed unanimously with minor modifications, the Bishop of New Westminster arguing that his diocese had in fact complied with the motion as it was finally presented. The most important portion of the motion called on:

1. dioceses and individual bishops not to undertake unilateral actions or adopt policies which would strain our communion with one another without reference to their provincial authorities, and

2. provincial authorities to have in mind the impact of their decisions within the wider Communion.

A turning point in the council that made the final debate relatively easy came as the Council reflected on the contributions of Dr. Ishmael Noko of the Lutheran World Federation. In his address, Dr. Noko drew heavily on the African notion of *ubuntu*, an understanding of community that begins in the recognition of our mutual dependency and the need for acceptance and hospitality as constitutive elements of community. In the group discussions and plenary response the council began to work with this notion as a way of understanding communion in a way that might reach beyond the debates about unity and diversity, which had cast the problems facing the Communion into a series of seemingly irreconcilable opposites. The Council clearly began to hope that there might be more productive ways of talking about our differences, including those around human sexuality, by renewing our emphasis on the nature of community, and the bonds of mutual responsibility and respect that make such community possible. Clearly, the majority of the Council was not going to condone the events in New Westminster, but they were equally not convinced that censure or severed relationships would be helpful ways forward at this time. In the end, the motion passed by the Council was about the processes and procedures that enable us to function together as a community and a call for restraint and calm on behalf of all as events continue to unfold.

New Westminster Revisited

After the study process initiated by the Diocese of New Westminster following the vote in 1998, the matter came to a vote in diocesan synod again in 2001. Once again the synod voted in favour of the motion, this time by 56.5 per cent, and once again the Bishop withheld his consent. No new process was set in place at this point, and the Bishop took no steps at that time to reintroduce a motion on this subject. However, when it became clear that motions were going to be introduced from parish vestries at the 2002 diocesan synod, the Bishop decided to offer a proposal that was endorsed by the synod (63 per cent). That proposal — described by the Bishop as permissive, not coercive — provided for a rite of blessing of same-sex relationships, the appointment of an episcopal visitor to offer pastoral care to parishes and clergy who desire it, and a conscience clause stating that no member of the diocese, lay or ordained, will be required to act against their conscience in the blessing of same-sex unions. Prior to the vote some conservatives had suggested that they would prefer that authority be effectively deferred to the parishes and blessings simply be allowed to take place without a formal diocesan or episcopal policy, but Bishop Ingham insisted that no blessing would take place without the consent of the diocesan synod.

After the vote representatives from eight parishes walked out of the synod and threatened conversations about the possibility of alternative episcopal or diocesan arrangements with Primates in other parts of the world, and indeed Archbishop Kolini of Rwanda wrote offering "ecclesiastical protection." Shortly afterward several of the parishes withdrew financial support from the diocese, although they sought to make arrangements to continue to support the General Synod directly. The parishes, grouped together under the heading of "The Anglican Communion in New Westminster," have made several proposals, including the suggestion of a non-geographical diocese, although this would not, in fact, be possible under the civil legislation of the Province of British

Columbia. None of the proposals offered to date by either side seems to have eased the logjam.

A great deal of hope was placed on the House of Bishops, but in the end their statement acknowledged the divisions that exist within the House on this matter and called on both sides to re-open conversation with each other in good faith, "before the fracture widens." At the same time the bishops agreed that, "we will not make individual decisions in any additional dioceses before General Synod, the church's governing body, meets in 2004." They referred the matter to General Synod "for discussion and, if possible, resolution." The statement also said that until the matter is resolved, "all bishops are asked to uphold the 1997 guidelines of the House of Bishops on human sexuality." The guidelines state that bishops "do not accept the blessing of homosexual unions." In open session it was made clear that this request applied to any further decisions.

With the encouragement of the House of Bishops, negotiations began and the Bishop of New Westminster offered to put any further developments on hold until a process of mediation was begun. A facilitator was appointed with the agreement of both sides. However, from the beginning it was unclear what approaches might lead to progress. Talks soon broke down acrimoniously with both sides accusing the other of negotiating in bad faith. It is likely that trust levels were low from the very beginning, and the significant obstacles to progress must have quickly become clear. Even before talks formally broke down, representatives from the parishes that called themselves the Anglican Communion in New Westminster (ACiNW) began talks with the Bishop of the Yukon and visited his diocesan Executive Council. The bishop, with the support of his synod, extended an offer of alternative episcopal oversight with jurisdiction. Bishop Ingham, however, refused this initiative and moved to inhibit any intervention by the Bishop of the Yukon within his diocese. From these events it became clear that the issue of jurisdiction was one of the sticking points in the negotiations between the Diocese of New Westminster and

ACiNW. The clergy representing the ACiNW were not satisfied with an arrangement that provided pastoral care under the jurisdiction of the Bishop of New Westminster even if that care extended to issues of clergy deployment. They wanted the right to church plant in the diocese, something that both the diocese and the House of Bishops clearly found unacceptable. They also expressed the view that a conscience clause was inadequate because, they asserted, this was a matter of gospel truth and not a matter of conscience.

Informal talks appear to have continued with individual parishes. At the same time a parish outside the eight asked to make use of the provision for an Episcopal Pastoral Visitor. After some negotiation, the Rt. Rev. Bill Hockin, the retiring Bishop of Edmonton, was approached and agreed to work with the parish. This provision was supported by the House of Bishops who went further to suggest a job description that was supported by Michael Ingham. They also asked Bishop Buckle of the Yukon to withdraw his offer of pastoral support. At the time of writing it is unclear how these issues will be resolved.

At the same time, a liturgy was published on the web site of the diocese for use by those parishes who had met the Bishop's requirements, which include the support of the annual vestry of the parish. The liturgy was used for the first time at the parish of St. Margaret's Cedar Cottage on 28 May. This event was greeted with delight by many supporters of change, anger by conservatives, and great caution by many observers. A part of the reaction may have been related to the timing of the publication of the liturgy. It appeared within days of the Primates' Meeting in Brazil. At that meeting, aware of events in the diocese, the Primates said

> The question of public rites for the blessing of same-sex unions is still a cause of potentially divisive controversy. The Archbishop of Canterbury spoke for us all when he said that it is through liturgy that we express what we believe, and that there is no theological consensus about same-sex unions. Therefore, we as a body cannot support the authorization of such rites.[11]

Clearly, many of the Primates were unhappy with developments in the Diocese of New Westminster. However, the statement as it stands contains some interesting ambiguities that likely reflect the diversity of opinion amongst the Primates regarding both the appropriateness of the action in New Westminster and what response might be made. Thus, the Primate of the Anglican Church of Canada states that the absence of consensus made it impossible for the Primates of the Anglican Communion to speak with one mind in support of the actions of the synod and Bishop of the Diocese of New Westminster. He went on to say,

> At the same time, reports that characterize the Primates' letter as a direct and unanimous repudiation of those actions are wrong. The Primates do not, at our meetings, either move resolutions or take votes. We seek the deepest possible expression of unity in whatever terms are available to us. In this case, our common mind accurately reflects the potential for division and the absence of theological consensus among us and within the churches that make up the Anglican Communion.[12]

Archbishop Peers goes on to point out that the action of Bishop Ingham was in response to the repeated request of the synod of his diocese. He clearly states that the statement of the Primates itself makes it clear that it is not intended to claim or exercise jurisdiction over the church in Canada, a jurisdiction it clearly does not and could not have. We can see this in the placing of the statement about the nature of communion immediately preceding the section on sexuality. There the Primates state that,

> ... all churches, and not just Anglicans, face challenges in applying the Gospel to their specific situations and societies. These challenges raise questions for our traditional teaching and understanding — questions which require of the Church a careful process of thought and discussion in order to discover a way forward that is true to our inheritance of faith in Christ and to our duty as Christians to care for all people.

They went on to remind their readers that similar threats to the communion of the church had been posed by the consecration of women to the episcopate. In 1988 the concern about potential disunity had been so great that a commission was requested and later set up under the leadership of Archbishop Robin Eames of the Church of Ireland. That commission lead to the production of the Virginia Report, which called for "the highest degree of communion possible with tolerance for deeply held differences of conviction and practice."[13]

In light of this the Primates committed themselves to two fundamental principles:

– to the recognition that in each province there is a sincere desire to be faithful disciples of Christ and of God's Word, in seeking to understand how the Gospel is to be applied in our generation;

– to respect the integrity of each other's provinces and dioceses, acknowledging the responsibility of Christian leaders to attend to the pastoral needs of minorities in their care.

In his conclusion Archbishop Peers commented on the pastoral letter and the situation we find ourselves in as follows.

Finally, the Primates' letter speaks of the life of the Anglican Communion in terms of having been "irrevocably called into a special relationship of fellowship with one another." Communion is not something we accomplish, but a gift from the Father, given through the death and resurrection of Jesus. Moreover, it is not something we choose, but a fact of our common life, a reality established among us at great cost. Finding a way to embrace that communion in times of profound disagreement and conflict is not likely to be easy. It is, however, the hard and holy work to which we are called as we follow Jesus on the way of the cross that leads to new life.

The difficulties of continuing to embrace the gift of communion are, of course, legion. The Archbishop of Canterbury expressed his sadness over the "inevitable tension and division" that would inevitably follow from the blessing of same-sex unions.[14] Certainly such division is taking place and will take place in the short term. As this chapter goes to press the Archbishop Peter Akinola of the Church of Nigeria has issued a statement severing relationships with the Diocese of New Westminster, though not with the Anglican Church of Canada.[15] Given the fact that such division seems to reflect some diverse interpretation of recent events, and of recently issued statements, it is unclear what the long-term consequences are going to be.

Conclusions

Since what I have been doing in this paper is telling a story, I am reluctant to overburden it by offering too much in the way of conclusions. What I do want to offer are two observations in terms of the way this debate has unfolded. First, it is clear that we are far from agreeing with each other on matters of biblical interpretation and on our understanding of the doctrinal significance of the events that are taking place. Revisiting this ground one more time is unlikely to be productive, and the Primates seem to have recognized this in their response to the unfolding of events. The very debate about whether or not this is a matter of doctrine is an interesting one. Clearly, for some it is, but the temptation is to move from this observation to claims about the doctrinal positions of others, and at that point the claims cease to be as compelling. They require us to cast this debate in terms of those who are maintaining historic doctrinal formulations and those who are not. What should be clear from this paper is that such a view is at the very least simplistic. We need to find a more helpful way of articulating both the differences and why those differences are disturbing. I would argue that the position taken by the Primates that this is a serious issue, but not, ultimately, a church dividing issue, is an attempt to reframe the way we understand each other across this disagreement.

Second, the story I have told is not simply the story of a debate, or disagreement. It is the story of a community wrestling with significant fracture and dislocation as a result of conflicts within its life. From that perspective any solution will have to arise from within the structures that shape our common life, structures that will to some extent determine the solutions available. We cannot hope to resolve our differences if we insist on expecting more from structures, or groups, or individuals, than they can possibly deliver. To ask the House of Bishops or the Archbishop of Canterbury to act in ways they cannot act will inevitably bring disappointment. It also follows that our will to resolve this issue is premised on our will to remain in community with each other. If that community were unimportant to any of us, the tensions would be less acrimonious and the hurts would run much less deeply. That people are hurt tells us that the communities that make up the Anglican Church, regionally and globally, matter to us and there is a great deal of desire to continue to work within them. Still, the question has to be raised, at what cost? At what point can we no longer continue to be in fellowship with each other? This is a difficult question. It is made even more difficult when we begin by fracturing the structural bonds through which we recognize each other as fellow Anglicans. Given this, we need to see any movement to fracture as a last resort and be extremely wary of the temptation to move precipitously to a position from which retreat will be difficult.

Let me therefore return to where I started. I have traced the history of a debate, a debate that has often been acrimonious. But is it possible to recognize in the outlines of that debate something that looks more like a dialogue? Is it possible to see across the divides to the common and shared community whose very existence makes us so prone to feelings of betrayal and makes this debate so hurtful and alienating? Is it not true, that were that community less important, or less real, the debate would have been shorter and the possibility of parting much less painful? It has been my experience that overwhelmingly, despite significant differences, when Anglicans come into conversation with each other they recognize family and understand instinctively that the body of Christ ought not to be fractured except for the most serious of reasons. Indeed, those reasons must be able to withstand the critique of another age that will have a more distanced perspective on the tensions we find ourselves in the midst of. What I find disappointing about recent events is that they have begun to overtake what I saw as a growing recognition of this underlying community. What I hope is that we might remember why it is that we are so hurt, before we make the fracture complete and final.

Notes

1   For discussions of the debates from those who were
    present, see J. Solheim, *Diversity or Disunity? Reflections on
    Lambeth 1998* (New York: Church Publishing Incorporated,
    1999), or P. Gibson, *Discerning the Word* (Toronto: ABC
    Publishing, 2000).

2   See, for example, ed. Timothy Bradshaw, *The Way Forward?
    Christian Voices on Homosexuality and the Church* (London:
    Hodder and Stoughton, 1997). In the Canadian context, the
    resource *Hearing Diverse Voices*, produced by the Anglican
    Church of Canada, represented an attempt to get beyond
    the simple repetition of opposed positions, and there is
    considerable evidence that it has proved helpful in those
    contexts where it was used, although some concerns were
    expressed that the resource was not as balanced as it should
    have been.

3   *Issues in Human Sexuality: A Statement by the House of Bishops*
    (London: Church House Publishing, 1991), p. 47.

4   *Ibid.*, p. 46.

5   *Ibid.*, p. 45.

6   Statement to Press, quoted in, "A Statement by the Angli-
    can Bishops of Canada," 1997.

7   Press release, 7 February 2000.

8   *A Communique from the Primates of the Anglican Communion*,
    Porto, Portugal, 29 March 2000, ACNS 2094.

9   *A Pastoral Letter and Call to Prayer.* Primates' Meeting,
    Kanuga, North Carolina, USA, 8 March 8 2001, ACNS
    2410.

10 *Anglican World*, Trinity 2002, 17.

11 A Pastoral Letter from the Primates of the Anglican Com-
    munion, Gramado, Brazil, 27 May 2003.

12 Primate's Statement on New Westminster Approval of a Rite for Same-Sex Blessings, Toronto, 29 May 2003.

13 Report of the Inter-Anglican Theological and Doctrinal Commission, 1997, chapter 1.

14 Statement by Archbishop of Canterbury, 29 May 2003, ACNS 3454.

15 Statement by Archbishop Peter Akinola, 30 May 2003. See ACNS 3455.

"Patience Leads to Character" *

The Polygamy – Homosexuality Analogy in Contemporary Debate

George Sumner

Among the rhetorical weapons in the church's battle over its teaching on human sexuality, an instrument of choice has been the moral analogy. The comparison with slavery, or polygamy, or usury, is lobbed at the opponent like hand-grenades from a fox-hole. In the midst of this war of attrition, as for the English and German soldiers in no man's land on Christmas Day, there come moments when we are called to the respite of conversation and civility, during which we may stop and reflect on those projectile analogies. The hope is that this collection of essays will be one such moment.

"Let us not talk falsely now; the hour is getting late," advised Bob Dylan to my generation. Anyone who still supposes, after decades of diocesan dialogues and contrived sharings, that the church will somehow dispassionately talk its way into agreement is either naïve or disingenuous. In the midst of political polarization church people must be clear where they stand while they try, even now, to hear their opponents. I view the movement to change

---

* Rom 5:4.

the church's teaching on homosexuality as a serious error, though I also value those respites of civility and analysis. In this spirit I offer an essay on the subject of the analogy between the problems of teaching on polygamy and homosexuality, with the following aims. First, I intend to show that the analogy is a helpful one, but that it leads to conclusions different from those drawn by its liberal proponents. Second, I believe that the lessons of polygamy acknowledge the messiness of the pastoral life of the church and the complexity of our thinking on that pastoral life and so point toward the ground where a fruitful engagement may be found, if some day we could find the humility, charity, and theological seriousness to pursue it. Finally I believe that moral analogies like polygamy are of real but limited help, and so the case before us opens up the question of how such analogies are meant to work in Christian moral reasoning in general.

Surely Bishop John Spong's suggestion of cultural evolution, and hence African inferiority, was one of the most odious moments of Lambeth 1998. But he also played another, more culturally relativistic note, which has been picked up by other liberal church voices with more approval. The Africans should recall their accommodation to polygamy before they get indignant with the Western church over homosexuality. The argument goes beyond the Lord's advice on specks and logs: the gospel must achieve contextual embodiment in each locale, and that will mean a church welcoming of polygamists in Africa, and a church welcoming of gays in America.

Such an argument leads to a major question in the theology of mission: what does it really mean to speak of the gospel being "incarnated" or "inculturated" or "contextualized" in a particular culture? Behind that question one can see, yawning wide, the danger of a sheer cultural relativism in which "the gospel" dissolves into a thousand instances, without the means to bring norms to bear or make judgements about appropriate features in different cultural settings. At the outset, we confess that these are "things that are too hard for me" (Ps 131:2). Whatever incarnating the gospel is, it ought to include attention to the facts on the ground. As a modest beginning, we ought first to inquire how the issue of polygamy was actually dealt with.

What does it mean to be "for" or "against" polygamy? At the level of teaching, one might believe that polygamy is inherently consistent, or inconsistent, with the Christian life. Does opposition mean that polygamy is totally sinful, or rather an inferior form of marriage to be avoided by Christians? But matters do not stop there, for even if one opposes polygamy, there remains the question of what the church will do about it — the question of sanctions. Does one refuse the man baptism unless he abandons all wives but one? And what about baptism for the wives? Until these questions are clarified, to speak of being "for" or "against" is hopelessly vague.

The Africa to which the missionaries came in the nineteenth century showed a variety of marital practices, among which polygamy was widespread, though in many societies practically limited to the more wealthy. By contrast, the missionaries, both Roman Catholic and Protestant, aware though they obviously were of polygamy's precedents in the Old Testament, came with a clear Christian teaching about monogamy. As a result, one cannot find within the mission churches any advocacy of allowing a second marriage to a baptized Christian. In this sense the churches, adversarial though they were on so many issues, presented a single, consistent front. It is precisely in reaction to this stand that one finds in some (though by no means all) of the independent churches that began to split off in the later part of the century, a sympathy for Christian polygamy. "Polygamy loomed large among these causes [as a reason for splitting off], and some of these Churches pride themselves on keeping all the discipline and worship of the parent body, with the sole exception of polygamy."[1] This essay focuses on the consensus view of the Church Catholic in Africa.

Over the question of what the church should then do, one finds, however, far more disagreement. If one looks beyond Africa for a moment, Bishop Milman of Calcutta advocated admission to baptism for a pagan who was already a polygamist, as well as his wives. The Bremen mission in the Gold Coast of West Africa followed this line until the early twentieth century. Likewise the controversial Bishop Colenso is sometimes reported to have been in favour of polygamy, but he was actually addressing this same issue of baptism for the pagan polygamist: "to put away all but one ... before Baptism is unwarranted."[2] (Of course it did not help that Colenso was viewed on other matters as a heretic.) The key point is that from the nineteenth century on, the debate over polygamy was a debate over what to do with the institution as a pre-existing reality. On the normative question of Christianity's sole commitment to monogamy there was no question, nor any on the question of blessing the taking of a second wife by a Christian.

If one studies the pronouncements of successive Lambeth Conferences, in conjunction with other theological deliberative bodies in Africa itself in the twentieth century, one does indeed find a gradual acceptance of the "liberal" position, but, again, it is a liberalism of pastoral accommodation to pre-existing realities. So at the Conference in 1888 the bishops pronounce unequivocally that "persons living in polygamy be not admitted to baptism," while "wives of polygamists may ... be admitted in some cases." By 1971 the Anglican Consultative Council at Limuru had acknowledged that some dioceses were allowing the baptism of polygamists, though it still advocated admission to the catechumenate. Earlier the All Africa Church Conference at Mindolo, Zambia, had advocated the baptism of polygamists, and even gone so far as to suggest that communion for post-baptism polygamists might be considered on a case-by-case basis. This last view has remained unusual, and even it was offered at the level of pastoral response, and not as a normative endorsement of polygamy. Finally the Lambeth Conference of 1988 approved the baptism of pagan polygamists, and so represented the "victory" of the "liberal" view.[3] Its resolution reads in this way: "This conference upholds monogamy as God's plan, and as the ideal relationship of love between husband and wife; nevertheless recommends that a polygamist who responds to the Gospel and wishes to join the Anglican Church may be baptized and confirmed with his believing wives and children on the following conditions: (1) that the polygamist shall promise not to marry again as long as any of his wives at the time of his conversion are alive...."[4]

To be sure, the fact that debate over polygamy has been a debate over pastoral response does not mean that one could not take up the stronger position in favour of polygamy *per se*. As a teacher in an Anglican theological college in Tanzania in the early 1980s I can recall an occasional student, wishing to be daring or provocative (as only theological students can!), taking up this stronger position. I also remember, incidentally, that older pastors would mutter in response that it was easy for a young one, with no real-life knowledge of polygamy with its jealousies and attempted poisonings, to make such a case. But the point remains that such positions were daring precisely because they were outside of the normal range of theological opinion.

Liberals who use the polygamy analogy mean to suggest that, just as this issue is being rethought in Africa after many years with the traditional view, so the issue of homosexuality can be rethought in the West. Hence African critics of the latter proposed change should rethink their opposition in light of the former. But, since the mainstream debate over polygamy has not been over the normative status of monogamy for Christians, the analogy deployed in this way breaks down. This does not, however, mean that the analogy is useless; on the contrary, in the light of the normative consensus over polygamy one can see the sense in which the analogy is most helpful.

Between the normative affirmation of Christian monogamy and the pastoral conundrum of how to deal with the families of polygamous converts there is a gap. This gap presupposes the moment of conversion, when the realities of the old life collide with the gracious demands of the new. To be sure, "In Christ it is new creation; the old has passed away, behold the new has come" (2 Cor 5:17). But to some extent we continue to possess that newness in hope while we wrestle with the stubborn vestiges of the old. To deal faithfully with that gap is to hold to the gospel norm while praying for the discernment to find an "interim" pastoral response that will not represent acquiescence once more to the old.[6] It is precisely that gap that is the point of similarity, the analogy between the African churches' struggle with polygamy and the Western churches' struggle with homosexuality. The gap is not a problem *per se*, rather it is of the very nature of the Christian life in this "in-between time," with its need to deal with the pre-existing realities of this broken world.

It is here too that a more careful historical sense of marriage in the West comes into play. Quite simply, the "strict constructionists" among the early missionaries and the African Church leaders themselves did not take sufficiently into account the extent to which the long history of Christian marriage in the West had struggled to live with that very same gap. St. Augustine was fully aware how polymorphously irregular his spiritual charges were, how widespread the concubinage and marital irregularity.[6] At a later date, the medieval church in England continued to teach that sex should wait until after the marriage in church, though in many cases it followed immediately on the earlier rite of espousal. At the brink of the Reformation the specific problem of concubinage among those sworn to celibacy seemed intractable. And of course more recently it has been observed that the West has not really foresworn polygamy, only taken to practising it serially. In the same period cohabitation prior to marriage has become, among Christians in a number of denominations in the West, more the rule than the exception. In each case the church has needed to craft a prudent pastoral response for the gap, for pastoral realities at once widespread and anomalous.

So in Africa, in a manner not so different from the West's own history, the Christian must be willing to recognize the full meaning of polygamy, and so the real difficulty in some circumstances in its abandonment. It is tied in with the need for children to support agricultural life, and offers an answer to the vulnerability of single or widowed status for a woman.[7] It may offer an answer to the desperate need for children for, from the pagan perspective, "to lack someone close who keeps the departed ... is the worst misfortune."[8] At the same time, as this last quotation indicates, some of the reasons for polygamy's social importance are bound up with the old religious world and need to be challenged by the witness of the gospel. Furthermore, with the rapid cultural change in contemporary Africa, the issue may now have more to do with the impoverished isolation of an urban shanty than the old solidarities or rural paganism. The real theological heart of the issue here is the same for Africa and the West: to find a pastoral practice that is at once charitable, realistic, and evangelical as well. Conversion requires both welcome and challenge.

It follows, then, that the analogy between polygamy and homosexuality amounts to a counsel of patience. For in the case of polygamy, the consensus on doctrine was maintained, but a pastoral willingness to "muddle through" in the messiness of inherited, "pre-conversion" anomalies was gradually demonstrated. To follow the analogy, the debate over blessing same-sex unions is misguided, for it misplaces the debate in the realm of doctrine. The polygamist is baptized, as are his wives, and they are then encouraged in the virtues of the Christian life, in spite of the fact that the shape of their sexual life continues to show "in the mean time" the contours of the "old man." The analogy counsels, then, a "third way" built on the virtue of patience, which abandons the rending political campaign for doctrinal legitimation and strives after the shared goal of pastoral care. The polygamist and the homosexual, their lives being inconsistent with the church's teaching, are particularly obvious cases of that inconsistency that pertains to all humans in the community of the new creation.[9]

The analogy of polygamy in Africa and homosexuality in the West works well in yet one more way. In both cases one could argue that today the issue is the "presenting problem" of the state of Christian marriage in society. In neither case does it help the disease for the doctor to bless the symptom. Poverty, disease, urbanization, adolescent pregnancy, and rapidly shifting social roles are placing great strains on marriage for the African in a manner not so very different from the history and experience of the West. In both social settings the shoring up of the role of the father and the maintenance of Christian norms amidst cultural flux are powerful issues lying behind the immediate moral question. Both issues testify to the confusion over the central issue of Christian marriage and so cannot be considered without regard to the effect on the more central crisis of which they are "presenting problems." Christian ethics of the family and sexuality begins with the central issue of Christian marriage, that "mystery of Christ and the church" (Eph 5:35), and other issues can only be rightly addressed if they are considered in the wake of that central issue. Both polygamy and homosexual unions present broken or distorted images of that relationship that serves for the whole community as a symbol of "the mystery of Christ and the church." For only Christian marriage, in the difference of its members, in their communion, in their covenant exclusivity, and in the openness to the world thereby allowed, can serve as the symbol. Questions such as polygamy and homosexual unions require compassion, but they are misunderstood if considered only in terms of the question, "What is permitted?" The question, "What conveys the gospel of Christ?" must precede, and the proper answer to that question involves, among other things, attention to Christian marriage.

Two things in an analogical relation are, by definition, alike in some ways, and different in others. In consideration of those differences we find the boundaries of the analogy's usefulness. First of all, we have seen that the analogy counsels patience. But one may ask in what sense patience has hope in the case of homosexuality? With polygamy, even should the practice continue in society, the expectation was that the Christian children of polygamous parents would be monogamous — the problem would last a generation. But the issue of homosexuality offers no such time limitation. One could argue for the pertinence of patience in an analogous sense only by means of a wider cultural argument that, as cultural trends and attitudes change, things may look different in a generation. While this is possible, there is no particular reason to think this so.

Whatever one's theological assumptions, both polygamy and homosexuality require that the Christian moral theologian sort out the claims of nature and grace, of creation and redemption. In the case of polygamy, one must decide if it can accord with the *lex naturae*, and so whether its prohibition for Christians derives from its very nature or rather from the fact that its time has passed in the new economy of salvation. The decision about homosexuality depends in large measure, for Protestant as for Roman Catholic, on the judgement that the complementary relation of man and woman in marriage is intended by God and so built into the fabric of our created natures, so that our redemption in turn respects the shape of our creation.[10] On this score it is interesting to note that Thomas Aquinas believed polygamy to be "sort of" in keeping with the natural order,[11] because it at least shares with monogamy the end of procreation. If we look to scripture, we find that the evidence about polygamy is mixed in the Old Testament, and even the *locus classicus* of Genesis 1 can be interpreted in a manner consistent with polygamy, though the unanimous voice of later tradition understood it in terms of monogamy. By contrast the scriptural evidence concerning homosexuality is consistently negative. On both scores the analogy between the two questions is weakened.

The latter question, that of scripture, reminds us of the real but limited value of an analogy like that of polygamy. As was suggested at the outset, different analogies will seem to bolster different sides of the argument, though each fits the question at hand only partially. The question of the relative weight due to each remains a matter of discernment. The advocate of same-sex unions insists that the proper analogy is liberation from slavery, and the opponent responds that the primary New Testament view of the institution is negative (Gal 3:26) though it is tolerated (Philem). The opponent of same-sex unions might suggest the analogy of divorce, which is treated pastorally but not itself blessed. The list could go on. The argument about homosexuality becomes a matter of duelling analogies.

Here one should observe how these analogies have in fact been functioning, although at times tacitly. We are asked to compare scripture's witness about slavery to that about homosexuality. We are asked to consider its full and variegated treatment of polygamy in relation to normative Christian marriage. Analogies ought to offer no independent evidence; they are not to be weighed somehow over against what Romans 1 has to say about the subject of homosexuality. Analogies are useful, rather, to the extent that they help to shape[12] our imagination as we read scripture.[13] Imagination is not, after all, some capacity by which we can boast of some access of our own to the divine, though a strain of romanticism, still influential today, would suggest this to us. Imagination and scripture are not to be set against one another, but rather the tutelage of scripture directs and empowers the imagination. One way that this flourishing of the biblical imagination may take place is by the juxtaposition and comparison of passages, since biblical interpretation is the art of listening for the coherence of scripture's witness amidst its diverse voices. Scripture can best be its own interpreter as new comparisons are sought, and analogies such as that of polygamy can offer just such a new connection.

There is a real debate to be had in the church on the subject of homosexuality, but it should be a struggle on different ground — not that of doctrine, but rather that of pastoral response. Such is the lesson of the analogy of polygamy. The real fruit for the moral imagination would be found, not in legislative victories, but rather in the virtues: among revisionists, a deeper humility that can foreswear political offensive, among the conservatives, a deeper patience for one particular legacy of the old Adam, one among many others shared by us all who are his progeny, who all are the redeemed as well.

Notes

1   Parrinder, Geoffrey, *The Bible and Polygamy* (London:
    SPCK, 1950), p. 2.
2   Adrian Hastings, *Christian Ministries in Africa* (London:
    SPCK, 1973), p. 13 and pp. 11–16.
3   *Ibid.*, pp. 23–25.
4   Derived from the Lambeth Conference web site.
5   For the St. Andrew's Day Statement, see ed. Timothy
    Bradshaw, *The Way Forward?* (London: Hodder and
    Stoughton, 1997).
6   Radner, SEAD Harvest Article.
7   Eugene Hillman, *Polygamy Reconsidered* (MaryKnoll, NY:
    Orbis, 1975), p. 119.
8   Benjamin Ray, *African Religions* (Englewood Cliffs, NJ:
    Prentice and Hall, 1976), p. 40.
9   This is the sense in which the sin of homosexuality is
    singled out by Paul in Romans 1 as a state that shows
    clearly the distortion and inversion of the created intent of
    God, in which all sinful human beings participate.
10 See Oliver O'Donovan, *Resurrection and Moral Order* (Lon-
    don: Apollos, 1986).
11 Supplement to the *Summa Theologiae* 65.1: "Pluralitas
    uxorum quodammodo est contra legem naturae, et quo-
    dammodo non."
12 See Ellen Davis, *Imagination Shaped* (Valley Forge, PA:
    Trinity International, 1975).
13 Here we may compare the frequent misuse of the "three-
    legged stool," as if scripture, tradition, and reason were
    entities that could be weighed over against one another.
    The original intent was surely that they formed, together,
    an account of the wise and reliable reading of scripture,
    namely by the exercise of our analytic powers as we listen to
    the great interpretive voices of the past.

Pastoral Care

Homosexuality and the Anglican Church in Canada

A Pastoral Approach

Patrick Yu

The official position of the Canadian House of Bishops regarding homosexuality, as articulated in their 1997 Guidelines,[1] revolves around a distinction between person and activity. Anglicans are urged to look beyond a person's sexual orientation and respond to the image of Christ in each one. A homosexual person, as a human being created in God's image, is deserving of respect and ministry. If that person is also a Christian, then s/he is a member of the church to be welcomed. Sexual orientation to the same gender is accepted as part of the make-up of the person. This is quite apart from homosexual activities, the innate goodness of which the majority of Canadian bishops were unable to affirm in light of scripture and tradition. They were therefore not willing to attest to the goodness of homosexual unions, even otherwise praiseworthy ones, by a marriage-like blessing. With the decision of the Diocese of New Westminster to implement a rite for the blessing of same-sex unions, the landscape has begun to change. But just as the 1997 Guidelines have not enjoyed overwhelming support, it is unlikely that a liberalized policy will command the kind of support that will quiet unrest, or diminish the possibility of schism.

The situation in Canada, in fact, is no different than that in many other parts of the Anglican Communion, which is to say that it is one of confusion and division. This situation is likely to continue until the mind of the church becomes clear, whether that is related to or independent of political decisions that may be made. This essay explores ways for Christians to walk and talk together in this confusing and tense time, ways that can do justice to God's call to his people to love one another.

I proceed from several assumptions. I believe, firstly, that the current disagreement within the church about homosexuality is both serious and multi-faceted. It is not simply a dispute between "gays and straights," as it were, but about different understandings of sexuality and the appropriate ways to follow Christ in this important dimension of human life. The differences go deeper than sexuality. Conservatives and liberals alike hold up the principles of justice, moral order, and inclusion, for example, but mean very different things by these words. Does justice mean equality, or does it mean the divine righteousness that casts down the mighty and raises up the meek? The first looks to human rights policies, the second to the saving action of God and to the *eschaton*. Does inclusion mean that God in Christ is calling the whole world, or does it mean that God accepts the world just as it is? One issues in evangelism, the other in pluralism. And what is the basis for moral decision-making, especially regarding sexual practice? To conservatives the natural law tradition is crucial, while liberals tend to appeal to human rights. The differences of approach run deep. So the issue of homosexuality actually involves the whole church in serious reflection about itself and about its understanding of the gospel.

Secondly, I reject the argument, often posed in debates, that in order to support gay people, it is necessary to support specific revisions of marriage and ordination rites, and, more importantly, of the theological constructs behind them. Pastoral counsel should never be taken apart from discernment of what is right and good because what is supportive will ultimately be what helps people live in the way of the good. So setting parameters of laudable action is always part of the church's pastoral ministry. This approach, however, pays close attention to "all sorts and conditions" of actual human situations. It seeks creative ways to act with generosity within given parameters even as it examines the validity of those parameters. Doing so will involve both theological and practical considerations, but will not predetermine which has to give way to the other.

Lastly, I agree with the assessment that there has been inadequate pastoral care for gay and lesbian members of the church. Various levels of the church have reacted with judgement rather than understanding, fear rather than faith, suspicion rather than trust. People who find it difficult to live with the parameters of the tradition have been left to fend for themselves. They were regarded as enemies to be defended against. In my assessment, this cautious approach has generated a belated sympathy in the church, making her more receptive of proposals outside her tradition. Since no room for tenderness toward homosexuals was to be found within the traditions of the church, or so it seems, the only alternative is to turn our collective back on that tradition. In the short history of open public debate in Canada, the will to remedy our record has been affirmed time and again. For example, in the discussion on sexuality at General Synod, 2001, half of the groups registered the importance of extending pastoral care to homosexuals and "traditionalists" alike. This essay is an attempt to steer a course through the artificial dilemma that demands either total rejection or total affirmation of homosexuality.

But what is pastoral care? Recognizing the imprecision of this term and the many images it may generate in people's minds, let us begin from a literal and biblical image. Pastoral care is a response to God the great shepherd. God reveals himself in two aspects: as the sovereign lawgiver who sets humanity's destination, and as patient helper in our often halting journey toward it. The scriptures are alive with stories of God walking with individuals and communities as they strive to fulfil their vocation in the world. Men and women strive to obey God's commands, yet they also know God's words of grace: his words of forgiveness, promise, and transformation. The scriptures make good reading because they are not simply a series of moral precepts illustrated by cardboard characters. Each episode is a study of people full of character, whose flaws we can identify with. God's grace to each one gives us hope.

Part of this grace is a certain flexibility, an attention to the individual situation. Jesus, for example, met people with a breadth of approaches. He in turn confronted, challenged, taught, healed, and pronounced forgiveness. These instances portray a God who meets men and women in their concrete, fallen situation. At the same time, God summons each and all to transformation into his own likeness. God's people, particularly designated leaders, also take on this shepherding role, which is to be modelled after God's own actions (Ezek 34). The charge to leaders is to seek the strayed, strengthen the weak, protect the vulnerable, heal the sick, and bind up the injured. The church's rich pastoral tradition grows out of this. It is a tradition that began in the Bible itself, the Wisdom literature and pastoral epistles being the most obvious examples, and continued in the church in a long history of pastoral works such as *The Shepherd of Hermas*, St. Gregory's *Pastoral Rule*, Martin Luther's *On the Cure of Souls*, and, in our Anglican tradition, the works by Jeremy Taylor *The Rule and Exercise of Holy Living*, and *Holy Dying*.

If God meets us in our concrete situations, in all our complexity as people, then a pastoral approach to homosexuality in the church will indeed give prime attention to the homosexual person. But it will give attention first to the person, and only secondarily to his/her homosexuality. A person is more than his or her sexuality. A person has unique gifts, personalities, roles, interests, contexts, vulnerabilities.... As such, a person is an integrated being not defined by any constituent element. To regard anyone only through the lens of sexuality is fundamentally flawed. That we are more than any one part of our nature is a theological understanding of personhood that should inform our self-definition and self-knowledge. The St. Andrew's Day Statement, a compact document by English Evangelicals designed to lay out the theological parameters for dialogue, states in its first principle, "In him [Jesus Christ] we know both God and human nature as they truly are."[2] Not only are we not reduced to any constituent part of our humanity, we are more than our history or our present. Each of us, in Christ, is created, fallen, redeemed, and destined for glory. The invitation to attend to the homosexual person is an invitation to broaden one's understanding of the human person, not to confine it. This invitation is also extended to the homosexual person, who is equally prone to see himself narrowly defined by sexuality.

Nor are we to consider each person in isolation, or homosexuals as segregated groups. The image of the body, so important to our understanding of Christian society, suggests that in Christ a community's different parts are nevertheless connected under one head. A common identity therefore underlies all of us. The concerns of any part of the Christian body are the concerns of all. This approach should free us from the "we/they" attitude, so prevalent in the debate. If all are created, judged, forgiven, and called, the struggle around sexuality can be considered as no more and no less important than any other area in which we strive to follow Christ. Just as Christians respond variously to the evangelical counsel in dealing with time and money, we should expect a range of responses to the evangelical counsel about sexuality. This is not to concede that all such decisions are morally indifferent, but to request the same patience in this as in other areas of life: "quick to listen, slow to speak, slow to anger" (James 1:19). R.F. Hurding identifies four elements in the church's tradition of pastoral care: the prophetic, the shepherdly, the priestly, and the physicianly.[3] In the church's approach to homosexual practice, the prophetic element, at least that aspect of it that reacts against a perceived sin, has overshadowed the other elements. It is time to bring about a good balance of all of these parts.

The goal of pastoral care is always "to re-affirm the good news of salvation in Christ, forgiveness of sins, transformation of life and incorporation into the holy fellowship of the church."[4] If the approach to homosexual people has overly emphasized the challenge of transformation, i.e., the prophetic element, it may come from a fear of compromise. Would repentance be circumvented without this emphasis, resulting in "cheap grace"? Can there be forgiveness without an awareness of sin? I take the position that God's forgiveness is more fundamental than our awareness and confession of sins. While each of us needs to come before God as sinners, it is a life-long journey for us to be made aware of particular sins in our lives and to deal with them according to the grace given to us by the Holy Spirit. The biblical pattern suggests that challenges come after deliverance and mercy. Jesus invited Zacchaeus, for example, into the circle of grace while he was still a tax collector, unreformed and presumably unrepentant. Zacchaeus's acceptance of God's invitation gave him both the moral vision and the moral power to be a new person, restoring fourfold the money he had unfairly taken. The challenge for those who uphold the traditional teaching of the church is to proclaim good news as Jesus did, embodying it as well as speaking it, welcoming before judging. The message to homosexual persons, for example, must address society's disproportionately harsh treatment of them. It should include a word of peace that shows understanding of their need for safety at many levels.

Embodying good news has to begin with establishing relationships. From the accounts given by homosexual persons, it would appear that such common courtesy and respect have been lacking in the way some Christians relate to them. But we are each bound to love our neighbour. In our baptism, we promise to "seek and serve Christ in all persons, loving [our] neighbour as [ourself]." A pastoral responsibility is enjoined on all Christians, and especially on those who have taken on leadership roles. It will include support, the willingness to listen, a commitment to learn about the subject, sensitivity in one's use of language, refraining from the rush to judgement, a comfortable awareness of one's own perspectives and their limitations, and discernment as to when to offer them. In this sense every Christian is a pastor, a helper invited to bear another's burden (Gal 6:2). This role is undertaken, however, with a clear sense that no one can take another's place in that person's ultimate responsibility for living his or her life before God (Gal 6:5). It is only in a relationship of mutual respect and trust that genuine discussions about one's sexuality can take place. Whoever wades into a sensitive area of another person's life must first decide to treat the person as a "thou" who is more than his or her sexuality — in other words, to be a friend. Friendship is not a means to an end but is to be celebrated in itself. It comes with many obligations in time and energy, and it often includes defending each other from harm. Moreover, in treading into another person's life one must be prepared to open one's own. This high regard for friendship contrasts with our society's prevailing values. In the context of Western industrialized societies, friendship is often submerged under other influences, becoming less important than sexual relationships. In my view, the sexualizing of human relationships is a reaction to the dominance of economic relationships between people. In a liberating but not dismissive sense, we need to discover what it is to be "just friends." Friendship commands an elevated status in the Bible, culminating in the honour of being called a friend of God. Jesus, in his final discourse in the Gospel of John, calls his disciples no longer servants, but friends (John 15:13–15).

The gospel message is fundamentally a message of grace, a "yes" God pronounced in Jesus Christ of God's judgement that our destiny is eternal life in Him. This is the horizon of our discipleship and proclamation. In our particular circumstances, however, we experience God's word as a mixture of "yes" and "no," a message of acceptance and a challenge to grow. Within the horizon of God's basic affirmation friends do help friends to discern, in particular attitudes and actions, both the "yes" and the "no." To be a friend does not entail giving up ever being a critic. Rather, friendship constrains one to point out things that are harmful in a person one cares about. It is also true that most people listen to challenges only from people they know are accepting and supportive of them. Within a solid bond of friendship and fellowship a mutual challenge can and indeed should arise in the differing options regarding sexual practice and differing attitudes toward it. In one sense, the trust inherent in friendship provides a safe context for this conversation. It can also be a very unsafe situation, though, since honest conversation between respected friends has a depth that cuts through caricatures and stale stances. To raise issues known to divide is to risk the relationship itself. In any friendship, deeper disclosure may lead to a greater sharing of interests and values, or it may reveal such fundamental differences that the relationship is arrested, or even becomes unsustainable. It is important to underline that this kind of parting of the ways, which involves discernment in each particular case, is not the same as categorical judgements that exclude certain people from being one's friends.

A pastoral approach strives to maintain relationships in good faith, even in the face of irreconcilable differences. Friends may make clear to friends serious objections to their action yet continue to stay in touch, even accompanying each other and offering support that does not compromise their own stance. In so doing they hold the bond of friendship above the demonstration of a stance. In this spirit, The House of Bishops' statement of the Church of England addresses dissidents with these words, "While unable ... to commend the way of life just described ... we stand alongside them in the fellowship of the Church." I believe that such an outgoing approach toward homosexual people is the condition under which traditional sexual teaching will be considered at all. An accepting and caring community is necessary for practising the discipline implied by that teaching. My judgement is that we are very far from both, and serious repentance is needed.

Much of what I have said addresses traditionalists within the church. The burden of maintaining fellowship through serious disagreement lies most obviously upon the shoulders of traditionalists — their position is at this point the teaching of the church. But patient friendship is also the responsibility of homosexuals in the church. I am very grateful for the friendship of my gay and lesbian friends, and I know that they, too, have to exercise patience and discernment in maintaining friendships within the church, and have done so. To ask for less from homosexual members of the church is the worst kind of prejudice. We must assume a common gospel, a common basis on which we stand before God, and a common call for self-sacrifice and discipleship, even as we face different visions of what that entails. In that spirit, what I ask from traditionalists I ask from the whole church, including Christian brothers and sisters from the homosexual community. I ask a generosity of spirit, refraining from caricature, an honesty that includes sensitivity, an eagerness to build bridges of friendship, partnership in genuine dialogue, and a refraining from coercion.

In addition to demonstrating care and acceptance, pastoral care needs to be understood more broadly. Homosexuality is experienced in the church in extensive and varied ways and may not even touch on either of the issues in terms of which the debate is framed, namely blessing same-sex unions and ordaining practising homosexuals. William Arnold listed the following scenarios one may encounter on a congregational level:

> a teenager struggling with the fear that he or she is homosexual; a college student or young adult struggling with how to tell her or his parents of a chosen homosexual lifestyle; a troubled spouse coming to acknowledge homosexual orientation and asking what to do about a marriage to a loving heterosexual partner; a troubled spouse who has discovered that his or her partner is gay or lesbian; an officer in a congregation who is gay and wants to know whether to resign his position; a member of a congregation who is asking for use of the church for a support group for homosexuals; parents who are troubled by the discovery that their child's fourth-grade teacher is lesbian.[5]

Members of General Synod had the right instinct when they called for more depth in pastoral care and the extension of that care beyond homosexuals. As the above list indicates, the pastoral task of the church is not limited to discernment regarding the essentially political options of ordination and same-sex blessings. The approach needs to be more wide-ranging and more flexible, and more open. Many people, in addition to those seeking ordination or the blessing of their unions, clearly could benefit from some kind of intentional accompaniment in their often lonely struggles around homosexuality.

To some extent, a more nuanced pastoral care is already happening — but to some extent it is not. A gay friend wrote, on the matter of being listened to and treated respectfully as a person, "On the whole, I feel supported in this way mainly by clergy … With congregations I'm not always so sure." While individual and confidential conversations with clergy are a welcome starting point, they are not enough. For one, acceptance and support for a person should come from the whole community, not just the clergy. For another, it allows members of a congregation to continue in all kinds of unexamined assumptions about homosexuality and homosexual people. Sexual conduct is a proper concern of the Christian community. Sweeping it under the carpet will not help. What we need are opportunities for thoughtful exploration of this issue that involve engagement with our Christian tradition and concrete life situations, including the situations of those who are uncomfortable with homosexuality. These conversations are a form of pastoral care, involving as they do challenge and support for those who are affected differently by and respond differently to homosexuality and homosexual people.

But most congregations have avoided the discussion so far. The reason given frequently is the attempt to avoid conflict. People sense that this is a hot issue involving a fundamental aspect of our humanity. The discussion will be passionate, therefore threatening. However, procrastination will prove costly for the church. One reason for taking up the discussion is that homosexuality is as close to a representative issue on sexual morality as we are going to get. In the age of mass media, silence from one part of the church gives people the freedom to impose upon it opinions from any quarter that bears the name Christian, however bizarre. Unless the church at the grass roots level owns this question and comes to a broad common understanding, we will be credited with the opinion of the articles that people read, or the TV shows they watch, ranging from the homophobic to the libertine. By common understanding I do not mean agreement in detail or on specific actions. I do mean an ability to articulate the issues involved and even the range of possible solutions. The world will judge our church by its stance on this issue. We have no choice on this. The question is whether we will be judged truly for what we have thought through and believe in, or for something that is mistaken for our tradition because we have not bothered to deal with it openly.

Another reason for pursuing the discussion broadly is that powerful forces in the church and in our culture will continue to ask the church for a decision. These matters are decided in the forum of General Synod. Often we hear complaints that decisions are made that do not represent the ethos of the average congregation. This will be true unless congregations take this up voluntarily and seriously. Only then can a solid public opinion about the matter emerge. Otherwise, the matter will be left to those who have the most passion about it. Unfortunately, groups with strong passions can be bound by their own history of conflict and may lose sight of the middle ground.

To engage in this discussion, however, requires that we recover some tools we have lost as a church. To begin with, we need to reclaim the confidence that our faith has relevant and helpful things to say about complicated ethical decisions. There seems to be a collective loss of nerve on the part of the Canadian church to engage in ethical discourse. This is certainly true on the congregational level. When we do not practise thinking through moral issues as Christians, we succumb to a host of unconscious and therefore unchallenged assumptions. In fact, the feeling in many of our congregations reflects a resignation, even a surrender to our cultural trends. The silence around sexual practices points to a wide acceptance of the secular notion that sexual choices are morally neutral and purely private. Even those Christians opposed to it have few tools other than a rigid legalism that sees the Christian life primarily as obedience to a list of rules arbitrarily imposed. This is a sad surrender of a rich tradition, and an unnecessary one. Christian moral decisions are not simply a series of isolated choices but flow out of the shape of a life that is ordered around the good news of God in Jesus. This life is given both as a gift and a calling. Christian ethics are therefore an integral part of proclaiming the good news. Part of the gospel is that God has given us light to discern the kind of action that helps us to flourish as human beings and human communities. This discernment is what ethical deliberation is about. In his essay "Christian Moral Reasoning" Oliver O'Donovan succinctly outlines the ethical task in a series of questions: "How should I act? How shall I advise others to act? How shall I use such public authority as I have to constrain the community to act?"[6] Understood in this way, we can see ethics not as some difficult subject but as something we engage in implicitly every day. We can see also its corporate aspect. The fourfold ethical tasks outlined above connect the individual to the community. Pastoral leaders will have to reclaim this engagement with ethics from the stance of faith. They can also equip their congregations, by preaching and teaching, to do the same.

The question, then, becomes one that every Christian shares. Since we are all sexual beings, we need to deal with questions such as, "How should I regard and act on my sexuality as a disciple of Jesus? From my own discipleship in sexual matters, how should I advise others to be a disciple of Christ in their sexuality, even when it expresses itself differently from my own? How does sexual behaviour affect society? Should there be external and public standards of sexual behaviour and if so, what are legitimate means of enforcing these standards? In what way should the church as a faith community act differently from society at large?" There are many resources that can be brought to bear to address these questions, including personal experience, scientific studies, and social theories, to name a few. There are also broad theological themes that will be relevant. Questions about sexual ethics touch on the fundamental themes of the biblical story, themes of creation and fall, of redemption and the possibility of holiness, of sacramental living. These are themes that touch all our lives. We know the goodness of sexuality as rooted in creation; we know the misuse of it, rooted in the fall. It seems obvious that heterosexuals are not markedly more successful in dealing with the gift of sexuality than are homosexuals. But we also know the promise that, in Christ, our sexual natures (like the rest of our lives) are caught up in God's redemptive purposes, to become a sign of the love and faithfulness of God towards his people. Within the present order, as we await full redemption in the consummation of the kingdom, the ways to appropriate the powerful gift of sexuality are a matter of discipleship for each person. Paul called it "working out your own salvation in fear and trembling" (Phil 2:12).

Finally, ethical thinking about sexual practice has to take into consideration the historical situation in which we find ourselves. The widespread use of birth control and the possibility of severing sexual intercourse from procreation has radically changed the landscape. The questions that flow out of that change are still in front of the whole church. Homosexuality is only one of them. Christians find themselves asked to rethink the relation between the procreative and unitive aspects of sex. For example, should the openness to offspring be part of every sexual act, as the Roman Catholic church insists, or should it be the general intention of every marriage, or should it be part of our general understanding of the purpose of sexuality, together with the purpose of uniting two people, even when procreation is not possible or not desired?[7] The least we have to do is to express the value of our traditional teaching in our own time, not just about homosexuality, but more broadly, in the face of serial monogamy and of a culture that elevates sexuality to idolatrous status, while degrading and exploiting it. In other words, the call to engage in sexual ethics is not simply "for" the homosexual, it is a common task for the whole church.

A pastoral approach to homosexuality, therefore, calls the Christian community to own the discussion as relevant to itself. It will help the community to realize the wide-ranging pastoral situations surrounding it; it will identify the gift of sexuality and the challenge of its use as a common concern that none of us has mastered; and it will equip the community with theological, ethical, and scientific knowledge. Finally, a pastoral approach challenges a Christian community to examine what it aspires to be. If, for example, a church understands itself to be a community apart, distinguished from the world by its distinctive standards in sexual behaviour, it will spend time and energy in inculcating those standards. That church will apply church discipline strongly and swiftly to sanction those falling short of those standards. On the other hand, if a church understands itself as being a haven for those on the margins of society, it will elevate the virtues of patience and tolerance. It may de-emphasize moral challenges or dispense with some altogether, claiming inclusion and acceptance as overriding virtues. The point here is not to force churches to choose an artificial mode that all their members have to fit into, but to bring to the surface deeply seated assumptions that fuel their passions. The often intemperate debate over homosexuality is partially energized, I believe, by holding onto part of what the church is, as if that should be all that it is. The church is always at the same time both a haven for the outcast and a place to form lives that are oriented toward the kingdom. That's what Jesus did so well — offering an unconditional acceptance as well as an uncompromising call for transformation. It is false to claim one or the other as the defining characteristic of the church. Rather, these two visions of the church have to be held together.

Certainly a fruitful debate will not materialize without attention to some of the community values implied by our faith, but also fashioned by our history as Anglicans and also by each particular congregational history. It is worth pointing out the fallacy of a superficial appeal to inclusivity in this debate. Inclusivity can be a slogan that divides, but unity is both a gift and a calling. A church that systematically misrepresents or manipulates dissent, thereby denying living space to dissenters, cannot claim to be inclusive. Just as genuine universalism refers to the scope of the gospel, but does not bypass faith in Christ, genuine inclusivity is an invitation to all people, but does not bypass evangelical discipline. The debate over what that discipline may or may not involve is a legitimate and productive one. But the selective appeal to inclusivity without reference to anything else is truly a bizarre claim, one that obscures the distinction between church and world.

From the foregoing discussion, I wish to propose five general directions with which the church can approach homosexuality pastorally.

1. The church should devote resources to turning the pastoral principles in our official documents into practical actions in ways that homosexual people find authentic. Such pastoral principles are remarkably similar throughout the Anglican Communion, and can be found, for example, in the Canadian House of Bishops' statement (1997), and the report on Human Sexuality to the 1998 Lambeth Conference. While upholding the parameters of marriage and singleness, these documents accept the presence of homosexual persons in society and in the church. In forming our pastoral responses we do well to note the consistency in mainstream Anglicanism around the world. There is a resolve to uphold the church's tradition regarding sexuality and marriage, and there is a consistent call for sensitive, even generous pastoral practices. Instead of being paralyzed by the anticipation or dread of some grand decision, the church can do much to put in practice specific ways to communicate its solidarity with homosexuals. The specific actions in the Canadian House of Bishops' statement include opposition to discrimination in society, acknowledging the presence of gay and lesbian people in the church, commending the gifts of gay and lesbian Christians in the church in a way that demonstrates mutuality of ministry.

The tendency of the church thus far, unfortunately, has been to appeal selectively to the authority of those documents. Traditionalists hold onto their opposition to homosexual practice, while ignoring the challenge to be generous and irenic. Since I am also a traditionalist, I can say that the onus is on us to show that our objections are based on principle and not prejudice. We must go the extra mile to demonstrate practical good will. Gays and lesbians must find evidence of welcome and friendship, which, as stated above, are particularly necessary in a culture that elevates sexual intimacy far above any other form of human intimacy. In this way conservatives should consider the manner in which their concerns are voiced. Just as homosexual acts appear to conservatives to be obviously immoral, judgemental and dismissive outcries may appear to homosexuals and those sympathetic to them just as obviously unloving. One controversial issue concerns programs of healing and change. Whether it is the claim that they "work" or the counter claim that they do not, care is to be taken to ensure that both claims and counter claims will stand up to objective scrutiny. Similarly, it is misleading for revisionists to portray official statements as being more permissive than they are. Such selective quotations will raise expectations and generate false hopes. There is a temptation to read the mind of the church selectively, or even to manipulate information, in order to give one's agenda an advantage. Such advantages, in my view, are short term and detract from a lasting direction that truly reflects the mind of the church.

2. An irenic and generous posture does not imply a *de facto* concession on the morality of homosexual relationships. On that question the church is at a genuine impasse. Even though the question has been on its agenda for a decade, it is only recently that we see signs of genuine dialogue, where different parties have gone beyond what are essentially monologues filled with caricatures of their opponents. But genuine dialogue is not possible in an atmosphere of suspicion or where there is an obvious imbalance of power. I believe that a premature decision at this time, whether it be the introduction of new practices or the foreclosure of such practices

from ever happening in the future, are simply impositions of power. While individual minds may be made up, the collective mind of the church is not ready to decide on the absolute rightness or wrongness of homosexual relationships.

This impasse does not, in itself, need to be an impediment to the church's exploring creative pastoral actions. The Lambeth report listed four positions toward homosexuality. One describes "those who believe that committed homosexual relationships fall short of the biblical norm, but are to be preferred to relationships that are anonymous and transient." The second part of that statement can be received as a practical judgement on the relative merits of long-term, committed relationships over short-lived and promiscuous ones. Pastoral counsel arising from such a relative judgement does not need to abandon the church's teaching on sexuality and marriage. It is a practical way to support people in concrete situations.

3. Such practical cooperation needs a great measure of good will from people who hold strong but divergent convictions. The church cries out for examples of costly truth-speaking, in unity, from its visible leaders. This agenda of facing the truth together will free the church from paralysis in its day-to-day work of pastoral care. All who are committed to that task will benefit from a commitment to face the reality of concrete situations, and to clarify what they are actually faced with. Even our comprehension of the phenomenon itself can be distorted by rhetorical considerations in debate. Same-sex relationships are portrayed by one side as monogamous, faithful, and deeply spiritual. They are characterized by the other side as promiscuous, exploitative, and dangerous.

We need to go beyond the public sharing of individual stories. This appeal to experience can be misleading. There is a similarity in form to these stories, stories by gays and lesbians on the one hand, and stories by "ex-gays" on the other. I am not questioning the subjective authenticity of those who are brave enough to share their lives in public; I am only questioning whether "experience" is ever acquired without an interpretive framework. Experience itself may be tolerant of more than one set of self-understandings. It depends on, among other things, the organization of those experiences. Within a social group, the way that experience is organized can be self-perpetuating. If the goal of pastoral care is supporting people rather than winning arguments, we would pay more attention to the nuances in each experience and strive to be accurate in our understanding and descriptions. Research conducted with some control on methodology and based on firsthand knowledge will be most helpful in setting the common ground for discussion. Such first hand, first person, information can be bolstered by insights garnered by those who are compassionately involved in pastoral care. Perhaps in that sharing, pastors will find similar observations, even common practices across dogmatic lines, that bear the marks of compassion, understanding, and caution. The common ground of pastoral practice will allay fears and facilitate referrals. Such conversations may even lead to formal pastoral guidelines that are based on real practices.

Another matter that needs to be clarified is the scope of the discussion. Even in the short time that the church has wrestled with the blessing of marriage-like same-sex relationships, the list of sexual activities seeking legitimation has grown longer. The coalition seeking change currently includes gay, lesbian, bisexual, transsexual, and transgendered persons. It will be helpful if the discussion is more focused. Those who wish the church's teaching to change can help the church to sharpen the question by defining their own boundary of morally acceptable sexual behaviour. There is a basic confusion, I believe, in the arguments employed in the debate. The argument about the moral rightness of a particular action quickly changes into the argument about the human rights of people engaged in that action. They are quite separate issues. The former question has to do with whether homosexual activity is in accordance with God's will as we have received it. The latter question concerns the legitimate freedom of a person in society to make choices, and the freedom and limitations that society has in promoting or sanctioning choices it deems wrong or harmful. This applies in a special way to the Christian community as a society apart with declared values. The conclusion that homosexuality is contrary to God's will does not free one from respecting the dignity of homosexuals. Conversely, the love and respect due each person does not necessitate agreement or blessing of his or her actions.

4. Attention should be given to the challenges raised by this discussion to congregational life. The church's response to homosexuality has uncovered important issues that go beyond the specific decisions in this controversy. It raises questions as to what kind of community we wish to be, how we in fact treat each other and outsiders, how we can be a distinctive witness in our culture. Other ongoing discussions are also brought into sharp focus, to wit, the nature of scripture and its authority in our moral deliberations. In order to respond adequately to these challenges, a more intentional teaching agenda, incorporating both practical and theological material, needs to be pursued among congregations. Practical skills will not be confined to clergy but must be shared to engender awareness, at least. They include self-reflective, active listening and conflict resolution skills. Theological awareness will build on the core doctrines of creation, fall, redemption and hope, with special encouragement to practise ethical discernment.

5. Finally, a pastoral approach to a community in conflict will wish to involve as wide a range of its members as possible. Unfortunately, synods of various kinds prove inadequate as primary forums for the kinds of discussions necessary. Synods involve but a small proportion of church members. They follow an impersonal procedure of debate in which motions are won and lost after arguments only a few minutes in length. Important issues such as this, as a group observed from General Synod, are "not able to be solved/resolved by the passing of a motion."[8] In my view, the mind of the church is not discerned without its first being engaged. In other

words, a snapshot poll of any kind is not helpful without some in-depth consideration of issues. The issues, however, cannot be truly comprehended if an imminent decision hangs in the balance. The Toronto synod discussion in 1995, from which these thoughts origi-nated, offers a creative process. The organizers took care to invite articulate presenters who have some standing among people of divergent viewpoints. They also gave each speaker about ten min-utes to make their case. Ten minutes is not a long time, but it is a vast improvement over the "sound bite" arguments that charac-terize most synod debates. The entire discussion was preceded by a "no motions" motion that prevented the possibility of any party exploiting the outcome of the discussion. This careful combina-tion of factors created a "space" within which the many facets of this complex issue could be talked about, even debated passion-ately, in a free, safe, and thoughtful manner. This process embodied some elements of the pastoral approach I envision: care, fairness, patience, listening, thoughtfulness, space.

Notes

1 House of Bishops Guidelines 1997. These reaffirm the original 1979 Guidelines.
2 Bradshaw *et al.*, "The Saint Andrew's Day Statement. An Examination of the Theological Principles Affecting the Homosexuality Debate," 1995, p. 4.
3 R.F. Hurding, "Pastoral Care, Counselling, and Psycho-therapy," in *New Dictionary of Christian Ethics and Pastoral Theology*, eds. David Atkinson and David Field (Leicester: Intervarsity Press, 1995), p. 79.
4 "Saint Andrew's Day Statement," p. 6.
5 William V. Arnold, *Pastoral Responses to Sexual Issues* (Louisville, KY:W/JKP, 1993), p. 136.
6 O.M.T. O'Donovan, "Christian Moral Reasoning," in *New Dictionary*, pp. 124, 5.
7 The 1962 Book of Common Prayer marriage rite is an example of the second position when it allows, in its rubrics, the omission of a prayer for children when that is impossible. The BAS marriage rite preserved this discretion by inserting a square bracket in the prayers, but it moved into a new understanding of the purpose of marriage by also putting a square bracket around procreation in the preface. This is the third position, which significantly changes the understanding of the purpose of marriage.
8 Report of Table 1 in "Sexuality Discussion: General Synod 2001 Transcript from Newsprint."

"The Gladness of the Gospel"

A Traditional Perspective on Pastoral Care

David A. Reed

P astoral care in today's church is complex business. Pastors often feel tossed around by every prevailing wind of culture.
Their ministry is exacerbated by the porous social boundary that
exists between mainline denominations and the surrounding culture.[1] This leaves the church to wrestle, sometimes fiercely, with
great diversity within its ranks. The foremost issue with which the
Anglican Church of Canada, a mainline church, has had to con-
tend for the past twenty years is the place of homosexual Christians
within its fellowship.

The porous boundary between the church and the culture has
often resulted in confusion and disagreement over what constitutes Christian pastoral care and how it is to be exercised. Part of
the dilemma can be traced to the current historical amnesia that
pervades much of church culture, both conservative and liberal.
Ours is a generation of Christians with little memory of its past
practice — awareness of "how it was done" — appreciation for its
cumulative wisdom, and respect for its authority. In addition, Christians today are influenced by a culture in which the primary
authority for ethical decision-making is the individual feeling of
whether an act feels "right," "good," "natural."[2] The effect has
been either to emphasize present experience and empirical method

in a way that threatens to undermine both the church's primary authority of scripture and its traditional pastoral practice, or to build a perceived impermeable wall around the church to shield it from the onslaughts of a hostile world.

It is increasingly clear that the ability of the mainline church to think Christianly about matters of faith and morals has been weakened. The effect on pastoral care is strikingly illustrated by Methodist theologian Thomas Oden, who shows how the pastoral writers of the twentieth century abandoned wholesale the wisdom of the tradition's spiritual masters in favour of the knowledge trumpeted by the new breed of psychologists.[3] As a result, pastoral care is often characterized as helping individuals sort out their problems through passive listening and value-neutral counsel.

The complex arena of sexuality is not immune to this trend, and perhaps for that reason deserves the church's urgent attention, especially in light of the recent gargantuan shifts in sexual attitudes and practices. Since the 1960s both society and the church have struggled with a cluster of issues relating to sexuality — divorce, abortion, AIDS, sexual abuse, homosexuality. In the frequent absence of clearly stated beliefs and policies, pastors have continued to carry the burden of people's lives that confront them daily, with ambiguities, moral failures, broken dreams, and the shattered lives of both innocent and guilty.

Of the cluster of sexuality-related issues, homosexuality is one of the church's most pressing challenges today. It has been hotly debated in church councils for now over twenty years, and the returns have been meagre at best. We have witnessed defections of members and congregations, rebellion by the disaffected, challenges to authority, and threats of schism. Perhaps most disconcerting is the apparent lack of rapprochement. Yet there are credible testimonies of change of heart, repentance for prejudice, compassion, and honest desire to discern God's will for the church.

The debate in the coming years will engage the church at every level, doctrinally, morally, and practically. The church will hopefully resist the temptation to allow other debates to hemorrhage into this one as a generic human rights issue.[4] It will be called upon to adopt a missionary stance that seeks compassionately to communicate its message to a foreign culture in a way that still retains the integrity of the Christian vision of life in both teaching and practice. The burden will be most keenly felt in the church's ministry of pastoral care.

Two Visions

Two visions of the identity and status of sexually active homosexuals in the church have for the past two decades been presented, theologically debated, and politically advocated in the church. What follows is a brief summary of these two positions, revisionist and traditional.

The *revisionist vision* may be held equally by theological liberals and those who in every other way adhere to creedal orthodoxy. But in the matter of sexuality, revisionists consistently argue that current empirical studies in sexual identity formation challenge traditional thinking; namely, that homosexuality is not necessarily immoral promiscuity but is fundamentally an inherited orientation. Homosexuality is "a predominant, persistent, and exclusive psychosexual attraction toward members of the same sex."[5] Variations include bisexuals, whose attraction is directed toward persons of both sexes. Since, the argument goes, we now know something about human sexual identity that we did not know before, the implication is that social attitudes and laws need to change in order to reflect this new knowledge and satisfy justice. The appeal is fundamentally that, since homosexuality is a "natural" human condition, society has a responsibility to guarantee it as a human right. Further, the repulsion toward gays that still prevails in parts of the culture needs to be rigorously and publicly resisted in order to create a safe and just environment for homosexuals.

For Christians, scripture is a chief battleground in the debate. Revisionists and traditionalists alike express commitment to biblical authority. The main difference lies in the interpretation of key passages and their relationship to the overall witness of scripture. The main argument in revisionist exegesis is that, whatever the scripture teaches about homosexuality, it cannot *ipso facto* refer to present-day homosexuals because it knows nothing of homosexual orientation. These passages are a prohibition against something else (e.g., idolatry), are referring to something other than homosexuality (e.g., promiscuity in the culture), or are condemning a number of practices, including same-sex. In the last category, the interpreter is permitted to locate the prohibitions within a larger theological framework of grace and new creation, thereby relativizing the prohibition and engaging in a wider theological reflection with voices from the culture. In all cases, the scripture's authority is preserved for what it intends to teach, and modern homosexuals are exempt from the burden of the specific prohibitions apparently relating to homosexuality, leaving them to work out their ethical life situationally and ecclesially.[6]

James B. Nelson, popular revisionist, is less committed to the primacy of scripture, pointing out that biblical scholars themselves cannot agree on what the scripture teaches. He is willing to include scripture as a source of authority, but insists that it is not enough: "We need to ask also ... what does our experience as sexual human beings tell us about how we read scripture, interpret the tradition and attempt to live out the meanings of the gospel?" Nelson concludes that there is no specific biblical sex ethic, only a situational love ethic "as the governing sexual norm."[7]

Occasionally revisionists appeal to the classical Anglican theological sources of authority — scripture, tradition, and reason. But they imply, and sometimes claim, that scripture is, in the image of a three-legged stool, but one authority among three by which the church governs its life. This is the position taken by Louie Crew, Episcopal priest and founder of the gay organization, Integrity: "In the Episcopal Church, our theology reveres Scripture as but one of three sources of authority, co-equal with Reason and Tradition."[8] It is clear throughout the essay that Crew perceives scripture and doctrine to play a "minimalist" role in decision-making, and that freedom to think in "new ways" and the democratic processes in church councils carry at least equal authority.

A foundational theological pillar that sustains the revisionist vision is *inclusivity*. In Crew's words, it is "the boundless love of God and its absolute inclusiveness."[9] One can turn to a number of places in scripture that announce the all-encompassing love of God for the world, beginning with John 3:16. With this there can be no disputing between revisionist and traditionalist. Both would also apply this divine principle to baptism as a sign of God's grace toward all who are called into that community of forgiven sinners who desire to follow Jesus as Saviour and Lord.

The revisionist, however, believes that this principle of inclusivity opens the door for practising homosexuals to every level of the church's life. Whether by design or accident, the theological appeal to inclusivity is often strengthened by or generated from the appeal to human rights.[10] One can only speculate that the traditional pastoral strategies are perceived to be too ineffective to produce the desired change, and that a human rights appeal has increasing plausibility and authority among many Anglicans as a means for understanding and implementing the theological virtue of inclusivity.

Homosexual practice is defended on the basis that psychosexual identity or orientation, rather than biological sex differentiation, defines personhood. It is this orientation, therefore, that determines what is "natural." Three implications follow. One is that if it is natural, one is morally entitled to exercise one's natural orientation within the parameters of loving concern for the other. Another is that biblical sexual limits within heterosexual marriage do not apply, since they do not address modern homosexual orientation. Finally, heterosexuality must not be privileged, since that would be reverting to a biological definition of sexuality.

Let us now turn to the alternative approach. The *traditional vision* grounds its beliefs and moral practices in what it perceives to be the church's consistent teaching on sexuality as set forth in scripture. Debates continue to swirl around the significance of current scientific studies of homosexuals for theological decision-making. One debate is the status of homosexual "orientation." While some traditionalists simplistically and prejudicially relegate homosexuality to the bin of human promiscuity and divine abomination, others now acknowledge the contribution of scientific studies that demonstrate that at least there is a sexual orientation that human beings do inherit, orientations that are varied and complex.

It should be noted, however, that the scientific community is less clear about the causes of homosexuality. The debate often bounces between biological and environmental influences, and the state of the research at present is inconclusive.[11]

The traditional vision does not consider orientation or cause to be definitive for ethics, since both reflect human "dis-order" in the world. Unlike some revisionists, traditionalists argue that homosexuality, even as an orientation, is one manifestation of the fallenness of the world, not an open option in God's original design for the ordering of human sexuality. Furthermore, traditionalists point out that sexual identity is not as fixed as revisionists propose. Even within a clearly perceived orientation, humans can and do adapt to a wide range of sexual practices (e.g., homosexual practices by heterosexuals in prison or the military). In early development, sexual identity is still being formed throughout the teen years; this development often extends into adulthood. This means that it is unstable and somewhat malleable depending in part upon external influences. A more sweeping proposal comes from a secular sociologist, David Greenberg, who concludes that human sexuality is all a social construction, that "human sexuality is extremely plastic and innately non-specific with regard to sexual objects. All of us . . . have the capacity to be sexually attracted to members of the same sex."[12]

For this reason traditionalists resist the notion that orientation by itself is a conclusive argument for affirming homosexual practice. Since humans are shown to be adaptive, there is at least a theoretical possibility for orientation to be changed or ameliorated by external influence, such as a caring and supportive community.[13] This, however, does not deny that many homosexuals can recall no other orientation from childhood, or that for many a homosexual orientation will persist throughout their lifetime.

The guiding theological principle for traditionalists is not inclusivity but *intentionality*. Ethical decision-making and life purpose cannot be ultimately determined by biological, psychological, or social causality. Humans will draw meaning for their sexual experience from relational or spiritual domains, whether it is recreational pleasure, romantic friendship, or an exclusive marital bond. What they decide will be for them "natural." But direct appeal to what is natural — or worse, feels natural — can never be the basis for moral action. Ethics by definition involves a wider set of claims upon humans. As theologian Stanley Grenz points out, traditional Christians seek to form their vision after the mind of the biblical authors for whom "the 'natural' is what is in accordance with God's purpose, goal, or *telos* for human existence."[14] "Natural" in this sense is the same as theological normativity for sexual practice.

Orthodox Anglicans, like the revisionists, turn to the classical Anglican sources of scripture, reason, and tradition to determine the divine intention for sexual practice. Unlike revisionists, Anglicans historically have always understood scripture to be the primary revelation mediated through reason and tradition.[15]

In matters of sexuality, scripture and the teaching of the church have been unwavering in two areas. The first is the boundary around coitus. Traditionalists affirm the heterosexual, monogamous marriage bond as the proper location for sexual union, and reject sexual activity in homosexual and non-marital heterosexual relationships. While empirical studies may confirm or deny the satisfactional superiority of any given arrangement, the biblical and theological vision is normative.

In the present climate of opinion, which is less than convinced of the personal and social goods of marriage and perceives sexual freedom to be a human right, it is particularly difficult to argue that reserving the exclusivity of the sexual union for heterosexual marriage is humanity's best offer for human flourishing. Christian teaching has been consistent, though it varies their priority, in setting forth the goods of marriage and commending them to society. One is that marriage is the human community in which mutual intimacy and joy can be experienced and honed to maturity in the midst of the uncertainties and infirmities of life (its unitive function).[16] The other is that marriage is the normative community for rearing children (its procreative function). Traditionalists believe that both are consistently set forth in scripture; and, acknowledging human failure and frailty, they believe this moral vision for the ordering of human community to be worthy of commending to society for its well being.

Traditional Christians also accept the biblical teaching that the "one flesh" of marriage mirrors in its form of human community the relationship between God and the People of God, especially that mystery of the relationship between "Christ and the church."[17] For all these reasons, there seems no clear pathway from the consistent biblical witness regarding sexual boundaries to one of non-exclusive sexual practice.[18]

The second consistent teaching of scripture on sexuality as understood by traditionalists is its view of sexual identity. Unlike the revisionist view, this view does not affirm same-sex unions, because they fail to conform to God's purpose or *telos* for sexual relationships. Most advocates for same-sex unions regard sexual unions as value-neutral, so that one form of union is not to be morally privileged. As Bishop Spong states, "homosexuality and heterosexuality are morally neutral."[19]

The crucial point of disagreement is whether or not sexual difference is constitutive or incidental (non-essential) to human identity. The revisionist insists that sexual expression is good because Christians theologically embrace the goodness of creation. This is intended as an incarnational affirmation against a spirit-flesh dualism. However, as ethicist Philip Turner points out, the revisionist stops short of affirming that humankind is actually constituted as male and female.[20] In other words, sexual difference is incidental to, not constitutive of, what it means to be human.

Practically, a revisionist view permits homosexual and various forms of trans-sexual relationships so long as they are loving, caring, and mutually fulfilling. Humankind is constituted as a psychosomatic-spiritual unity, but sexual difference is extrinsic to that identity and is determined by psychological orientation, not biology. The revisionist result is a dualistic androgynous ideal that is more in keeping with Greek than with biblical anthropology.

The traditional vision can find no biblical basis for affirming same-sex unions. Though many conscientious conservatives would desire to justify their acceptance, scripture, and the church's consistent traditional interpretation of it, provide no ground for same-sex practice. On the contrary, a strong case can be made for locating sexual differentiation within the *imago Dei* itself.[21]

The popular argument that same-sex unions belong biblically to the same generic category as divorce and the ordination of women — and therefore should likewise be approved — is reductionistic in that it disregards the peculiarities of each. Scripture simply does not treat them alike. Rather, it is possible to discern, as theologian Ray Anderson proposes, a hermeneutical distinction between precedence and antecedence. In the cases of the acceptance of Gentiles in the church, the role of women in the church, and the status of those divorced and remarried, there was no direct historical precedent. However, in each case there was a biblical antecedent: Abraham was accepted by faith before his circumcision, women were judges and prophets, and in remarriage God creates a new thing as "a gracious recovery of the biblical *antecedent* that marriage itself is given by God as a possibility within the divine image." Homosexuality, unlike the others, stands alone with no biblical antecedent. "Those who argue for the normalizing of homosexual relationships and full acceptance by the church must do so on other grounds."[22] Here then we have the second non-negotiable pillar of a traditional vision of human sexuality: normative sexual practice is heterosexual because sexual complementarity as male and female is intrinsically bound up with being human.

In summary, there are two boundaries between the revisionist and traditional vision that are at present irreconcilable. One is the boundary of general sexual permission. The revisionist approves of sexual practice outside the boundaries of marriage under the conditions of a situational love ethic that preserves the virtues of mutuality, care, and justice toward the other. The traditionalist believes that limiting sexual practice to marriage is the best arrangement for human flourishing and witnessing to the divine mystery of God's mission in the world through the church.

The second is the boundary of sexual difference. The revisionist affirms the essentiality and goodness of bodily sex for human identity but rejects the view that male-female complementarity is necessary to that identity. The traditionalist holds that a biblical anthropology demands sexual difference as constitutive of humanity.

A Traditional Pastoral Care Approach

How does pastoral care in a conflicted church carry out its ministry in a way that embodies God's inclusive love and concern for the world and yet preserves the divine intentionality for God's creatures as set forth in scripture? It is clear to me that there will continue to be learning, growth, and change on all sides — and undoubtedly some damage — as the church wrestles with these questions into the future. But I believe that attentiveness to the church's traditional ministry of pastoral care will eventually yield the more faithful and fruitful account of God's purpose for humanity. To that task we now turn.

Pastoral care has always functioned with two fundamental theological assumptions. One is that it has understood its ministry to be carried out within a particular framework that shapes its basic vision and subsequent action. That perspective is provided in the four movements of salvation history narrated in scripture — creation, fall, reconciliation, and final redemption. Undergirding the narrative is the conviction that this movement from creation to redemption is the work of a gracious, loving, and benevolent God whose action on behalf of humanity is now and always carried out for its good. Hence, the biblical vision is definitive even in the face of life situations that at first appear to belie a benevolent deity. Also, the narrative persists when challenged by other worldview narratives that arise from culture, even when they present themselves as more compelling, loving, and compassionate than the traditional narrative.

The other foundation for traditional pastoral care is that it is carried out, not simply in, but *as* the church. Pastoral care cannot be reduced to value-free service for an individualistic culture.[23] It is the church itself that is caught up, sometimes feebly, in the ministry of Christ, bearing faithful witness to him and offering the resources of grace. Therefore, it should come as no surprise that traditional pastoral care will be vulnerable to misunderstanding and even hostility when it resists expectations imposed upon it by a culture, including many in the church, that runs counter to its calling. Thomas Oden offers a description that reveals the complexity and comprehensiveness of the church's ministry of pastoral care:

> Pastoral care is a unique enterprise that has its own distinctive subject-matter (care of souls); its own methodological premise (revelation); its own way of inquiring into its subject-matter (attentiveness to the revealed Word through Scripture and its consensual tradition of exegesis); its own criteria of scholarly authenticity (accountability to canonical text and tradition); its own way of knowing (listening to sacred Scripture and the historic church); its own mode of cultural analysis (with worldly powers bracketed and divine providence appreciated); and its own logic (internal consistency premised upon revealed truth).[24]

Such an approach prescribes the shape and method by which pastoral care is exercised. It cannot be reduced to a set of rules, but it provides a means of discerning the will and purpose of God. It seeks the mind of Christ within the Christian community, not because it has lost confidence in the scriptures, but precisely because this community does have confidence in the Bible as the Word of God, knows that it cannot circumvent it, and understands its calling to seek diligently until it finds. Neither church nor creation is an independent path for knowing the mind of Christ.

Pastoral care, then, is a distinct activity of the church that is "directed towards the elimination and relief of sin and sorrow and the presentation of all people perfect in Christ to God."[25] It would be a serious misrepresentation of this task to perceive it simply as narrow and exclusive. From a traditional perspective, pastoral care is inclusive within the framework of salvation history and the divine purpose. It cannot be satisfied with any horizon narrower than the love of God for the world created and redeemed.

It is the human rights appeal, however, that is too exclusive as a basis for pastoral care, since it denies the church its right of self-determination. Specifically, it misunderstands the essential distinction between the church's ordering of its internal life and its relationship to the world, by conflating the former into the kind of inclusivity that the church advocates on behalf of those in society who do not share its views. The cross of Christ is the basis upon which the church can allow its own vision for the world to be rejected, knowing that the resurrection and God's vindication are ultimately assured. But that is not the same as asserting that, because the church supports the rights of practising homosexuals in society, it must order its interior life in exactly the same way.

The companion to the cultural appeal of inclusivity is *compassion*. Any action that is perceived to be lacking in compassion will receive swift and severe censure. But as in the case of inclusivity, a mantra does not a virtue make. This is not to suggest that we ignore the church's record of heartlessness throughout history. Periods and regions give a grim account of the corporate sin of the church. The Epistle of James reminds us that compassion is an elusive virtue that requires constant vigilance.

Compassion is woven into the very fabric of traditional pastoral care through the character of a loving God who knows the weakness of every human being. In the salvation-history scheme none are strong; all are a universal fallen humanity in need of saving. This leaves no room for pharisaism, a position that excludes some from weakness. But compassion is theologically a richly textured virtue that does not yield to simplistic charges when it does not conform to popular expectations.

The tradition of pastoral care writing is replete with appeals to compassion and concern, even when one is being exhorted to confess and repent. This is well illustrated in the advice given by Chrysostom (d. 407) to a fellow priest:

> Show thy charity towards the sinner. Persuade him that it is from care and anxiety for his welfare and not from a wish to expose him, that thou puttest him in mind of his sin…. Urge him to show the wound to the priest; that is the part of one who cares for him, and provides for him, and is anxious on his behalf.[26]

Pastoral care writers in the Reformation tradition embraced the range of human frailty that called for pastoral attention. German theologian Martin Bucer advised pastors to "draw to Christ those who are alienated; to lead back those who have drawn away; to seek amendment of life in those who fall into sin; to strengthen weak and sickly Christians; to preserve Christians who are whole and strong."[27] A century later, Puritan pastor Richard Baxter identified four groups that call for pastoral attention: the immature, those with "particular corruption which keeps under their graces," "declining Christians," and strong Christians.[28] One cannot doubt that the vision of pastoral care in the tradition is deeply formed by Paul's counsel: "admonish the idlers, encourage the faint-hearted, help the weak, be patient with all of them."[29]

Compassionate pastoral care needs to demonstrate patience, knowing the depth of the human struggle and allowing time for the Holy Spirit to work in the soul. Nor does a traditional approach need to deny the relative benefits that come from various arrangements other than marriage. As Turner states, "There is no need ... for the church to prove either lacking in compassion or punitive in its discipline. There is without doubt much good in many of the "relationships" that people ... now so frequently enter."[30]

But a traditional vision of pastoral care understands these relationships as limited experiments. It will not function with integrity if it relinquishes the normative vision, the *telos*, which guides its work. Its invitation is not to instant perfection but "Come, walk with us," as fellow journeyers who know their own frailty but diligently seek to mould their lives according to the good purpose of God as revealed in salvation history. It is this spirit that one discerns in the statement released by a group of conservative Anglican bishops on the eve of the 1998 Lambeth Conference:

> God's dealings with his world is a story of sensitivity and compassion. The church needs to reflect God's love to all people. The story of God's concern offers hope for all of us, that all of us become progressively more human as our lives unfold in response to his grace. With such encouragement the church must welcome all in pain. The persecution and ostracism of homosexual persons as well as sexual hypocrisy are evils and have no place in the church.[31]

Since traditional pastoral care lays claim to the qualities of inclusivity and compassion, it is woefully inadequate to charge traditionalists with homophobia and prejudice simply on the grounds of their disapproving same-sex unions. When set within the tradition of salvation history, the church endeavours to witness to the world something of God's all-encompassing love and compassion. It does that best when it sets forth God's intention for humanity and invites fellow strugglers to grow into it. Failure on our part may discredit but cannot nullify the vision, because it belongs to God and is God's gift.[32]

Traditional pastoral care is a complex and demanding activity involving doctrine, spirituality, the ecclesial community, and normative moral vision. It calls for sensitivity and knowledge in many areas. In matters pastoral, one size does not fit all. But there have been identifiable constants throughout history. In their classic study, *Pastoral Care in Historical Perspective*, Clebsch and Jaekle name four pastoral care functions that have been continuous: healing, sustaining, guiding, and reconciling.[33] Therefore, it is appropriate to reflect briefly on the pastoral challenge of homosexual practice from the perspective of these enduring pastoral functions.

Healing "helps a debilitated person to be restored to a condition of wholeness, on the assumption that this restoration achieves also a new level of spiritual insight and welfare."[34] Christianity is a transformative religion, and the assumption in pastoral care is that healing can occur. Change, personal and social, is possible. The hoped-for change may not occur immediately. But the achieving of spiritual insight implies that what is not accomplished physically or emotionally may occur spiritually. And what is not accomplished now is promised eschatologically, as the person is given the hope of resurrection life.

This means that there needs to be room in the church for ministries that support change of practice, and perhaps orientation, for homosexuals. Healing ministries are an offensive presence for revisionists, who often claim that healing is impossible or believe that the presence of these ministries undermines the call for homosexuals to be accepted in the church without such change. But to refuse their presence is to deny this fundamental pastoral conviction that change can occur, even if that transformation is gradual, filled with struggle, primarily spiritual, or physically delayed until the resurrection of the body.

Healing is also directed to the Christian community itself. The church stands under judgement for its prejudice and maltreatment of homosexuals, a hostility that was most intense from the late medieval period to the nineteenth century.[35] Healing of individuals can occur only within a community of credibility and trust. And that cannot occur until the community has been healed, transformed, of the spirit that excludes certain persons from its life. The recent challenge to acknowledge the presence of homosexuals in and on the margins of the church is being met not only by revisionists but also by some conservative Christians who feel the sting of judgement for the church's hypocrisy. It may include public declarations of sin and acts of repentance.[36]

Sustaining "consists of helping a hurting person to endure and to transcend a circumstance in which restoration to his former condition or recuperation from his malady is either impossible or so remote as to seem improbable."[37] This function speaks directly to homosexuals for whom change of orientation has been elusive. Revisionists in effect circumvent the struggle by proposing the judicious acceptance of sexual practice outside marriage. When one embraces a traditional sexual ethic, the struggle is not eliminated but becomes the place of possibility for a deeper transformation. What needs healing is the burden of shame and guilt that so frequently haunts the inner life of the homosexual. The gospel holds forth the promise to homosexuals that like other Christians who have discovered strength and healing in suffering they may transcend their painful "circumstance" and find their burden transformed into joy through the grace of the cross. But this sustaining function of pastoral care will also require a church that has the courage to embrace both this vision and an unconditional friendship for the homosexual.

The pastoral task is to assist homosexuals, along with all Christians, to be counter-cultural in a way that helps them sustain their faith and manner of living in the midst of a culture that communicates powerful messages to the contrary. This will require of a church the kind of baptismal identity that knows itself to be "not of the world" but also not out of the world; a church with the capacity to welcome "all sorts and conditions," to befriend and provide a powerful antidote to the loneliness and alienation that marks those that are already marginalized by society. The sad commentary is that most churches are far from equipped, spiritually and relationally, to be that kind of sustaining community suited to live in a post-Christendom culture.

Guiding "consists of assisting perplexed persons to make confident choices between alternative courses of thought and action, when such choices are viewed as affecting the present and future state of the soul."[38] The revisionist tends toward the modern "client-centred therapy" of Carl Rogers, in which a person is guided to discover and shape decisions out of one's own set of values. This stands in sharp contrast to a traditional approach in which persons are counselled to sort out their difficulty within the context of a normative vision rooted in salvation history.[39] Traditional pastoral care neither avoids nor denies the painful struggle of homosexuals, but circumscribes it within the larger redemptive purposes of God. It may acknowledge the provisional relief and well-being found in monogamous same-sex unions. But its counsel is ultimately grounded in the conviction that conformity to the normative vision is in the end more fulfilling. This belief must also be a warning against any temptation to be censorious toward those who choose not to embrace a normative ethic. Good counsel will call for teaching, encouraging, and motivating all who desire to follow Jesus to strive joyfully to live into God's purpose for humanity.

Finally, *reconciling* "seeks to re-establish broken relationships between man and fellow man and between man and God."[40] In the homosexuality debate, both revisionist and traditionalist have much to be forgiven. But reconciling the offence of sexual impropriety is not the same as approving *a priori* a sexual practice that is both universally and consistently excluded in scripture and the church's teaching. To deny that homosexual practice is a moral failure may temporarily relieve struggle but cannot be justified by traditional pastoral care.

For those who acknowledge the struggle and seek reconciliation and amendment of life, forgiveness is assured. For some who either resist or otherwise do not acknowledge their failure, pastoral care may exercise some form of discipline by which persons are urged to be reconciled. Discipline is the exercise of boundary setting, in belief and practice, with the intention that persons be restored to that amendment of life which seeks to conform to God's purpose.

It is here that the church may rightly exercise its "discipline," by denying current proposals to officially bless same-sex unions and ordain practising homosexuals. This is the theological moment in which the church balances its mission of compassionate care for "all sorts and conditions" of persons and its responsibility to be a faithful witness. Public and official liturgical acts validate practices in ways that both approve of those practices and contradict the received teaching on sexuality. For the church to exercise properly its reconciling function means in this case not to admit such liturgical acts but to describe, by refusing them, a different and normative vision of God's purpose for sexual relationships. Holding up, in its sacramental life, this alternative vision is the discipline the church can exercise in its work of reconciliation. The challenge for the church is to be deliberate in ridding itself of systemic homophobia so that homosexuals who are being drawn by the Spirit to follow Christ may find a welcoming fellowship to guide and sustain them in that journey. But the church will need to do this in ways that do not obscure its normative vision.

What are some ways of being this kind of church? The "revisionist" model churches are well known, such as the Metropolitan Community Church, founded by Mel White, a formerly Pentecostal gay minister. A number of congregations within the mainline denominations publicly present themselves as "affirming congregations," congregations that welcome homosexuals and affirm homosexual practice, including same-sex couples. Their belief and practice on homosexuality is most compatible with the revisionist vision.

In recent years a number of conservative congregations have made an effort to reach out to the homosexual community. They denounce the church's homophobia and affirm homosexual persons as equally loved and accepted by God. But there are at least two recognizable types of congregations. The first is what might be called the "non-issue" congregation. It operates attitudinally with an unspoken policy that sexuality will be a non-issue in the pulpit. The church is to be a safe place for homosexuals, including those in partnerships, to participate without fear of embarrassment or censure. The premise is that teaching on sexuality, though important, is secondary to other spiritual and pastoral goods needed in this particular time and place. The leadership may argue that in the present climate of hostility against homosexuals, the church needs to set its priority on compassionate evangelistic and pastoral ministry to those marginalized by society and shunned by the church. The obvious deficit is that the non-issue congregation, though conservative, effectually rules out the possibility of teaching publicly on traditional sexual morality. An appropriate alternative may be to address such matters, including heterosexual practices like cohabitation, in the more discrete settings of personal counselling or marriage preparation.

The second type, more public in addressing the topic of homosexuality, is the "transformational" congregation. A movement called "transforming congregations" publicly challenges the church to repent of its homophobia and welcomes homosexuals into its midst.[41] Many of the healing ministries directed to assisting homosexuals who desire to change are represented.

But what if healing and change do not occur? This can still be a church that advocates for justice and fairness for homosexuals in society, works to relieve the congregation of its homophobic attitudes and practices, creates a community of friendship and support for homosexuals, treats homosexual practice as in no way different from other human failures (such as adultery and divorce), openly teaches the traditional normative vision for sexual life, practises at all levels the life of grace that comes through forgiveness, and opens the church structures to celibate homosexuals at every level, including ordination.

Who is helped and hindered in these two congregations? The non-issue congregation will attract homosexuals across the spectrum of practice, including those in partnerships. But it will not be particularly helpful for those who seek to live a celibate life or pattern their sexual lives heterosexually within marriage, because the congregation will implicitly view such decisions as a lifestyle choice, not a normative standard.

The transformational congregation will not likely attract homosexual partners because of its traditional position. But it will be home for homosexuals who are in marriages, or single and strive to remain celibate. They know they need a spiritual and moral community that upholds traditional sexual morality, one that knows how to practise forgiveness and is communally skilled in friendship, support, and counselling for all who struggle in grace.

Most of our churches, however, do not fit well into any of the above categories but reflect a familiar pattern in the historic churches: publicly maintaining a consistent traditional position while benignly ignoring a contrary practice. In most situations this is prudent, as it respects an appropriate boundary between what the church publicly endorses and the personal and private struggles all Christians endure. This practice has integrity as long as the normative vision continues to be morally compelling for its people. However, a critical line is crossed when private practice wields more power than and erodes the credibility of the church's teaching. The consequences for the church's moral life can be extreme: witness the residential schools crisis in Canada, and the long line of sexual abuse cases by church leaders (with cover-up policies rather than remedial help or removal).

But there are more common and subtler ways in which the practice has the effect of muting the teaching voice of the church. It may be expressed passively in a lack of attentiveness to the normative practice, or felt when efforts to promote or strengthen a public virtue in practices or policies are resisted. A recent study by W. Bradford Wilcox on the attitude of religious institutions to marriage illustrates this critical tension. His conclusion is that "houses of worship" that historically have had a high investment in the institution of marriage "have been both unable and unwilling to foster the beliefs and virtues that make for a strong marriage culture."[42] Wilcox's striking discovery, however, is that the reasons are not to be found in the official beliefs but in the countervailing practices that lie beneath the surface: fear of provoking public dissent, distraction by other social issues, discomfort due to the clash between official beliefs and questionable practices in the pew, and the tendency to sentimentalize marriage rather than help couples prepare for it.

It is never easy to discern when the integrity of the church's teaching is eroded and the critical line is crossed. But by neglecting such discernment the church risks transmitting to future generations an impotent gospel.

"The gladness of the gospel"

One who embraces the traditional vision of pastoral care does not find an easy path of ministry to the homosexual community. Neither easy accommodation nor intolerant isolation will do. The pastoral task is to appropriate the kind of adaptation to the present situation that most faithfully preserves the normative vision. It is difficult to see how a revisionist proposal can satisfy that demand, in that affirming same-sex unions effectively neutralizes the normativity of the heterosexual marriage bond. And a merely conservative rendition easily devolves into moralism.

The debate frequently becomes one of seeking ways to alleviate the burden borne by homosexuals. What is missing in much of the discourse on both sides is the belief that there can be gladness in denying oneself the benefit of existential relief. But it is a joy that comes only by believing that the cross leads to fullness of resurrection life. As Oliver O'Donovan states, we must begin with the "redemptive energy of God" that shifts the centre of action from the will to the affections. The affections become the bridge between what we believe to be right and our will to do it, because they "at one and the same time discern reality and incline towards it." Affections that are grounded in the gospel "incline our hearts," motivate us, to fulfill the purpose of God for our lives. This peculiar "gladness of the gospel" disposes the disciple of Christ gladly to exchange the unlimited possibilities pledged by a culture of self-fulfillment for "those defined possibilities that are offered us in what God has done."[43] The homosexual can "gladly" embrace the cross of self-denial and accept the divinely offered order for sexual relationships in full confidence that this moral order is "itself made new in Christ."[44]

Jesus teaches that "those who love their life (psuchē) lose it, and those who hate their life in this world will keep it for eternal life (zoē)."[45] Psuchē life refers to those good things that make for quality of life beyond survival needs. It would also describe the kind of life that includes the companionship, intimacy, and sexual satisfaction offered in a same-sex union. But as such this is not the way of Christ, but the choice of a provisional good. To embrace the moral order set forth in scripture is to accept the cross of letting go of psuchē in order that only that kind of life offered by Christ, zoē, can be grasped.[46]

Without confidence in this gospel life we can take no pleasure in offering our homosexual sister or brother its "limited possibilities." But gospel gladness grasps the redemptive power that gives us courage to see in the stone of stumbling a rock upon which to stand. We believe — some way, somehow, somewhere, some time — that good will be mysteriously born out of this pain, that the pain will be healed, and that God's final benediction will not be thwarted.

Notes

1   "Mainline" denominations refers to the historic Protestant churches that were transplanted in North America from Europe and England, in contrast to the "new" or "young" denominations that were formed on this continent during the nineteenth and twentieth centuries.

2   A recent study conducted by Barna Research reveals that most Americans are likely to base truth on their feelings. The Bible or teachings of the religion were primary for only a small percentage. The primacy of individual feelings of rightness was even more pronounced among teens. For the full report, see www.barna.org.

3   Oden illustrates this shift in a stunning comparison of authorities quoted by representative nineteenth- and twentieth-century leading pastoral writers. The latter made no reference at all to the Christian spiritual masters (Augustine, Luther, etc.), but quoted twentieth-century psychologists (Freud, Jung, Berne, etc.) with precisely the same frequency as the nineteenth-century writers referred to the spiritual and pastoral writers. See chapter 1, "Recovering Lost Identity," in Thomas C. Oden, *Care of Souls in the Classical Tradition* (Minneapolis: Fortress Press, 1984). For an excellent historical treatment of the influence of psychology on the practice of pastoral care, see E. Brooks Holifield, *A History of Pastoral Care in America: From Salvation to Self-Realization* (Nashville: Abingdon Press, 1983).

4   One of the weaknesses of applying the argument of human rights to the homosexuality debate is its tendency to reductionism. That is, other issues such as racial equality and the ordination of women are treated as merely subsets of rights values. The theological or moral appeal of a

particular issue is *ipso facto* made inconsequential to the appeal for recognition.

5   A definition taken from the *Encyclopedia of Bioethics*, cited in Stanley J. Grenz, *Welcoming But Not Affirming: An Evangelical Response to Homosexuality* (Louisville, KY: WJK Press, 1998), p. 32.

6   For a review of the different approaches to the text, see Dierdre J. Good, "Reading Strategies for Biblical Passages on Same-Sex Relations," web site: www.gts.edu/academic/faculty/good/djgarti.htm.

7   James B. Nelson, "Needed: A Continuing Sexual Revolution," *The Christian Century* 105/18 (1 June 1988), p. 540.

8   Louie Crew, "Changing the Church: Lessons Learned in the Struggle to Reduce Institutional Heterosexism in the Episcopal Church," at web site: http://andromeda.rutgers.edu/~lcrew/gayhist.htm.

9   Crew, "Changing the Church." I am aware that other moral goods, such as compassion, love, mutuality, fidelity and justice, are included in the appeal. But inclusivity often appears to be the gate of entry, and is often applied as a synonym of God's grace, or in Tillich's famous words, "accepting that you are accepted."

10   An example: a resource book published by the Anglican Church of Canada, *Our Stories/Your Story: A Resource by the Working Group on Gays and Lesbians and the Church of the Human Rights Unit of the Anglican Church of Canada* (Toronto: Anglican Book Centre), 1991.

11   For an excellent survey of various contemporary approaches to homosexuality, see chapter 1 of Grenz, *Welcoming*, pp. 13 ff.

12   As summarized by Don Browning, "Rethinking Homosexuality," *The Christian Century* (11 October 1989), p. 911.

13   For a brief discussion of whether or not sexual identity is "static" or "dynamic," see Grenz, *Welcoming*, pp. 28–33.

14 Grenz, *Welcoming*, p. 101. This is the heart of Grenz's argument, which he sets forth in chapter 5, pp. 101ff.

15 A fourth source, experience, is frequently added to the other three. Borrowed from the Methodist tradition, it completes the "Wesleyan Quadrilateral." Albert Outler, American Methodist patriarch, coined the term but in later years regretted having done so as he witnessed it being used to distort Wesley's view of scripture. See Albert Outler, "The Wesleyan Quadrilateral in John Wesley," *Wesleyan Theological Journal* 20/1 (1985), p. 11.

16 Recent studies are drawing attention to the harmful effects of divorce on children, even into adulthood. These studies also show that in most divorces support for the parents' decision has had little credibility with those children affected. See especially Judith Wallerstein, *The Unexpected Legacy of Divorce* (New York: Hyperion, 2000), and Linda J. Waite and Maggie Gallagher, *The Case for Marriage: Why Married People are Happier, Healthier and Better Off Financially* (New York: Doubleday, 2000).

17 Ephesians 5:32.

18 Because the revisionist locates the moral basis for coitus outside the exclusive marriage bond, the character of the sexual activity is defined by other ideals, be they hedonism, relational intimacy or limited covenant. Even Bishop John Spong's effort to provide a Christian moral foundation for same-sex unions stops short of lifelong, exclusive vows, though we recognize that many same-sex couples intend their commitment to be lifelong. He describes their relationships as, "faithful, monogamous, committed, life-giving and holy," in *The Koinonia Statement to the Members of the House of Bishops*, 25 August 1994.

19 *Koinonia Statement*.

20 For Turner's critique that revisionist sexual ethics is fundamentally dualistic, see chapters 1 and 2 in Turner's *Sex, Money and Power* (Cambridge, MA: Cowley Publishers, 1985).

21 Genesis 1:27. Among others, Karl Barth argues that the image of God is the creation of humanity *as* male and female and male or female.

22 Ray S. Anderson, *The Soul of Ministry: Forming Leaders for God's People* (Louisville, KY: WJK Press, 1997), pp. 126–27.

23 Revisionist ethics is not a significant advance over a value-free paradigm, as a situational love ethic is sufficiently generalized and compatible with the best of a secular ethical vision; namely, it has little specificity to challenge sexual behaviour. For instance, the same ethical appeal to intimacy and care for the other is articulated by advocates of polyamorous (lit., many loves) sexual relations, heterosexual and homosexual. For a Christian situationist ethic, it is difficult to see why a monogamous relationship should be compelling if the culture in fact testifies that polyamorous relationships can also be wholesome and "life-giving."

24 Thomas C. Oden, *Pastoral Counsel*, vol. 3, in *Classical Pastoral Care* (Grand Rapids, MI: Baker Books, 1987), p. 4.

25 Stephen Pattison, *A Critique of Pastoral Care* (London: SCM Press Ltd., 1988), p. 13.

26 Cited by George H. Williams, chapter 3, "The Ministry in the Later Patristic Period (pp. 314–451)," in eds. H. Richard Niebuhr and Daniel D. Williams, *The Ministry in Historical Perspectives* (New York: Harper & Row, 1983), p. 70.

27 Cited in Kenneth Leech, *Soul Friend: The Practice of Christian Spirituality*, (San Francisco: Harper & Row, 1980) p. 85.

28 Cited in Leech, *Soul Friend*, p. 86.

29 I Thessalonians 5:14 (NRSV).

30 Turner, *Sexual Ethics — And the Attack on Traditional Morality* (Cincinnati, OH: Forward Movement Publications, 1988), p. 20.

31 "The Dallas Statement," www.AmericanAnglican.org/News/News.cfm?ID=58&c=2.

32 I understand that both revisionist and traditionalist can

assert biblical grounds for their positions. I have indicated my preference for the traditional vision, and my reasons for it. My purpose in this paper is, in a limited way, to show that a traditional vision of pastoral care "makes sense," is not by definition homophobic, and is compelling for those seeking diligently to follow Christ.

33 William A. Clebsch and Charles R. Jaekle, *Pastoral Care in Historical Perspective* (New York: Harper & Row, 1967).

34 Clebsch, *Pastoral Care*, p. 8.

35 See Grenz, *Welcoming*, pp. 68–72.

36 For example, see the web site set up by evangelical Christians to promote justice and respect for homosexuals within the Christian community: www.justice-respect.org. See also web sites, www.messiah.edu/hpages/facstaff/chase/h/frame.htm, and www.transformingcong.org/. The mission of Transforming Congregations is to help churches "adopt a redemptive and pro-active response to the homosexual issues of our day."

    One conservative pastor, Pastor Bob Stith, openly confessed, on behalf of the church, the sin of homophobia to an openly gay person as a representative of the homosexual community, November, 1998: www.justice-respect.org/essays/repentance.html.

37 Clebsch, *Pastoral Care*, p. 8.

38 Clebsch, *Pastoral Care*, p. 9.

39 Clebsch, *Pastoral Care*, p. 9.

40 Clebsch, *Pastoral Care*, p. 9.

41 See the Transforming Congregations web site: www.transformingcong.org.

42 Wilcox is research fellow at Yale's Institute for the Advanced Study of Religion and professor at the University of Virginia. The study was reviewed by Michael J. McManus, "Churches Unable and Unwilling to Support Marriage," www.smartmarriages.com, 14 February 2002.

43 Oliver O'Donovan, "Evangelicalism and the Foundations of Ethics," chapter 8, in eds. R.T. France and A.E. McGrath, *Evangelical Anglicans: Their Role and Influence in the Church Today* (London: SPCK, 1993), p. 99.

44 O'Donovan, "Evangelicalism," p. 104.

45 John 12:25 (NRSV).

46 For an excellent biblical treatment of the dimensions of life, see chapter 4 of J. Robert Nelson, *Human Life: A Biblical Perspective for Bioethics* (Philadelphia: Fortress Press, 1984).

ABC Publishing
ANGLICAN BOOK CENTRE

Discerning the Word
The Bible and Homosexuality in Anglican Debate
Paul Gibson
Focusing on the 1998 Lambeth Conference resolutions on scripture and sexuality, Paul Gibson examines the way cultural norms influence our understanding of biblical authority. He issues a challenge to the church, and proposes a way forward that honours scripture, tradition, and our evolving culture.
1-155126-320-3 $14.95

An Honourable Estate
Marriage, Same-Sex Unions, and the Church
Christopher Cantlon and Pauline Thompson, editors
An informative resource for Christians concerned about non-traditional relationships and homosexuality and the church's response. Includes open-ended questions, suggested scripture passages, and case studies to assist thoughtful discussion.
1-55126-158-8 $16.95

Hearing Diverse Voices, Seeking Common Ground
Anglican Church of Canada
Attempts to take seriously the biblical record and current biblical scholarship; Anglican tradition; current scientific research and understanding; and the witness of gay and lesbian Anglicans.
1-55126-112-X $16.95

Anglican Essentials
Reclaiming Faith within the Anglican Church of Canada
George Egerton, editor
1-55126-095-6 $14.95
Study Guide by Michael Knowles
1-55126-137-5 $9.99

The Challenge of Tradition
Discerning the Future of Anglicanism
John Simons, editor
Fresh perspectives on a wide range of hotly debated issues.

*Available from your local bookstore or
Anglican Book Centre, phone 1-800-268-1168
or write 600 Jarvis Street, Toronto, ON M4Y 2J6*